PANTYFEDWEN LEC

RELIGION IN THE INDUSTRIAL REVOLUTION IN SOUTH WALES

E. T. DAVIES

CARDIFF
UNIVERSITY OF WALES PRESS
1965

PRINTED IN GREAT BRITAIN

TO

SIR DAVID JAMES, LL.D.

Founder of the Pantyfedwen Trust
and benefactor of the
people of Wales

By the same author

The Political Ideas of Richard Hooker

Episcopacy and the Royal Supremacy in the Church of England in the Sixteenth Century

An Ecclesiastical History of Monmouthshire (Part I)

Monmouthshire Schools and Education to 1870

PREFACE

When I was invited by the D. J. James Pantyfedwen Trust to deliver the Annual Lecture for 1962 the subject chosen was one on which a certain amount of work had already been done by me. This was the place of religion in a society which had a well-defined beginning during the second half of the eighteenth century, and which was obviously in a process of certain fundamental changes by the end of the First World War.

The area chosen was the scene of the eighteenth-century industrial revolution, which changed the technique of iron production and set up an iron industry in a belt extending some eighteen miles across north Glamorgan and north Monmouthshire. This was followed by the deep-coal-mining industry after 1860 which spread industrialism throughout the valleys of Glamorgan and Monmouthshire. This choice had many advantages: industrially it was virgin territory except for iron and tinplate production which had gone on around the eastern rim of this area for some generations before 1760; it threw up a number of industrial communities which were composed largely of immigrants, both Welsh and English, and it presented the churches and the chapels with a sphere of work which in its extent and nature had not been pre-empted by either the Established Church or the older Welsh Nonconformist denominations. If the former had been in these areas centuries longer than the latter, the Nonconformist chapels had taken root since the seventeenth century. In 1750 this area was very sparsely populated; by 1800 the iron industry had been established at the head of every valley, and, ecclesiastically, the new society would be captured by the religious bodies which would best take advantage of their new opportunities. The vested interests, in the form of long-term possession of this territory, were evenly balanced, and the future belonged to the boldest.

This sudden dramatic development with its rapid changes had no parallel elsewhere. If we compare the Welsh scene with the contemporary English scene we see that the problem of language affected the former profoundly, whereas, of course, it did not enter into the religious situation of the latter. Furthermore, the whole religious situation became merged with the political and social struggle which dominated Wales for the second half of the last century: indeed, the tension between church and chapel was not only theological and ecclesiastical but was profoundly political and social as well. This division between church and chapel affected every community in Wales in the last century. Hitherto attention has been paid to this tension in the rural areas where it originated; this present study traces the church and chapel issues in an industrial community. There were, therefore, factors in the Welsh industrial situation which were completely absent from England, and consequently the general picture is very different. The Welsh industrial picture did not begin to approximate to its English counterpart in matters of religion until a generation before the First World War.

The Lecture was given at University College, Cardiff, on 2 May 1962 under the chairmanship of Sir Frederick Rees, a former Principal of the college. Under the terms of the D. J. James Pantyfedwen Trust the lecturer must be an Ordained Minister or a Clergyman in Holy Orders, and the Annual Lecture is to be given on 'Religion generally or on some religious subject approved by the Trustees', and it has to be extended and published, with the condition that 'as the object of the Lectureship is to further the cause of religion, presumably by appealing to as wide a circle as possible of fairly well-educated and cultured people, a too technical treatment should be avoided'.

The reader must be prepared from the outset for a feature of this present study which he may feel is unsatisfactory and inconclusive, viz., those parts of it which deal with denominational statistics. The difficulty here is threefold: statistics are not always available; when they are available they do not refer to the same units, but rather to county associations, dioceses, rural deaneries, or an archdiocese, so that a basis of comparison is not always present, but most important is the fact that various religious bodies assess their numbers on different bases. The outstanding difference lies between the Roman Catholic church which produces imposing figures based on infant baptism, and on the other hand the Baptists, who count only adult baptisms. The Independents' and the Calvinistic Methodist statistics are based on those received into 'full membership', while the Church in Wales produces the figures of its communicants, and usually those who communicate at Easter. Not only is there no means of reconciling these different assessments, but underlying them is a different theological approach to figures; thus the statistical differences between Roman Catholicism and the Baptists reveal a fundamental difference in their conception of the nature of the Church. As there is at present no reconciliation of these theological extremes it follows that figures do not carry the same meaning. The historian must accept the situation and warn the reader.

It is both a duty and a pleasure to place on record my debt and my gratitude to those who have helped me in this work. To the librarians and staffs of the National Library of Wales, Aberystwyth, and of the public libraries at Merthyr Tydfil, Aberdare, Newport, and of the Monmouthshire County Library I offer my thanks. My debt to the librarian of the Cardiff Public Library and to the staff of the Reference Department of that library is particularly heavy and my thanks are correspondingly great. Mr. John Creasley, of the Dr. Williams' Library, London, has supplied me with transcripts of certain documents used in this book. There are others with whom I have had correspondence and conversations throughout the time taken for the preparation of this work: The Reverend R. Ivor Parry and Mr. W. W. Price, both of Aberdare; Mr. Walter Morgan, of the National Library of Wales, Aberystwyth, and the Reverend Islwyn Jenkins, of Cathays High School, Cardiff. All these friends have one thing in common: an intimate knowledge of the localities dealt with in this book, based largely on personal experience, which has enabled them to recall the flavour and characteristics of communities which have seen great changes in the past few generations; and this is an experience which I myself share. I offer them my thanks, as I do also to the D. J. James Pantyfedwen Trust for inviting me to give the Annual Lecture for 1962 and for making possible the publication of this book. Last, but by no means least, my acknowledgements and thanks are due to my wife for the patient work she has done in preparing my manuscript for publication. In view of such help and kindness from so many quarters it follows that all the mistakes that remain, both of judgement and presentation, must be my own.

No doubt this tale has more than one moral, but, for me, the most significant can best be expressed in the words of Evelyn Underhill: 'The spiritual impulse must not be allowed to become the centre of a group of specialized feelings, a devotional complex, in opposition to, or at least alienated from, the intellectual and economic life.' Every religious body, to some degree or other and in different ways, overlooked this principle in the work they did in the society of the early industrial revolution in south Wales.

E. T. DAVIES

Llangybi Rectory
Usk, Mon.
June 1964

CONTENTS

I

THE FORMATION OF A NEW SOCIETY

IN 1756, Richard Pococke, Bishop of Ossory, visited Pontypool, and described the industry carried on there by the Hanburys:

> I went five miles to Pontepool in a very romantic situation between the hills on a rivlet which falls into the Uske at Caerleon. Here Major Hanbury, father of the present possessor and of Sir Charles Hanbury Williams, ambassador in Russia, set on foot great iron works of many kinds, which occasioned a little compact town to be built here. The houses and buildings belonging to this manufacture are scatter'd, and extend for above a mile along the river. Here they work iron from the ore into several sorts of utensils. They make wire, nails, and plates of iron for tin. This latter secret was learned in Saxony, but immediately improved, for they did it by hammers, but Mr. Hanbury invented two iron rollers, which can be scrued together at any distance. They take a piece of red hot iron about four inches broad and five long and put it between the rollers, which roll it thinner; then they double it and heat it, and so continue doubling and putting it between the rollers until it is thin enough for the purpose; the thinnest they make is for tags for Manchester laces used by the ladies, 450 of them go into a box 5 inches and ¾ deep; these plates being soak'd in a composition of thin sal armoniac, and some other things are dip'd into fire, which, especially in the thin plates, incorporates with the iron. What they call double block tin is done with a finer tin, and is less apt to rust, as well as the very thin sort. Of a thicker kind of plate they make salvers and candlesticks and many other things which they japan. . . . They have a particular way of procuring iron ore; they make holes in the mountains for rivlets to run into, which bring down iron ore when there are floods, and when the waters fall they pick it up; sometime agoe the rock open'd in the bed of a river, and the

water took its course down the hole, but this carrying off the water, the country people fill'd up the hole, and the rivlet took its usual course. The manufacturers and the miners all over the country wear crimson flannel shirts and no other garments over them, which looks very well, and is proper to dry up the sweat of those who work at the fire, which it is said would otherwise prejudice their health.[1]

Such was a description of the only industrial centre at that time in the area soon to be transformed by the first phase of the industrial revolution which took place in north-east Glamorgan and north Monmouthshire. In 1756 the parish which became the centre of the iron industry, Merthyr Tydfil, had no better use for its iron-ore than 'the repair of the parochial road adjoining, when it became impassible for the farmer's car';[2] and in 1710 the number of baptisms in that parish was seven, rising to twenty-seven in 1750.[3] Hitherto in these parts there had been iron-smelting on a small scale, the mining of outcrop coal, and the conversion of timber into charcoal for the use of the older iron industry in south Glamorgan and Monmouthshire. The coal had been used locally, both for domestic purposes and for the burning of limestone, and also sold in the market centres of Brecon and Abergavenny. It was an area which had little contact with the south, and far more contact with the Usk and Neath valleys. It was served by parish roads, and lacked communication with the southern part of Glamorgan and Monmouthshire until the canals were built during the last decade of the eighteenth century. The canals were later succeeded by tramroads, but access by road to the new industrial areas was not possible until the construction of the Abergavenny–Merthyr road in 1812; indeed, it was easier to reach these communities by road from the north than from the south

[1] Richard Pococke, *The Travels through England* (Camden Society, 1888–9), ii. 209–10.

[2] Walter Davies, *General View of the agriculture and domestic economy of South Wales* (London, 1815) ii. 458.

[3] Ibid., ii. 462.

until well into the second half of the nineteenth century. The description of one particular parish in this area, that of Aberystruth, could well be applied to this whole district, from Hirwaun to Blaenavon, except that when this description was written, the Glamorgan end of this area was beginning to change.

Edmund Jones (The Old Prophet: Yr Hen Broffwyd), who ministered to the Independent congregations in the Ebbw Fawr and Ebbw Fach valleys, published a valuable account of the scene of his ministry. The parish of Aberystruth contained 'neither town nor village', and it had but 150 houses in all, 30 of them in the Ebbw Fawr valley, and the remainder in the Ebbw Fach valley; while the whole area contained a population of about 500. The land was poor and barren, and was of little value: a large meadow of 120 acres was let for £4 per annum. There were cornfields on the eastern sides of the lower slopes of the valleys where oats were grown. The parish was not self-supporting, for the poor had to buy their corn in Abergavenny, which was the market centre for this area. The chief source of income came from cattle and sheep, together with the sale of timber for iron-smelting in the adjoining parishes.[1] The houses were scattered here and there in the bottom and sides of the valleys. They were built of stone and timber, 'not of Earthen-sides and timber, as in some parts of Wales', and some were mean and others well built.[2] Others of these houses were delightfully situated. There was Tŷ yn y Llwyn where the Independents held their religious meetings. This was a 'delicate house, both the Kitchen and the Hall. A person delighting in Study, and being alone, need not desire a better place than the Hall, with its delightful Garden before it toward the South, the door of entrance to it from the Hall, and the delightful woody Mountainous prospects about it'.[3] The rainfall was heavy, the hillsides were thickly wooded, the rivers

[1] Edmund Jones, *A geographical, historical, and religious account of the parish of Aberystruth* (Trevecka, 1779), pp. 39–40. [2] Ibid., p. 50. [3] Ibid., p. 57.

provided good fishing, and the tops of the mountain good grouse-shooting.

With the exception of Merthyr Tydfil at the head of the Taff valley, and Blaenavon at the head of the Afon Lwyd valley, this description could well apply to that series of valleys which extends across north Glamorgan and north Monmouthshire: the valleys of the Cynon, Taff, Rhymney, Sirhowy, Ebbw Fawr, Ebbw Fach, Afon Lwyd, and, to extend the area into the contiguous part of Brecknockshire, the Clydach valley. These were the parts, because of the abundance of iron-ore, outcrop coal, water power, and supplies of limestone, which saw the establishment of the new iron industry between 1757 and 1800. After being the abode of Welsh upland farmers for centuries the process began which ultimately transformed this area into a number of thriving industrial communities. A new society was born with its own distinctive way of life, its own language and religious outlook, and practices which differed from the communities in the south of both counties. Glamorgan and Monmouthshire experienced a cleavage between two societies which grew up within their boundaries, a cleavage between the old, historic, rural communities and the new ironworks communities, and this cleavage, although narrowed by to-day, is still apparent between, for example, the Caldicot Moors and Nant-y-glo in Monmouthshire, and the Vale of Glamorgan and Dowlais in Glamorgan.

Up to the end of the eighteenth century, these new communities, with the exception of Blaenavon and Merthyr Tydfil, developed but slowly. It is fortunate for us that William Coxe, rector of Bemerton, who toured Monmouthshire in the autumn of 1798 and again in the following spring, unlike the majority of those who visited the county in those days and afterwards wrote a description of it, was as interested in the mountain regions of the north as he was in the lowlands, and so did not neglect to visit the scenes of the new iron industry. Since Edmund Jones had written in 1779 the iron industry had come to Nant-y-glo, and 'gave activity and life to this solitary region'.[1] When Coxe visited this area the works were closed, but he describes how 'a long range of stone cottages, built against the sides of a rock, was constructed for the workmen; each cottage consisted of two stories, which form two tenements, without communication; the entrance to the lower part is in front, and the doors of the upper tenements open to a ledge behind, which is cut in the rock, and runs the whole length of the range'.[2] The fullest description of all is reserved for Blaenavon which Coxe visited three times. The works here had the appearance of a small town, 'surrounded with heaps of ore, coal, and limestone, and enlivened with all the bustle and activity of an opulent and increasing establishment. The view of the buildings, which are constructed in the excavations of the rocks, is extremely picturesque, and heightened by the volumes of black smoke emitted by the fumes'.[3] The works, established in 1789, employed 350 men, and around them had grown a community of over 1,000 souls, which was the largest community at that time in north Monmouthshire. Coxe mentions the ironworks in the Ebbw Fawr valley, at a place to be known later as Ebbw Vale, but then known as Pen-y-cae, after a local farm which was the site of the earliest iron furnace. His excursion through the Sirhowy valley was made within a year or so of the beginning of the iron industry in Tredegar; and Coxe did not visit the Rhymney valley where the first iron furnace was worked in 1800.

Had our clerical traveller crossed the Rhymney river and visited Glamorgan he would have had a very different scene to describe in the parish of Merthyr Tydfil, for since 1759 the four great iron works of Dowlais, Cyfarthfa, Plymouth and Penydarren had been established and were maintaining a community of 7,705 by 1801. Had Coxe crossed from the Taff valley to the head of the Cynon valley he would have

[1] William Coxe, *A historical tour of Monmouthshire* (London, 1801), p. 250.
[2] Ibid., p. 251.
[3] Ibid., p. 227.

found a well-established iron industry in Hirwaun, but lower down the valley the Abernant and Gadlys works were yet to be opened; and, in any case, the prosperity of Aberdare was to be based more on the coal than on the iron industry. The population of this area, comprising the old parish of Aberdare, was 1,486 in 1801.

With the exception of Merthyr Tydfil, which grew rapidly, these industrial areas developed slowly at first, and it should not be overlooked that they were never merged into one industrial mass, but preserved their distinctions, separated as they were from each other by mountains which gave them for a long time to come a semi-rural character which they have not completely lost to this day, and which probably modified the worst rigours of the early industrial revolution. It was possible to write in 1809, with reference to the upper Afon Lwyd and Ebbw Fach valleys: 'In this unfrequented district, which was formerly called the wilds of Monmouthshire, only noticed for the cover it afforded for game, and the sport it furnished for the gentry for grouse shooting, and amid scenes, not inferior to the celebrated ones of the Swiss Alps, stands the village of Aberystwith'[1] [Aberystruth]. In the same year Pontypool had 'only two principal streets, yet is a large straggling place, containing many neat houses and numerous shops which give it an air of thriving prosperity; but the buildings being annoyed with the smoke of the adjoining forges, put on a dusky appearance'.[2] Unlike all other parts of the old ironworks area, Pontypool had endured the smoke from its forges since the second half of the sixteenth century.

This, then, was the region, from Hirwaun to Blaenavon in the north, and south to Pontypool, which saw an unprecedented and unparalleled increase in population during the first half of the nineteenth century. The population of Monmouthshire rose from 45,568 in 1801 to 157,418 in 1851, a

[1] J. Evans and John Britton, *A typographical and historical description of the County of Monmouth* (London, 1809), p. 101.

[2] Ibid., p. 106.

rise of 245 per cent. This figure was largely due to the increase in the new industrial areas of the west and north, and those of the north were part of the Abergavenny Union for census purposes. This Union was divided into sub-districts: Llanarth, Llanvihangel, Abergavenny, Blaenavon, Aberystruth, Tredegar, Rock and Bedwellty, and it increased in population from 10,513 in 1801 to 59,229 in 1851, an increase of 463 per cent. But it is an analysis of the sub-districts which reveals what was taking place in the valleys of north Monmouthshire in those days, for while the Abergavenny sub-district increased by 112 per cent., the Llanvihangel sub-district by 21 per cent., and the Llanarth sub-district by 39 per cent. in this period, the Blaenavon sub-district increased its population from 1,469 in 1801 to 5,855 in 1851, an increase of 298 per cent.; Aberystruth sub-district from 805 to 14,383, an increase of 1,687 per cent.; Tredegar sub-district from 1,132 to 24,544 an increase of 2,067 per cent., and the Rock and Bedwellty sub-district went up in population from 302 in 1801 to 2,639 in 1851, thus showing an increase of 773 per cent. Thus the greatest increases in the Monmouthshire valleys were in the Aberystruth [Blaina] and Tredegar districts. To these figures must be added the Pontypool sub-district of the Pontypool Registration Union, whose population increased by about 700 per cent. in the first fifty years of the last century, from 2,570 in 1801 to 20,614 in 1851.

The Newport Registration Union consisted of the sub-districts of Caerleon, Newport, St. Woolos and Mynyddislwyn, and showed an increase of population during the same period of 299 per cent., from 10,896 in 1801 to 43,472 in 1851. But the Newport sub-district showed an increase of 1,325 per cent. in the same period, from 1,423 to 20,279.

These increases were not uniform. The greatest decennial increase was that of 249 per cent. in the Tredegar sub-district between 1801 and 1811. This rate dropped to 36 per cent. and 57 per cent. in the two successive periods, and then went up to 134 per cent. between 1831–41, to drop to a 21 per cent. increase in the following ten years. Generally speaking, the two periods of greatest increase throughout the industrial areas of Monmouthshire were the decades 1801–11 and 1831–41, the two exceptions to this rule being the Rock and Bedwellty sub-district which saw its greatest decennial increase (of 111 per cent.) between 1821 and 1831, and likewise the Pontypool sub-district with an increase of 105 per cent. during the same period.

If this study were primarily concerned with the economic aspect of this new society it could be shown that these figures and fluctuations were by no means fortuitous, but are closely connected with the establishment, expansion and contraction of the iron industry. Apart from the Newport Union the rate of growth of population in the industrial areas up to 1851 showed a close correlation with the opening and closing of iron furnaces.

The other area with which we are concerned in this study, the industrial area of north-east Glamorgan, was covered by the Merthyr Tydfil Registration Union, subdivided into Merthyr Tydfil Upper, Merthyr Tydfil Lower, Aberdare and Gelli-gaer. The first two divisions made up the old parish of Merthyr Tydfil, and the third was conterminous with the old parish of Aberdare, and it is with these units only that we are now concerned. The parish of Merthyr Tydfil increased in population from 7,705 in 1801 to 46,378 fifty years later, an increase of a little over 500 per cent.; while the parish of Aberdare showed an increase of over 900 per cent. within the same period, viz., from 1,486 to 14,999. It is obvious that the parish of Merthyr Tydfil had grown rapidly in population before 1801, and the increase continued until 1821, then slowed down between 1821 and 1831, picked up again in the next ten years, and showed an appreciable decrease in growth from 1841 to 1851. Aberdare's population showed a net drop in the ten years following 1811, and its great increase took place between 1841 and 1851, a period which saw the beginnings of large-scale coal-mining in the lower Cynon valley.

When it is recalled that Edmund Jones had estimated the population of the Ebbw Fawr and Ebbw Fach valleys as 500 in 1779, it is clear that this tremendous increase in the population at the heads of these valleys by 1851 was caused largely by immigration into these parts. These were the areas later described by Dr. Thomas Jones, himself a notable product of this new industrial society, as 'the magnetic south into which multitudes of men, women and children had been drawn from North and Mid Wales, and from the West of England. They came from distant rural areas on foot and in carts; they came as Christians and as pagans, thrifty and profligate, clean and dirty; and gradually sorted themselves in their new surroundings according to tradition and habit'.[1]

The census of 1851 gives us an idea of the extent to which this new society was being formed largely by immigrants. It showed that in Monmouthshire there were 12,245 people who had been born in an English county,[2] and 25,866 people who had been born in a Welsh county. Of the latter, 18,517 were to be found in the Abergavenny Registration Union which, it will be remembered, extended across north Monmouthshire to the borders of Glamorgan, 2,773 were found in the Pontypool Registration Union, and 4,516 in the Newport Union. Likewise, most of the English immigrants settled in Newport and the new industrial areas. The greater part of the Welsh immigrants came from Glamorgan, Brecknockshire, Carmarthenshire, Cardiganshire and Pembrokeshire, in that order; while most of the English immigrants came from Gloucestershire, Somerset and Herefordshire. When it is remembered that these figures referred only to first-generation immigrants, and did not include the Monmouthshire-born children of earlier immigrants, it is clear that the new industrial areas of Monmouthshire, the ironworks districts, formed a new society, not only in the sense that the inhabitants

[1] Thomas Jones, *Rhymney Memories* (Newtown, 1938), p. 5.

[2] This figure excludes the Gloucestershire parishes contained in the Chepstow Registration Union, together with the Herefordshire parishes contained in the Abergavenny and Monmouth Registration Unions.

adopted, or were forced to adopt, a way of life not hitherto known in the county, but also in the sense that they were people whose roots and traditions lay elsewhere than in their adopted county. Together with the adjoining parts of Glamorgan these areas were in a real sense the 'frontier' of Wales in the nineteenth century, and it is probable that some of the characteristics of their religion arose from this fact.

The same factor of immigration had been at work in Merthyr Tydfil and Aberdare, except that there the overwhelming majority of the newcomers were Welsh, from Glamorgan itself, Carmarthenshire, Brecknockshire and Pembrokeshire. To the end of the nineteenth century and beyond a new Welsh society arose in an area that for centuries had been sparsely populated, and the same was true, but not to the same extent, of the Monmouthshire industrial society. It, too, was largely Welsh in speech and character, but it was to change earlier than the contiguous areas of Glamorgan. We shall see later that the domination of these parts by Welsh Nonconformity was conclusive evidence of the widespread use of the Welsh language in north Monmouthshire for the better part of the last century. It was not until the last decade of that century that a language census was taken which will be referred to later, but we are fortunate in having reliable information about the use of the Welsh language in the Pontypool–Blaenavon district in 1840. Investigation showed that 51 per cent. of the inhabitants of Trevethin parish spoke Welsh,[1] the majority of these being bilingual, while in Blaenavon, only six miles away but less exposed to rural Monmouthshire which was now becoming almost entirely English in speech, the proportion of Welsh-speaking inhabitants was 61 per cent. Although the decline of the language was greatly to affect Nonconformity in industrial Monmouthshire later, it can be safely assumed that the communities which grew up at the heads of the valleys were

[1] G. S. Kenrick, *The population of Pontypool and the parish of Trevethin* (London, 1840), p. 6.

preponderatingly Welsh-speaking in 1851. A far greater number of Monmouthshire people spoke Welsh in the nineteenth century than ever before.

To conclude: the second half of the eighteenth century saw the establishment of new iron industries in an area extending from Hirwaun in Glamorgan to Clydach in Brecknockshire, and these industries formed the economic basis of a society largely peopled by immigrants, intensely Welsh in speech in the Glamorgan sector of this area, essentially Welsh in speech and sentiment in north Monmouthshire, but by 1840 showing signs of an anglicizing influence as this society came into contact with rural Monmouthshire in the Pontypool area. The purpose of this book is to examine the place and fortunes of religion in this society, to describe the social conditions within which the various religious bodies worked, and to analyse the social influences which affected the fluctuations of belief and practice in these parts.

Although Monmouthshire was the home of Welsh Protestant Nonconformity, religion had sunk to a low level in the county by the end of the eighteenth century, and in assessing the strength of Nonconformity at that time the same difficulty confronts us as throughout the nineteenth century in the interpretation of Nonconformist statistics. In March 1773 it was stated that there were 5,000 Nonconformists in Monmouthshire distributed among thirteen churches.[1] This convenient round number, itself the aggregate of thirteen other convenient round numbers, gives rise to suspicion. The purpose of this enumeration was to support a grant to Nonconformist ministers from parliament, the famous *Regium Donum*; and there is certainly a wide disparity between the figures quoted in this document and those given for the same churches by denominational historians. Examples of

[1] *An Account received March 1773 of the Ministers and Numbers of auditors that usually attend at the several Dissenting Meeting Houses in Monmouthshire* (Josiah Thompson MS.).

three historic Nonconformist churches, namely Llanfaches, Pen-maen and Llanwenarth, will show wide discrepancies in figures. The Llanfaches congregation (the original Nonconformist congregation in Wales) worshipped in 1773 in Carw Hill, in the parish of St. Bride's, Netherwent, and they shared a pastor with Mill Street, the oldest Nonconformist congregation in Newport. The figures given for this joint church ('Newport & Carw Hill') in the 1773 document is 400. Yet the denominational historians have said that the cause at Carw Hill had sunk so low by the end of the eighteenth century that there was only one communicant left,[1] and there were 106 members in Mill Street in 1806 when it was the only Nonconformist church in a growing town.[2] Likewise with the Independent cause in Pen-maen, in the parish of Mynyddislwyn: 400 is given as the number in the 1773 document, but the denominational historians tell us that the membership was 102 in 1772.[3] Edmund Jones has also left testimony to the state of affairs in the old parish of Aberystruth where there were three places of worship, the parish church, the Baptist chapel at Blaenau Gwent, and the Independents' Meeting-house in Tŷ yn y Llwyn, an offshoot of Pen-maen. He says that the number of communicants among the dissenters, and especially the Independents, 'is much less than it hath been'. The Baptists were more numerous; and Jones estimated that, of a population of 500, there were 80 professors of religion, and could not resist adding: 'and among these not unlikely some hypocrites, tho' I hope not very many.'[4]

The last example of great disparity in statistics concerns the historic Baptist church at Llanwenarth. The numbers were returned as 600 in 1773, but in 1795 they were given as 125.[5]

These great differences in numbers present a difficulty which we shall encounter in a more acute form later. There

[1] T. Rees and J. Thomas, *Hanes Eglwysi Annibynol Cymru* (Liverpool, 1871–5, 1891), i. 8. [2] Ibid., i. 57. [3] Ibid., i. 20. [4] Edmund Jones, op. cit., p. 109.
[5] Joshua Thomas, *Hanes y Bedyddwyr ymhlith y Cymry* (ed. Benjamin Davies, Pontypridd, 1885), p. 418.

is no suggestion of dishonesty or collusion: throughout this study the problem of assessing the strength of Nonconformity depends on whether the members, or communicants only, are enumerated, or whether the 'auditors' of 1773 and the 'hearers' (*y gwrandawyr*) or 'adherents' of the nineteenth century are counted in addition. Closer attention will be paid later to this class on the perimeter of Welsh Nonconformity, but it is significant that the problem should have arisen in the eighteenth century. Even if the 'auditors' of 1773 are admitted, there would seem to have been no great increase in Welsh Nonconformity in its home county during the eighteenth century. A list of 1715 (again compiled for the same purpose as that of 1773) gives the total number as 2,991.[1] This is a more detailed list than that of 1773, and from the details given it is natural to presume that only communicants are included in the enumeration. If this supposition is correct, it is probable that Nonconformity actually lost ground in Monmouthshire from 1700 to 1800.

Even in the first two decades of the nineteenth century when the population was increasing at an unprecedented rate, the progress of Nonconformity was slow. The Baptists were to become the most powerful Nonconformist denomination in the new industrial areas, but their advance was not rapid. In 1791 the Baptist churches in Glamorgan east of Aberavon, and those in Monmouthshire and the adjoining areas of Brecknockshire, formed the 'Association of the South East' (*Cymmanfa Dde-Ddwyreiniol*),[2] an area which included the newly developing ironworks' industry. Over a period from 1791 to 1828 there was a net increase in the membership of the Association of 8,977, an average annual increase of 225. Growth from 1791 to 1803 was slow; in 1801 there was an actual decrease of 54 in membership, and an increase of

[1] Thomas Rees, *History of Protestant Nonconformity in Wales* (2nd ed., London, 1883), pp. 259–60.

[2] William Jones, *Hanes y Bedyddwyr Neillduol yng Nghymru, o'i dechreuad hyd y flwyddyn 1790, yn nghyda pharhad o hanes y Gymmanfa Dde-Ddwyreiniol o'r flwyddyn 1790 hyd 1831* (Caerdydd, 1831), p. 32.

only three in the following year. It was in 1816 that numbers began to grow more rapidly: 285, 338, 419, in the years 1816, 1817, and 1819 respectively, to be followed by greater increases in the period 1827–31 which were years of religious revivals in the industrial areas. By 1831 this Association of the South East consisted of 83 churches,[1] and in the following year the 'Monmouthshire Baptist Association' was formed with 30 churches and 13 branches,[2] but the *Circular Letter* of that year does not indicate the membership except to say that there had been a decrease of 33 during the year. It was not until the Monmouthshire Baptist Association met in Llanwenarth in 1840 that the membership was given as 4,926.[3]

In the year before the Association met at Llanwenarth a Baptist historian had published a history of his denomination in South Wales,[4] and this gives us valuable information about Welsh Nonconformity's most powerful denomination in these parts at that time. There were 34 Baptist churches in Monmouthshire,[5] 20 of these being Welsh, and the remainder English. The account of membership is in some cases an approximation, and the total amounted to between 4,000 and 4,100, which might be increased to 4,600 to cover those churches whose membership is not given.[6] As might have been expected, it was those churches in the industrial areas which had the highest membership: Tredegar, 350,[7] Pen-y-cae [Ebbw Vale], 330,[8] Rhymney and Nant-y-glo, each with 200 members,[9] Merthyr Tydfil, 300,[10] Dowlais, 254,[11] and Aberdare, 114.[12] But while the Baptists had strong churches in this industrial belt, there were also a large number of small causes which could not have kept their doors

[1] Ibid., pp. 65–66. [2] *Llythyrau Cymmanfa Mynwy* (Beulah, 1832).

[3] *Llythyrau Cymmanfa Mynwy* (Llanwenarth, 1840).

[4] David Jones, *Hanes y Bedyddwyr yn Neheubarth Cymru* (Carmarthen, 1839).

[5] This number did not include the branches (*y canghennau*).

[6] No membership figures are given for the last nine churches dealt with by Jones, but as these were all in rural Monmouthshire an addition of 500 errs on the side of generosity. [7] David Jones, op. cit., p. 739.

[8] Ibid., p. 742. [9] Ibid., pp. 744, 747.

[10] Ibid., p. 585. [11] Ibid., p. 595. [12] Ibid., p. 598.

open unless they had depended on what was virtually a part-time ministry. Welsh Nonconformity was establishing a hold on north Monmouthshire and north-east Glamorgan, but to enumerate the number of chapels is not in itself a sufficient guide to the strength of any particular denomination. When Benjamin Heath Malkin visited Merthyr Tydfil in 1803, and again in 1806, what he saw might suggest that everyone in the town attended a place of worship: 'There are about ten dissenting and meeting-houses, and their denominations are thus divided: three baptists, two presbyterians [unitarians], two independents, two in the connection of Wesley, and one, if not two, in that of Whitfield'[1] [i.e. Calvinistic Methodists]. This sounds impressive, but nearly forty years later two of the Baptist churches had only 50 and 86 members respectively.[2]

The spread of Nonconformity can be traced by examining the records of the registration of 'Dissenters' Meeting Houses' between 1750 and 1850 in the Merthyr Tydfil–Aberdare area and throughout Monmouthshire:

	1750–1800	1801–10	1811–20	1821–30	1831–40	1841–50
Merthyr Tydfil	3	10	5	2	5	5
Aberdare	—	4	2	2	2	4
Monmouthshire	23	54	139	94	53	48

If we take the three main Welsh Nonconformist denominations, the picture is as follows:

	Baptist	Independents	Calvinistic Methodist
Merthyr Tydfil	12	7	6
Aberdare	5	4	1
Monmouthshire	137	98	29[3]

There are two observations to be made on these figures: it is unlikely that all applications for registration have been preserved, and, what is of greater importance, many of

[1] Benjamin Heath Malkin, *The scenery, antiquities, and biography of South Wales* (London, 1809), i. 174.

[2] David Jones, op. cit., pp. 590, 594.

[3] *Schedule of the Church in Wales Records, Diocese of Llandaff*, iv. 130–77.

them were duplicated. This was especially true of the earlier registrations which were issued for dwelling-houses, and later the dwelling-house would be exchanged for a larger room, and, ultimately, for the first chapel to be built by that particular congregation. In many cases two, and possibly more, registrations would be applied for by the same congregation.

But events were to show that this new industrial society was strongly Welsh Nonconformist in tone, even though the degree of allegiance on the part of thousands was very tenuous. It has been shown that the state of Nonconformity at the beginning of the nineteenth century was not promising, but its later growth was due to successive generations of immigrants who came to work in the old ironworks districts and so created a Welsh Nonconformist society. The early beginnings of a new 'cause' cannot be better described than by quoting the opening paragraph of the history of a Nonconformist church in Merthyr Tydfil:

> Tua y flwyddyn 1794, yr oedd y gweithfeydd haearn yn Merthyr yn cyflym gynyddu, a'r bobl o bob cwr o'r wlad yn dyfod i'r lle, ac yn eu plith y personau canlynol, y rhai a nodwn yn ol trefn yr hen bobl: O'r Groeswen: Lewis Foster a Chatws ei wraig, Gabriel ei brawd, a Jack Salathiel. O'r Defynog: David Nicholas Thomas a Letice ei wraig. O Penmain: Shenkin Andrew a Barbara ei wraig. O'r Mynyddbach: Thomas Rees. Wedi i'r brodyr a chwiorydd ddyfod i'r lle, yr oedd eisiau byw yn grefyddol; mae y dyn duwiol, pa le bynag y bydd efe, yn myned a'i grefydd gydag ef.[1]

These words relate how Lewis Foster and Catws, his wife, Gabriel, her brother, and Jack Salathiel, all from Groeswen, together with David Nicholas Thomas and his wife, Lettice, from Defynnog, Jenkin Andrew and Barbara, his wife, from Pen-maen, and Thomas Rees, from Mynyddbach, met in Merthyr Tydfil in 1794 and desired to practise their religion. The author then went on to say that, rather than join an already existing Independent church in the town, they gathered

[1] R. Griffiths, *Hanes Eglwys Crist yn Zoar, Merthyr er ei dechreuad yn y 'Long Room' tu cefn i'r Crown Inn, yn y flwyddyn 1794, hyd yn bresenol* (Merthyr Tydfil, 1869), p. 5.

a separate congregation, consisting of nine members, in the Long Room of the Crown Inn; and this was the beginning of Zoar church. This account, with appropriate changes in details, could serve as the opening paragraph of the history of scores of Welsh Nonconformist churches in the new industrial communities; and it illustrates both the strength and weakness of Nonconformity at that time: lay initiative on the one hand, and on the other hand that lack of central control which led to the formation of too many churches and the building of too many chapels. Successive immigrants would move into the district, join the small congregations, and in due time a small chapel would be built to replace the cottage or Long Room where they had hitherto worshipped. The early Calvinistic Methodists in Ebbw Vale worshipped in a shed placed at their disposal by Messrs. Harford, the ironmasters: the first chapel was built in 1825 and was known as 'The Old Forge Chapel', and the first Calvinistic Methodist Association (*Sasiwn*) to meet in Ebbw Vale held its meetings in a disused brickyard.[1] This church was founded by people who came to Ebbw Vale from the Blaenannerch–Aber-porth district of Cardiganshire, and its growth was due largely to successive immigrations into the town from the same district.[2] Similarly, Wesleyan Methodism was greatly strengthened in the Rhymney area by an influx of iron-ore miners from the Llanidloes–Llangurig area.[3] Welsh Nonconformity, given an impetus by the formation of a new denomination, the Calvinistic Methodists, in 1811, was created in rural Wales and was brought to the scenes of the industrial revolution by tens of thousands of men and women escaping from conditions then prevalent in the Welsh countryside. It persisted in its new home as long as immigration continued and as long as the newcomers retained their native tongue.

[1] Evan Price, *The history of Penuel Calvinistic Methodist Church, Ebbw Vale* (Wrexham, 1925), pp. 22–25. [2] Ibid., p. 22.

[3] Llewelyn Morgan, *Hanes Wesleyaeth Cymreig yng nghylchdaith Tredegar* (Monmouth, 1914), p. 41.

This Nonconformity was essentially working-class in character as long as these industrial communities were dependent upon the iron industry. The Welsh immigrants were largely of peasant stock and could bring only unskilled labour to these new industries. But more important was the fact that the higher positions in the iron industry were occupied by Englishmen, and the industry itself was built by Englishmen and English capital. Throughout the industrial belt of north Monmouthshire only four Welsh names appear in the early history of these iron works: Walter Watkins, of the Llangrwyney Forge, near Crickhowell, who was one of the founders of Ebbw Vale in 1786, and David Evans, Thomas Williams and John Ambrose, who with Richard Cunningham founded the Union Iron Works in Rhymney in 1800. It is significant that all four names soon disappeared from the scene, being unable to hold their ground in competition with the English capitalists. Consequently, the early Welsh Nonconformists who came to work in these parts occupied the more lowly positions in the iron industry. It should also be noted that they were working for masters who were, at least nominally, Anglican in religion. The Crawshays of Dowlais, the Baileys of Nant-y-glo, the Kendalls of Beaufort, and Hills and Hopkins of Blaenavon, were Anglican, as were many other ironmasters. The outstanding exceptions were the Guests of Dowlais, who were Methodists, and the Harfords of Ebbw Vale, who were Quakers.[1] It is certain that, in this environment, and beyond the middle of the century, Welsh Nonconformity in these parts was essentially working-class in character. We shall see later that the change from the iron industry to the deep-coal-mining industry had a greater effect on the chapels than is generally realized.

[1] The only place where the Nonconformists were able to benefit by the fact of ownership in the old iron industry was Abercarn where Nonconformists had been actively engaged in that industry during the second half of the eighteenth century. This industry passed into the hands of Benjamin Hall (later Lord Llanover), who was far more sympathetic to Welsh Nonconformists than he was to his fellow Anglicans.

Contemporary observers emphasized the working-class character of the communities in which Welsh Nonconformity flourished. In general terms this truth was expressed by R. R. W. Lingen, one of the education commissioners of 1847, when he described the social composition of Merthyr Tydfil and Dowlais: 'It contains no middle class. . . . For although the absence of the truck-system from my district is allowing the growth of shopkeepers, yet these are only an offshoot. The works themselves contain no middle class. There are the proprietors and their agents of administration on the one hand, the mass of operatives on the other. The elimination of a middle class is rendered more complete when, to the economical causes tending to reproduce it, is superadded the separation of language.'[1] This working-class character and lack of middle-class leadership showed itself in Nonconformist institutions, and especially in the Sunday-school. In the spring of 1840, Seymour Tremenheere visited the industrial area between Merthyr Tydfil and Pontypool as representative of the newly established Committee of the Privy Council on Education. Interest in these areas had been aroused by the Chartist attack on Newport on the preceding 4 November, and although Tremenheere was instructed to inquire into the educational provisions of the area, including the Sunday-schools, he was also to report to the Lords of the Council how it had been possible for the Chartists to assemble in such secrecy on the hills of Monmouthshire, unknown to the magistrates.[2]

Tremenheere reported that middle-class leadership was beginning to make itself felt in those areas where truck-shops did not exist, or did not exercise a monopoly; and where this class existed, 'the scholars have the benefit of a more serviceable instruction' in the Sunday-schools. But where

[1] *Reports of the Commissioners of Inquiry into the state of education in Wales* (London, 1847), i. 21.

[2] A general account of Tremenheere's report, and one which emphasizes the educational aspect of it, can be read in E. T. Davies, *Monmouthshire schools and education to 1870* (Newport, 1957), pp. 79–81.

these schools were conducted entirely by labouring men, they confessed their inability to do justice to the work they undertook, yet they persevered. When asked how they were able to give instruction in their Sunday-schools, the general answer was that it did not extend far beyond teaching to read: 'We can read, and we can teach others; but for the understanding, we do come far short.' In another interview it was said: 'We teachers do meet together at times, and we do endeavour to expound the Scriptures the one to the other, so far as we do understand them.'[1] Tremenheere went on to emphasize the very important fact that the Sunday-schools of Dissent were attended by large numbers of adults as well as by children. 'It was gratifying to observe so many of the former, both male and female, intermingled with the children, and receiving instruction in classes from individuals much junior to themselves.'[2]

Jelinger C. Symons, who conducted the inquiry into the state of education in Monmouthshire in 1847, also gave high praise to the work of Nonconformist Sunday-schools, saying that they were superior to the Church Sunday-schools in every respect as means of religious instruction. The laity were far more active in them than were the Church laity in their schools. 'In 120 Dissenting Sunday-schools there were 15·3 teachers to every 100 scholars; in 30 Church Sunday-schools there were only 8·9 teachers to every 100 scholars.' The clergy in the industrial parishes were very active, 'but the Church laity do very little for the religious education of the poor—with a few bright exceptions, next to nothing.'[3] R. R. W. Lingen, who conducted the 1847 inquiry in Carmarthenshire, Glamorgan and Pembrokeshire, reported on Sunday-schools in those areas in terms which could be applied to these institutions elsewhere, emphasizing not only the value of the instruction given, but their social importance.

[1] *Annual Report and Minutes of the Committee of Council on Education* (London, 1840), p. 169.

[2] Ibid., p. 170.

[3] *Reports of the Commissioners of Inquiry into the state of education in Wales*, ii. 290.

'The universality of these schools, and the large proportion of persons attending them who take part in their government, have very generally familiarized the people with some of the more ordinary terms and methods of organization, such as *committee*, *secretary*, and so forth'; and these schools

satisfy the gregarious sociability which animates the Welsh toward each other. They present the charms of office to those who, on all other occasions, are subject; and of distinction to all those who have no other chance of distinguishing themselves. The topics current in them are those of the most general interest; and are treated in a mode partly didactic, partly polemical, partly rhetorical, the most universally approached. Finally, every man, woman, and child feels comfortably at home in them. It is all among neighbours and equals. Whatever ignorance is shown here, whatever mistakes are made, whatever strange speculations are started, there are no superiors to smile and open their eyes. . . . Whatever Sunday-schools may be as places of instruction, they are real fields of mental activity.[1] The Welsh working-man rouses himself for them. Sunday is to him more than a day of bodily rest and devotion. It is his best chance, all the week through, of showing himself in his own character. He marks his sense of it by a suit of clothes regarded with a feeling hardly less sabbatical than the day itself. I do not remember to have seen an adult in rags in a single Sunday-school throughout the present district. They always seemed to me better dressed on Sundays than the same classes in England.[2]

In accounting for the success of Welsh Nonconformity in these parts a high place must be given to the institution of the Sunday-school, not only, and possibly not primarily, for the quality of the instruction given, but for the opportunity it afforded to the rank and file of the laity to exercise gifts which could not find expression elsewhere, and for creating

[1] On 21 March 1847 one of the Commissioners of Inquiry visited the Calvinistic Methodist Sunday-school in Newport where he listened to an adult class discussing 'where the seat of the soul is'. Some thought it lay in the blood, others in the brain, and others in the heart. (Ibid., ii. 309.)

[2] Ibid., i. 6.

a form of organization which expressed the democratic character of these new industrial communities. These opportunities were not confined to the Sunday-school, for the same principle was at work in the diaconate of these chapels and also in the prominent place given to lay-preaching in those days. Dr. Thomas Rees wrote to the *Nonconformist* on 26 December 1866: 'The services of lay preachers in Wales are not confined to preaching-rooms and small Congregations. They are frequently invited to occupy the pulpits of the most respectable congregations while the ministers are engaged at the out-stations or elsewhere. No minister in the Principality would hesitate to engage a pious tradesman, mechanic, or labourer, who could talk common sense in the shape of a sermon, to supply his pulpit in his absence.'[1]

It is little wonder that Jelinger C. Symons should have said in 1847: 'Dissent has a firm hold on the affections of the people' in his report on the state of education in Monmouthshire.[2]

The first half of the nineteenth century saw the triumph of Welsh Nonconformity in north Monmouthshire and north-east Glamorgan. This was its heroic age in these parts, made possible by the self-sacrifice of tens of thousands of working-class people. The history of the Established Church, however, was very different for the greater part of this period, and Nonconformity benefited, not only from its own strength, but also from the weakness of the Church up to 1850.

As the failure of the Church in the industrialized part of the old diocese of Llandaff arose out of the nature of the ecclesiastical Establishment, it is necessary to examine the administrative and economic structure over which the local Church had no control and was powerless to reform. In common with all the other dioceses in the Church in those days, the diocese of Llandaff had no income of its own, no central fund which could be applied to diocesan purposes.

[1] T. Rees, *Miscellaneous Papers on subjects relating to Wales* (London, 1867), p. 28.

[2] *Reports of the Commissioners of Inquiry into the state of education in Wales,* ii. 290.

It was a poor diocese which had suffered greatly in the pre-Reformation period and after, and what income it had was vested in parishes and in the Llandaff Chapter; and up to 1836, until parliament began an administrative reform of the Church of England which was, in some respects, centuries overdue, these incomes could not be applied to other purposes however urgent; and, in any case, locally there was nothing to spare. Even after 1836, when the Ecclesiastical Commissioners were appointed with wide powers over the finances of the Church, so far from diverting moneys to other purposes in the diocese, they had to augment the local finances very considerably from the Common Fund.

The bishopric, like the diocese, was the poorest in the Church, and this made it necessary for all post-Restoration bishops of Llandaff to hold other appointments as well, usually an English deanery or a canonry of Christ Church. Richard Watson (1782–1813)[1] was a noted pluralist, but his successors, Edward Marsh (1813–16), William Van Mildert (1816–26), Charles Richard Sumner (1826–7), and Edward Copleston (1828–49) all held other appointments, the last three in turn being deans of St. Paul's. This was a serious matter for the diocese, especially during the episcopate of Copleston.

In addition to the financial exigencies which made these men virtually part-time diocesans, their rights of patronage were very slight. Throughout the whole of their diocese they had only four livings in their gift: Basaleg, Mynyddislwyn, Bedwellty and Bedwas, together with the chapelries attached; and of these only the second and third were in industrial areas during the time covered by this study. The parish of Merthyr Tydfil was in the gift of the Marquess of Bute (and in that of his trustees after he became a Roman Catholic), while Aberdare was attached as a chapelry to Llantrisant, whose patron in the Middle Ages was the abbot of Tewkesbury, and, after the dissolution of the abbey, the dean and

[1] In every case these are the years of the episcopate.

chapter of Gloucester. The other parishes which saw the spread of industrialism and the consequent great growth in population were likewise not in the gift of the bishop of the diocese: the earl of Abergavenny was the patron of Aberystruth and Llanhiledd, the ironmaster Thomas Hill was patron of Blaenavon as a 'donative chapel', and the dean and chapter of Llandaff had the gift of Trevethin, in which Pontypool was situated.

But the question of patronage was by no means the only, or the most serious, problem affecting these parishes which underwent such a transformation in the industrial revolution. Up to 1819, with the exception of Blaenavon, this area, with a rapidly increasing population, was divided into large upland parishes which had been formed in the Middle Ages, and, to make matters worse, they were served in all cases, except in Aberdare and Merthyr Tydfil, by churches built on the tops of the mountains: Bedwellty, Trevethin, Aberystruth, Mynyddislwyn, and Llanhiledd; while the new communities were settling in the beds of the valleys, being ministered to by the scores of Nonconformist chapels which were being built. This situation could be still more complicated, as for example in the case of Ebbw Vale, where an important township grew where four parishes met: Bedwellty and Aberystruth in Monmouthshire and the diocese of Llandaff, and Llangattock and Llangynidr in Brecknockshire and the diocese of St. David's. The old parish of Bedwellty was a particularly awkward case: to the west it followed the Rhymney river, while to the east it followed the Ebbw Fawr, thus enclosing the upper Sirhowy valley and the western slopes of the Ebbw Fawr valley. These boundaries were to prove very unmanageable when the provision of new churches and the formation of new parishes came to be tackled.

It need hardly be said that these mountain parishes had small incomes. Their tithe value in the pre-Reformation period was low, and the tithe commutation awards did not make them desirable places financially, even with grants from the Governors of the Corporation of Queen Anne's Bounty. Many of them were impropriated parishes, and so did not enjoy their full ecclesiastical income. One exception, the rectory of Merthyr Tydfil, was worth £884 in 1835;[1] Aberdare as a 'perpetual curacy' was worth £108 per annum; Mynyddislwyn and Bedwellty, two of the bishop's churches, were worth respectively £117 and £168 in 1835.[2] Aberystruth and Llanhiledd were rectories with incomes respectively of £265 and £112. Trevethin with Mamhilad and Llanover was worth £591, and supported three curates and an absentee incumbent; and Blaenavon, then virtually independent of the ancient parish of Llanover, was valued at £78 per annum.[3] Such sums did not make it feasible to divide these large parishes into many smaller units, each to share in what was already a small income. If the principle of supplying the parson with a 'freehold' and an assured income in the new parish was to continue, such a provision was quite beyond the resources of the diocese. Tribute has already been paid to those Nonconformists who sacrificed to build their chapels and maintain their ministers (albeit very shabbily indeed for a long time), yet it must be emphasized that the building of a new church presupposed, in most cases, the establishment of a new ecclesiastical district with an assured income. The pastoral work of the Church was, and is, based on the parish, and not on a congregation.

It is no exaggeration to say that the old diocese of Llandaff was confronted with a problem in the industrial parishes without parallel in the Established Church in those days, and was less able to solve it than was the case in any other diocese. The essence of the problem was the provision of places of worship. Thousands of people moved into the industrial valleys annually only to find that the Church had made no provision for worship in their immediate locality,

[1] *Report of the commissioners appointed by His Majesty to inquire into the ecclesiastical revenues of England and Wales* (London, 1835), p. 626.

[2] Ibid., pp. 626, 614.

[3] Ibid. ii. 614–15, 622–3.

and consequently they joined, or at least attended, the nearest chapel. Whatever were the causes of the rise and growth of Nonconformity in the rural areas of Wales, its spread in the industrial areas was due primarily to the fact that the Established Church lost nearly fifty years before beginning to provide adequate ministration to the newcomers. Even when the Church began to wake up, the procedure was cumbersome and slow, and contrasted very unfavourably with the speed with which the Nonconformist denominations could and did act. The description given of Sheffield could well apply to the old diocese of Llandaff in those days: 'Where the National Church required an Act of Parliament, a grant of money, an educated gentleman, and a crop of lawyers, the Methodists required only a friendly barn and a zealous preacher';[1] and the results were the same in both areas: industrial communities dotted with chapels before the Church was ready to begin.

In the parish of Merthyr Tydfil the problem had already become serious before the end of the eighteenth century. In the bishop's visitation of 1763 it was reported that there were about one hundred families living in the parish

> who are all farmers but mostly Rack Tenants, and dispersed throughout the parish are many cottages of the labouring poor. We have likewise besides these in the village of Merthir near 40 families, ¾ of these are Presbyterians professing themselves for the most part Arminians, with a few Calvinists, and fewer Anabaptists, and among all these I am afraid too many Deists; and in order to instruct the foregoing over-righteous Sects, about 16 or 17 years ago a Pompous Meeting House was erected on the northside of the village, not far from the Church.

Only 10 or 12 church communicants 'at most' were claimed.[2] In 1774 it was reported that an evening service in English was held 'at the request of the English men belonging to the

[1] E. R. Wickham, *Church and People in an industrial city* (London, 1957), p. 80.
[2] LL/QA/1.

Iron Works here.'[1] It was obvious that Nonconformity was greatly on the increase in this new industrial area before the end of the eighteenth century. When Bishop Watson visited the parish in 1809 for a Confirmation (which he claimed was the first ever to be held there), he wrote: 'In my time, this place has become, from a small village, a great town, containing ten or twelve thousand inhabitants, occupied in the fabrication of iron; and I thought it my duty not only to go to confirm the young people there, but to preach to those who were grown up, that I might, if possible, leave among the inhabitants a good impression in favour of the teachers of the Established Church, when compared with those of many of the sectarian congregations into which the people were divided.'[2] It was on this occasion that Watson lodged with Richard Crawshay, the ironmaster, who told him: 'If ever you have occasion for five or ten thousand pounds, it shall be wholly at your service.'[3] It is a pity that the bishop did not close with this offer on the spot, for it was to be a long time before an industrialist made a similar offer to a bishop of Llandaff.

When B. H. Malkin visited Merthyr in 1803 he noted that the parish church was filled with worshippers in an overwhelmingly dissenting society. By the time of his second visit four years later the church was being rebuilt on a larger scale and a 'spacious and elegant chapel of ease' had just been built.[4] But the bishop's visitation of 1817 revealed that Merthyr Tydfil, with a population of 11,104 could claim only 40 communicants;[5] and when Bishop Van Mildert made his primary visitation in August 1821, he said that in the church there was accommodation for only one-fortieth of the population, for although the building of a gallery had doubled the accommodation in the parish church, still only

[1] LL/QA/6.

[2] Richard Watson, *Anecdotes of the life of Richard Watson, Bishop of Llandaff* (London, 1818), ii. 367–8. The author of this book was Chancellor Richard Watson, son of the bishop.

[3] Ibid. ii. 371.

[4] B. H. Malkin, op. cit. i. 275–6.

[5] LL/QA/26.

900 could be accommodated out of a population of 18,000,[1] and he concluded that 'while Meeting-Houses for Dissenters spring up on every side, many of our own flocks are almost driven from Communion with the Established Church by this lamentable deficiency'.[2]

The earliest attempt to remedy this state of affairs was by an appeal to the ironmasters, on the ground that, as it was they who had brought thousands of people into these parts for their own private profit, they had a responsibility for their spiritual welfare. Apart from Bishop Watson's encounter with Richard Crawshay, it was Bishop Van Mildert who made the first appeal to the industrialists. 'A letter in my possession', said Bishop Ollivant nearly forty years later, 'shows that he [Van Mildert] had applied to some of our Iron-Masters at that time . . . but little, if any, result followed.'[3] Mildert's successor, Sumner, had better luck with J. J. Guest, of Dowlais, but Guest, a Methodist, did not see eye to eye with the bishop over the patronage of a church he undertook to build in Dowlais. The difficulty was ultimately solved, and Dowlais church was completed in 1827, its consecration being the last episcopal act of Sumner before being translated to Winchester after a stay of only one year in Llandaff, six months of which were spent in residence in St. Paul's deanery, London.[4]

Edward Copleston, who succeeded Sumner in 1828, visited Merthyr Tydfil in the September of that year, and there he learned that Guest had already spent £3,000 on Dowlais church and that he intended to add a tower, 'which will give it less the air of a meeting house'.[5] This parish had to wait until 1846 before a Welsh church was built there, and Copleston had obviously failed in an appeal he made to

[1] William Van Mildert, *Primary Visitation Charge to the clergy of the diocese of Llandaff* (Oxford, 1821), p. 7.

[2] Ibid., p. 8.

[3] Alfred Ollivant, *Seventh Visitation Charge* (London, 1869), p. 12.

[4] But Sumner was a most vigorous diocesan. Had he remained in Llandaff, the subsequent history of the diocese might well have been different.

[5] Letter from Copleston to Bruce Knight, 29 September 1828.

Crawshay (probably William Crawshay II), for he wrote later: 'If I can move the iron master—if I can "draw iron tears from Pluto's cheek", I shall be a worthy rival of Orpheus, and may take my place even before the Welsh Bards.'[1] He had occasion again to complain of the Merthyr ironmasters when the building of the Welsh church of St. David's was being contemplated. Anthony Hill and Guest were withholding a promised subscription of £500 because they could not appoint the architect: 'What the meaning of the word *honour* is in these gentlemen's dictionary, I am at a loss to conjecture', wrote Copleston.[2]

The growing parish of Aberdare was left without additional church building until after 1850, by which time it had become the parish where the fortunes of the old diocese of Llandaff were at their lowest.

The Monmouthshire industrial areas fared better than those of north-east Glamorgan in the matter of building new churches. Thomas Hill and Samuel Hopkins, ironmasters of Blaenavon, built a church in that township in 1805 in pursuance of an Act of Parliament, and this was followed in 1819 by the building of St. James's church, Pontypool, which, built for an English congregation, must have been the first church in the county to be built for worship in the English language. In the same ancient parish of Trevethin Tal-y-waun church was built in 1832 and Pontnewynydd church in 1844. In the old parish of Bedwellty the Tredegar Iron Company built St. George's, Tredegar, in 1836, and in 1843 the Rhymney Iron Company built a replica of this in Rhymney. The Ebbw Vale Company had built a church room in that township in 1836, to be replaced later by a much grander structure, and Crawshay Bailey built a church near Beaufort in 1842, while a church was built in Nant-y-glo in 1844.[3] But although Monmouthshire fared better during

[1] Letter from Copleston to J. M. Traherne, 9 January 1837.

[2] Copleston to J. M. Traherne, 24 September 1842.

[3] This list does not include churches built outside the ironworks district, the most important being St. Paul's, Newport, and Holy Trinity, Abergavenny.

the first half of the last century than the industrial areas of north-east Glamorgan, churches sprang up in these parts at a far slower rate than they did in England.[1] Bishop Copleston wrote to Sir Thomas Phillips on 7 July 1845: 'It is the mineral region, (consisting of some eight or ten parishes) not the diocese, which calls for aid. . . . It is hardly necessary for me, who have so often borne testimony to your munificence, and to that of Mr. Homfray, and of the Rhymney Iron Company, and of a few others, to say that I did not only except you from blame, but that your example shines the brighter for being contrasted with the gloomy picture exhibited by the parish of Bedwellty and Aberystwith(*sic*), and some others.'[2]

In comparison with the efforts of Nonconformity, those of the Established Church up to 1850 were very meagre, and, in consequence, the former captured and retained its hold upon this industrial society throughout the nineteenth century and the first two decades of the present century. For this, Bishop Copleston, in view of his long episcopate, must bear much of the blame. He was an eminent man in Church and State, but he perpetuated the eighteenth-century tradition of part-time bishops in the old diocese of Llandaff until his death in 1849. He lived in the diocese, first in Llansantffraed (Mon.), then near Cowbridge, and lastly, in Hardwick Court, Chepstow, but he spent six months of every year in St. Paul's deanery, London. He never understood his diocese: he was a Devonian, one of a long line of Devon squires, and the squire-tenant relationship was understood by him, but not so the new relationship of ironmaster and worker which affected the greater part of the population of his diocese. His tastes and interests were those of an eighteenth-century gentleman, and he spoke a different language from that of the ironmasters. He was known as a 'university

[1] From 1831 to 1851, virtually the years of Copleston's episcopate, 2,029 churches were built in England and Wales.

[2] W. J. Copleston, *Memoir of Edward Copleston, D.D.* (London, 1852), pp. 200–1.

bishop', and he would probably have been happier if he had remained in academic circles. It is significant that his work for education in his diocese was more fruitful than his work in church building. He formed the Diocesan Board of Education in 1839; and by 1847 there were 103 church day schools in Monmouthshire[1] and 86 in Glamorgan[2] (some of which, of course, were in the diocese of St. David's). It may be asked why he did not organize the work of church extension on a diocesan basis as did his successor, with outstanding results.

The answer has already been given: church extension on any significant scale could only be accompanied by the reorganization of the large upland mountain parishes into smaller units, and a financial provision made for them; and this was a problem which the diocese had neither the legal authority nor the financial means to accomplish. It was a task for which the Ecclesiastical Commissioners for England were responsible.[3]

We have already seen that Blaenavon had virtually become independent of its parent parish, Llanover, early in the nineteenth century, although it was not until after the middle of the century that it was constituted a separate parish; likewise St. James's, Pontypool, was separately endowed by the Governors of the Corporation of Queen Anne's Bounty, and had become, in effect, a separate ecclesiastical district, and Dowlais parish had been formed from Merthyr Tydfil in 1837 following the building of its church. Between 1844 and 1850 five new ecclesiastical districts were formed in the ironworks area by the Ecclesiastical Commissioners. In 1844 the ecclesiastical district of Nant-y-glo was formed out of the parish of Aberystruth,[4] and a year later Pen-maen

1 E. T. Davies, op. cit., Appendix X.

2 *Reports of the Commissioners of Inquiry into the state of education in Wales*, i. 101.

3 6 & 7 Will. IV, c. 77. Among the powers of the Commissioners was to constitute 'any part or parts of such parish or parishes, chapel or chapelries, district or districts, or any extra-parochial place or places, or any part or parts thereof . . . a separate district for spiritual purposes'.

4 *First General Report from the Ecclesiastical Commissioners for England* (London, 1846), Appendix, p. 61.

was formed from Mynyddislwyn. In 1846 Beaufort was formed out of the parishes of Aberystruth and Bedwellty in Monmouthshire and the diocese of Llandaff, and Llangattock and Llangynidr in Brecknockshire and the diocese of St. David's, while in the same year Cyfarthfa was separated from Merthyr Tydfil.[1] No other districts were formed in this industrial belt until after 1860.

Two more measures were taken by the Ecclesiastical Commissioners which were strictly necessary if the old diocese of Llandaff was to be equipped for the immense task which lay before it. On 12 December 1838 the income of the bishopric was fixed at £4,200 per annum, to commence at the next avoidance of the see (thus promising the diocese a full-time bishop), and a house was bought for him in 1851. Then, in 1843, the archdeaconry of Monmouth was created, and William Crawley, rector of Bryn-gwyn, became its first incumbent. Thus, by the end of the first half of the nineteenth century, the diocese was in a better state than ever to perform its mission. But the locusts had, by now, eaten many years.

A picture of the industrial parishes in the old diocese is shown in the Returns to the last visitation of Bishop Copleston in 1848. J. C. Campbell, rector of Merthyr Tydfil (and later bishop of Bangor), reported that in his parish three bilingual services and two English services were held every Sunday, with week-night services, and a monthly communion with about 200 communicants. The vicar of Aberdare, John Griffith, who had only recently come to the parish, had but one curate for a parish which extended ten miles by six and contained a scattered population of 12,000. He said that he had to restrict his ministry to the township of Aberdare where there was one church (the only church in the parish), and this was full. Trevethin had about 200 communicants, Aberystruth, 60–70, Blaenavon, 93, and Nant-y-glo, 60 communicants. Undoubtedly the best industrial parish in the whole diocese was Rhymney, with bilingual Sunday services,

[1] *Second General Report*... (London, 1847), Appendix, p. 23.

two weekly services, monthly communions and about 400 communicants.

These Returns indicated that the Established Church was a small minority in comparison with Nonconformity. Definite figures are not available except in a few cases: e.g., Dowlais, where there were 900 Independents, about 400 Baptists, a similar number of Calvinistic Methodists, 160 Wesleyan Methodists and about 200 church communicants. Most incumbents declared that Nonconformity was strong in their midst: 'exceedingly numerous' in Mynyddislwyn; '30 chapels in this district', said the vicar of Trevethin; 'Nonconformity strong but not growing' (Pontnewynydd); 'numerous, but not increasing' said the vicar of Rhymney; 'strong, but not increasing' (Tredegar), and for Merthyr Tydfil: 'Nonconformists are very numerous, especially the Baptists and Calvinistic Methodists.'[1]

Within three years of Copleston's last visitation the position of religion in this industrial area and the relative strength of the Established Church and Nonconformity were to become public knowledge.

On Sunday, 30 March 1851, a religious census was taken throughout England and Wales. Upon that day, everyone who went to church or chapel was counted. On the day before this census was to take place, one of the local papers in Monmouthshire referred to it in a leading article: 'The religious statistics, if correctly given, will be very interesting and useful. The "estimated number", however, of persons attending divine service, will be very inaccurate.'[2] On the same day the local Merthyr newspaper also referred to the coming census in very uncomplimentary terms:

The attention of the Clergy is specially called to a form or schedule for Returns of certain particulars regarding their Churches and Chapels, with which they will be furnished with the Householder's Schedule, under the Census Act, and which they will be required by the appointed officers to fill and deliver

[1] LL/A/35, 36, 37.

[2] *The Monmouthshire Merlin and South Wales Advertiser*, 29 March 1851.

up to them on Monday next. It is well to bear in mind that the enquiries contained in the *former* paper have no authority or obligation whatsoever,—they are perfectly inquisitorial in character—and when made are not to be relied upon as credible unless the facts in reply to them are '*verified*' by '*the officers*' whose '*duty*' it will be to test them '*as far as possible*'.[1]

This, the newspaper maintained, was a gratuitous insult to the clergy, for it implied that their statements were not to be trusted unless verified by officials. In practice, census forms were signed by the clergy and ministers in almost all cases, and no doubt was cast on the accuracy of the returns.

The census figures for Monmouthshire and north-east Glamorgan are here given for the separate registration unions or districts:

CHEPSTOW[2] (excluding the Gloucestershire parishes). Population, 13,369. There were 21 Anglican Returns, and 23 Nonconformist. The number of worshippers came to 4,625—35 per cent. of the total population. The total of Anglican worshippers that day was 2,536, being 18 per cent. of the population and 54 per cent. of the worshippers. Nonconformity, with a total of 2,089, represented 16 per cent. of the total population, and 45 per cent. of the worshippers.

MONMOUTH.[3] Population (excluding the Herefordshire parishes) 16,083. There were 29 Anglican Returns and 31 Nonconformists. The number of worshippers that day amounted to 6,447, being 41 per cent. of the population, and of these the Anglicans returned 3,858, being 60 per cent. of the worshippers and 24 per cent. of the population, while the Nonconformist figures came to 2,589, 40 per cent. of the worshippers and 16 per cent. of the population.

ABERGAVENNY.[4] The population here was 59,229, and there were 33 Anglican Returns, and 88 Nonconformists. The latter, with 32,339 worshippers, represented 54 per cent. of the total population and 86 per cent. of the worshippers, while the Anglicans with 6,222 returned percentages of 10 and 14 respectively. The total number of worshippers was 38,561, this being 65 per cent. of the population.

[1] *Cardiff and Merthyr Guardian*, 29 March 1951.
[2] H.O., 129/26/576.
[3] H.O., 129/26/577.
[4] H.O., 129/26/578.

PONTYPOOL.[1] The total population was 27,993, and there were 26 Anglican Returns and 55 for Nonconformity. The worshippers that day totalled 20,489, being 74 per cent. of the population; and of these Nonconformity with 15,790 worshippers accounted for 76 per cent. of the worshippers and 56 per cent. of the population, while the Anglicans with a total of 4,699 represented 17 per cent. of the population and 23 per cent. of the worshippers.

NEWPORT.[2] Population 43,472. There were 35 Anglican, and 75 Nonconformist Returns, with a total number of worshippers of 14,605, representing 34 per cent. of the population. The Nonconformists returned a total of 10,464 worshippers, being 26 per cent. of the population and 74 per cent. of the worshippers, while the Anglican total came to 4,141, which accounted for 9 per cent. of the population, and 28 per cent. of the worshippers.

MERTHYR TYDFIL[3] (including the old parish of Aberdare). The population was 46,907, and there were 55 Nonconformist and 8 Anglican Returns. Nonconformist worshippers totalled 27,790 on Census Sunday, and the Anglicans 2,207. The former were thus nearly 60 per cent. of the population and over 90 per cent. of the worshippers, while the Anglicans barely accounted for 7 per cent. of the worshippers and 5 per cent. of the population. The total worshippers made up about 64 per cent. of the population.

In addition to a census of worshippers that day an account of the seating accommodation in churches and chapels was also given. Taking Monmouthshire as a whole, the Established Church had provided accommodation for 22·9 per cent. of the population (and most of this was in the ancient churches in the rural areas), while Nonconformity had catered for 73·8 per cent. of the total population.[4] This fact clearly illustrates what had been believed for the preceding 25 years or so, that communicants and worshippers were

[1] H.O., 129/26/579.

[2] H.O., 129/26/580.

[3] H.O., 129/26/582. A number of returns in this section are ambiguous, and there were some notable absentees from the Anglicans, e.g. no returns were made for the parish of Merthyr Tydfil or Cyfarthfa. But the general picture is reliable.

[4] Horace Mann, *Religious Worship in England and Wales* (London, 1853), pp. 136–7.

being lost to the Established Church in the industrial districts primarily because of the lack of church buildings.

Before drawing more general conclusions from the figures which emerged from the census, it is important to compare the ecclesiastical picture of south Monmouthshire, rural and agricultural, and by 1850 largely English-speaking, with the north of the county, Welsh and industrialized. The percentage of worshippers in relation to population throughout Monmouthshire (i.e. 52 per cent.) was higher than it was for England and Wales that day, except for the Chepstow Registration Union which equalled the national average of 35 per cent. But the industrial areas excelled themselves: 74 per cent. for Pontypool Union (and this included a number of rural parishes), 65 per cent. for Abergavenny Union and 64 per cent. for the Merthyr Tydfil Union. The Welsh-speaking Nonconformist areas were well ahead of the English-speaking Anglican areas. This was partly due to the nature of the rural area in Monmouthshire: it is probably true to say that the old diocese of Llandaff reached its lowest point in the deanery of Netherwent in this county at the end of the eighteenth, and the early years of the nineteenth century. But language also had an effect on the religious scene: English Nonconformity in the south was not as virile as Welsh Nonconformity in the north: and we shall see later that there were those who believed at the time that the anglicizing of a district resulted in a decline in public worship, particularly in chapel-going.

The religious census figures of 1851 lead to another conclusion which is at variance with the national picture. Writing of the 1851 census, a contemporary authority said: 'It is observable how absolutely insignificant a portion of the congregation is composed of artisans. . . . From whatever cause in them or in the matter of their treatment by religious bodies it is sadly certain that this vast intelligent and growingly important section of our countrymen is thoroughly estranged from our religious institutions in their present aspect';[1] and a modern investigator has written that the industrial revolution did not so much cause, as reveal, the loss of the working-classes to the churches; they never belonged to them.[2] This generalization is not true of the industrial areas with which we are now dealing, and it did not need the census of 1851 to reveal this. Nonconformity from its beginnings in this society was essentially working-class in character, and there was evidence before 1851 that the workers in the old iron industry were 'religious' in the sense that they had some connexion with the chapels. Thus, in 1840, 75 per cent. of the community which grew around the Varteg Iron Works attended a church or chapel regularly or occasionally;[3] and the inquiry carried out in the Pontypool–Blaenavon area in the same year showed that, of a population of 5,115 in the latter place, the regular attenders at a place of worship were 1,135, and there were 490 people who said that they did not go anywhere;[4] while in Pontypool parish the regular attendance was 5,565, and the occasional attendance 2,226, and there were 5,311 who said they never went anywhere.[5] But there were a good many who attended only one service per Sunday. The general conclusion was that 'the Welshman is naturally of a religious dispositon'.[6] On 7 May 1850 Thomas Rees wrote to the *Christian Witness* about the 1849 Revival, and said that the Welsh were the most religious nation on earth. 'Nine-tenths of the middle and working class are either professors of religion or constant attendants on the means of grace';[7] and on 26 December 1866 he wrote an article to the *Nonconformist* on 'The Working classes of Wales and religious institutions'

1 Horace Mann, op. cit., p. 93. 2 E. R. Wickham, op. cit., Int., p. 13.

3 *Report of the Privy Council on Education* (London, 1840), p. 172.

4 G. S. Kenrick, op. cit., p. 23.

5 Ibid., p. 19. On p. 6, however, the number of those who said they did not attend a place of worship was given as 2,161. Obviously far more people absented themselves in practice than were prepared to admit, and at least one-quarter, and probably nearer one-third of the population disclaimed any kind or degree of religious allegiance.

6 Ibid., p. 13.

7 T. Rees, *Miscellaneous Papers* (London, 1867), p. 96.

in which he said that Nonconformity in Wales had captured 90 per cent. of the working-classes, and even 75 per cent. of the Welsh-speaking masses in anglicized districts, whereas these classes in England were irreligious.[1] There is no doubt that the new industrial society was 'religious' in the sense that the majority of people had some connexion with places of worship, but not even the religious census of 1851 bore out Rees's claims in the industrial areas, even when the most favourable interpretation possible to Welsh Nonconformity is placed upon it.

Without in any way modifying the conclusion already reached, that the communities which grew up in the old ironworks areas were predominantly Nonconformist, it is necessary still to inquire into the real strength, or the core, of the Nonconformist denominations in these parts, because there is a very great disparity between the figures of 1851 and those given by these denominations themselves. To take a few examples: David Jones, a Baptist historian, in a book already quoted, gave the total Baptist membership in Monmouthshire at not more than 4,600, whereas the total figure for the same denomination in 1851 was 30,726; moreover the Baptist membership in 1882, thirty years after the religious census, was given as 11,757,[2] a little more than one-third of the 1851 figure. The Calvinistic Methodist figure for 1851 was 8,867; yet the total membership of that denomination in Monmouthshire was given as 2,067 at the Association held in Ebbw Vale a year later.[3] The figure for the Independents in 1851 was 17,660, but ten years later, when the population of the county continued to grow, it was officially returned as 7,459.[4]

Trickery, dishonesty, or collusion, can be ruled out as an explanation of these wide differences in figures. Had there been any such practices protests would have been made, in

[1] T. Rees, op. cit. pp. 24–29.
[2] Quoted by Thomas Rees, *History of Protestant Nonconformity in Wales*, p. 462.
[3] Evan Price, op. cit., p. 42.
[4] Quoted by Thomas Rees, op. cit., p. 450.

view of the high feeling which then existed between church and chapel, and among the Nonconformist denominations themselves. But no such protests can be traced; and, furthermore, many of the signatories of the returns, both clergy and ministers, declared that their congregations were by no means abnormal on 30 March 1851; indeed the complaint among the rural clergy was that the census was held on an inconvenient Sunday, mid-Lent, Mothering Sunday, on which it was the custom to visit relatives rather than go to church; and a few ministers made the same point. It is true that in one or two cases the total congregations in some chapels must have greatly taxed the official seating capacity, but such cases were few.

There are three reasons which account for this great disparity in figures. In the first place there was the basis on which the census was taken: every worshipper was counted; if he attended once that Sunday, he was counted once; if twice, then twice; and if three times, his presence inflated his denomination's statistics accordingly. There is now no means of knowing how many separate persons attended church or chapel that day; and for that reason, if for no other, a great doubt must be thrown on the value of the census because of the basis of enumeration. When preparations were being made for the census of 1861, the Government of the day proposed to make a religious census an integral part of the general census, subject to the same legal penalties for default. At the Committee stage of the Census (England) Bill, on 11 July 1860, Sir George Lewis, the Home Secretary, said that the Nonconformist pressures against the proposed arrangement were so great that the Registrar-General had advised him that there would be a general resistance to it, and so the proposed clause was withdrawn, and no religious census was held in 1861, or since. Viscount Palmerston, in winding up the debate, said: 'To ask, as was done in 1851, how many people attended on a given Sunday in different places of worship would procure no information from which any useful conclusion could be drawn.'[1] Among the protesting bodies against the [revised] religious census proposed for 1861 was the Glamorgan Baptist Association in its meeting in Aberdare in 1860, when it passed the resolution: 'That this association disapproves of the project to compel all heads of families to state the religious profession of every individual in their houses on a certain night, as an oppressive measure, opposed to religious liberty, and ineffectual to secure a correct census; and cordially approves of the petition now read to be sent to the House of Commons against the bill in its present form.'[2]

In the second place, the question may well be raised how far the pattern of church and chapel attendance affected the figures on census Sunday. For generations, if not for centuries, Anglicans had had to be content with one service per Sunday, either in the morning or afternoon, except for the towns where there would be two services, but there was never an evening service except for those few new churches in the industrial areas. This gave a pattern of one attendance per Sunday which has persisted to this day. On the other hand, the good Nonconformist attended twice per Sunday, and it is only recently that this custom has been changed. This factor in the figures of 1851 cannot be proved statistically, but it is almost certain to have affected the results.

But the most important element in the Nonconformist figures was the presence of the 'hearers', the 'auditors' of 1773. Attention will be paid to this class in the next chapter, but it is certain that around the core of Welsh Nonconformity was this class, amounting to thousands more than the members themselves, who were Nonconformists in sympathy but not in membership, but could be relied upon throughout the century to support Nonconformity. It will be shown later how Nonconformists themselves regarded this class as being

[1] For the debate, see *Hansard's Parliamentary Debates*, (Third Series, London, 1860), clix. 1695–1742.

[2] *Glamorgan Baptist Association Circular Letter* (Aberdare 1860), p. 5.

on their fringe. These people (*y gwrandawyr*) inflated Nonconformist statistics quite beyond the real strength of Nonconformity; and one of the great changes has been their virtual disappearance in these industrial areas. But, in spite of these criticisms of the results of census Sunday, it remains true that we are dealing with a predominantly Welsh Nonconformist society in this study.

The reasons for the success of Nonconformity have been given, and those for the failure of the Established Church up to the middle of the nineteenth century have been touched upon: the nature of the Establishment in those days which delayed reform until it was almost too late; a largely non-resident episcopate which resulted in a lack of episcopal oversight and leadership; and the appointment of Copleston who was ill at ease in his diocese during a critical period of twenty years. Church income was small, at best, and much of it left the diocese to impropriators and appropriators, secular and ecclesiastical. Taking the old diocese of Llandaff as a whole, the tithe commutation income in 1866 amounted to £59,518. 1*s.* 4½*d.*, of which £13,748. 11*s.* 0½*d.* was paid to ecclesiastical appropriators outside the diocese, £11,265. 8*s.* 8½*d.* to lay impropriators, £453. 2*s.* 5½*d.* to schools, charities, &c., leaving the remainder £34,050. 19*s.* 2*d.* to the parish clergy, £16,855. 15*s.* 3*d.* for those of the archdeaconry of Llandaff, and £17,195. 3*s.* 11*d.* for those of the archdeaconry of Monmouth.[1] But the greatest weakness of all was the virtual absence of lay witness at a time when the Nonconformist layman played such an important part in the affairs of his chapel and denomination. Apart from such activities as the Diocesan Education Board and the Society for the Improvement of Church Music, it is true to say that the layman, except for the two churchwardens, had no opportunity of serving his church, even in the parish. There was no forum in the parish or the diocese where the layman's

[1] *Tithe Commutation Return by the Land Commissioners for England* (London, 1937), pp. 283–6.

voice could be heard. If we sum up the defects of the Established Church by saying that, until the parliamentary reforms of the years following 1835, it was still essentially a medieval institution in its administrative and financial structure, such a statement is the sober truth.

The laity were not obliged to assume responsibility for their church even in financial matters, because for generations the expenses of maintaining the fabric, ornaments and vestments of the parish church had fallen upon the church rate which was part of the parish rate in most cases. This originated at a time when the parish church was the responsibility of all in the parish, for all would use it sooner or later. The rise of Nonconformity, with the consequent necessity of maintaining chapels, made little difference to the church rate until the early years of the nineteenth century, and it was in the second quarter that the agitation against it got under way. Its abolition was one of the major aims of Nonconformity. In 1833 between 800 and 850 householders in Newport refused to pay the rate and it was never again levied in the town. Bishop Copleston wrote: 'Church rates must, I fear, be sacrificed.'[1] But the rate went on being levied and being paid; by far the greater part of the money handled by churchwardens from Easter 1853 to Easter 1854 came from the church rate.[2] But its day was slowly coming to an end: it had been abandoned in Newport; it had become a voluntary rate in Trevethin parish after 1845; the parish of Dowlais, after its separation from Merthyr Tydfil, had never levied it; it ceased to be collected in Merthyr itself in 1854; and in Aberdare it had been refused since the final decision in the Braintree Case.[3] Elsewhere throughout the ironworks

[1] Letter from Copleston to William Bruce Knight, 6 January 1834.

[2] *Church Rates. Abstract of Return to an Address of the Honourable The House of Commons dated 10 August 1854* (London, 1856), pp. 238–41.

[3] Church Rates. *Abstract of Return to an Address of the Honourable The House of Commons dated 17 July 1855* (London, 1856), pp. 215–16. In the Braintree Case (1837) the Court had laid it down that churchwardens could not act against the majority of the vestry, and this decision, with the increasing political pressures, finally brought about the abolition of the church rate.

district it seems to have been levied and collected until it was finally abolished in 1868. When it is remembered that the clergy income was derived from tithe commutation, rent of glebe, rent received from investments made by the Governors of the Corporation of Queen Anne's Bounty, and fees and dues, it will be realized that being even a faithful communicant in a parish in those days implied no greater direct financial responsibility than to make a contribution at the offertory in Holy Communion which was to be applied to charitable purposes. In its work in the new industrial areas the Church had to inculcate a sense of financial responsibility into her laity which Nonconformity took for granted. Gradually this lesson was learned, first, naturally, in the new industrial parishes, but it was to be a long time before most of the country parishes absorbed it.

II

WELSH NONCONFORMITY IN AN INDUSTRIAL SOCIETY

WALES was plunged into industrialism with no warning or preparation such as was afforded in certain parts of England where there had been a growing urban development based on a long tradition of industrial craftmanship. The new Welsh society sprang up within two generations with little, if any, foresight or consideration even for the decencies and amenities of life, but was saved from the worst horrors of the early industrial revolution by its setting amid magnificent mountain scenery which remained largely unspoiled. We have a picture of this society in a survey made by the representative of the newly formed Committee of Council on Education who visited the parishes of Bedwellty, Aberystruth, Mynyddislwyn, Trevethin and Merthyr Tydfil early in 1840, when the Chartist march on Newport in the preceding November had left a sufficient impression to cause the Lords of the Council to make an inquiry into the state of elementary education in those parts.[1] It was these first four parishes which had furnished the body of men who had marched on Newport, and they came from a society where people were 'collected together in masses of from four to ten thousand. Their houses are ranged round the works in rows, sometimes two to five deep, sometimes three stories high. They rarely contain less than from one to six lodgers in addition to the members of the family, and afford most scanty accommodation for so many inmates'. These were colourless working-class areas relieved only by the presence

[1] *Annual Report and Minutes of the Committee of Council on Education*, pp. 155–72.

of 'ten or twenty members of the establishment' and 'a few small shopkeepers',[1] with a population of 85,000, composed largely of immigrants. The inspector, Seymour Tremenheere, estimated that of these there would be 17,000 children, 11,334 of whom would need instruction in day schools, and 8,026 of whom received no such instruction in any of the 47 schools which served this area.[2] A large proportion of the adult population could neither read nor write; not all could read the Bible which was to be found in most cottages. In a survey of 20 families 'adjoining extensive works', 17 were Welsh, 13 of them had a Welsh Bible and in two there were religious tracts, but in none other were there any other books.[3]

Within these five parishes the Established Church had eleven places of worship and Nonconformity 93, and this disparity was even greater in the number of Sunday-schools of which there were 80 Nonconformist to 6 Church; the latter providing for 940 pupils. Nonconformity was clearly the religion of the great majority of the population. 'The exertions of this portion of the religious community have been great in endeavouring to provide spiritual superintendence and places of worship for these masses of population which have sprung up on spots in most cases distant from the parish church, and so rapidly as far to outstrip the means of spiritual care provided by the Establishment.'[4] Tremenheere, in his Report to the Lords of the Council on Education, quoted the figures of the investigation made by the proprietor of the Varteg works to show that, of a population of 8,598 of the district, only 24·24 per cent. did not go to any church or chapel. It did not need the census of 1851 to reveal that these communities consisted of Welsh Nonconformist, chapel-going folk.

In 1847 one of the Commissioners of Inquiry into the state of education in Wales visited the industrial areas of

[1] Ibid., p. 156. [2] Ibid., p. 158.
[3] Ibid., p. 160. [4] Ibid., p. 170.

Monmouthshire, and reported on the social scene as he saw it. To him it was a lawless, criminal, and dissolute society: 'it contains a larger proportion of escaped criminals and dissolute people of both sexes than almost any other populace; I know of none which, from what I could gather, contains so many'.[1] Evil in every shape was rampant, said the Commissioner, and all good influences were comparatively powerless. 'The whole district and population partake of the iron character of its produce; everything centres in and ministers to the idolatry of profit; physical strength is the object of esteem, and gain their chief God.'[2] Drunkenness was widespread, and this was encouraged by the payment of wages in public houses which abounded in these districts; and was further accentuated by the truck-shop system which was directly, or indirectly, associated with the ironworks, and what credit was left over after clearing the books of the truck-shop was spent in public houses which were sometimes held by mining agents. Relations between masters and men were bad; and the former were not anxious that their workers should develop provident habits. 'I want them to spend their wages and not to hoard them', said one employer. This truck-shop system, at first a necessity, at worst a tyranny, and at best an irritant, was the greatest single cause of discontent in these areas. It was calculated (indeed, in some places, organized), to keep the workers in a perpetual state of debt, and it was a deterrent to the growth of a trading class which could have modified conditions in these ironworks districts. Although abolished in 1831 (the truck system had always been illegal), it persisted in a refined form until the Truck Amendment Act (1887) gave it its death blow.

There can be no doubt that the greatest social evil in these ironworks communities was drunkenness, and this lay at the root of many other social problems because it accounted for too great a proportion of the workers' earnings. Malkin,

[1] *Reports of the Commissioners of Inquiry into the state of education in Wales,* ii. 290.
[2] Ibid. ii. 291.

writing of Merthyr Tydfil, said: 'The men employed at these works are too much addicted to drinking; but in other respects no great immoralities are to be found among them; far less indeed than might have been expected, considering the tide of dissoluteness which is usually found to flow in upon a place, from the rapid increase of vulgar population.'[1] Merthyr later became known as the hell of the Principality; and, a little more hopefully, as the California and Australia of Wales to which swarmed the dregs of every country.[2] The investigation carried out in the parish of Trevethin in 1840 showed that it was 'drunkenness which distinguishes the iron district of South Wales above every part of this besotted country'; and in the parish at that time there were 38 public houses and 132 beer shops for a population of 17,196,[3] patronized largely by lodgers who had no other places to resort to except their beds, which were occupied when they were at work by mates working a different shift. Dr. Thomas Rees also testified that immoderate drinking 'is the root of all the ignorance, poverty, irreligion, and dishonesty in dealing, of which tradesmen constantly complain'.[4]

But there were many to testify that the inhabitants of these places were generous and benevolent. They married early, often in poverty; children came rapidly and regularly, and so they remained in poverty. But judges acknowledged that serious crimes against the person or property were rare, and the illegitimacy rate was lower here than in rural Wales in spite of the custom for women to do outdoor jobs surrounding the ironworks. Moreover, although thousands of these families lived in very bad conditions, there is general agreement that the interior of their houses were kept clean in spite of adverse conditions.[5]

1 B. H. Malkin, op. cit. i. 273.

2 David Edwards, 'Nodweddion Brodorol Dosbarth Gweithiol Gwent a Morganwg', *Y Traethodydd* (Treffynnon, MDCCCLVI), xii. 456.

3 G. S. Kenrick, op. cit., p. 24.

4 T. Rees, *Miscellaneous Papers*, p. 21.

5 No doubt there were thousands of workers in these parts who answered to

How adverse these conditions were was shown by an inquiry made into the sanitary condition of Merthyr Tydfil in 1849. There was an almost complete absence of drainage; a complete absence of a public water supply—this was the 'crowning evil'[1]—most roads were unmade, and the infant mortality rate was very high. During the period 1841–7, of a death rate of 1,111 persons per year, 542 were those of children under three years of age, and 719 of persons under twenty years of age,[2] so that the expectation of life among the working class was very low: 'the average duration of life among the lower classes is 17 years'.[3] The report can be summed up thus:

Although Merthyr Tydfil has long been reported to be in an unsatisfactory condition as regards drainage, cleansing, and water supply, I was certainly not prepared for so bad a case as my own senses and the testimony of numberless witnesses proved to be actually existing here, Merthyr having sprung from a village to a town, without any precautions being taken for the removal of the increased masses of filth necessarily produced by an increased population, nor even for the escape of the ordinary surface-water; without regulation for the laying out of streets, or the building of tenements; and, above all, having among its population few or none of that class of individuals in easy circumstances who, in most other large towns, either by example or authority, in some degree check the wholesale accumulation of nuisances; from all these circumstances combined, a rural spot of considerable beauty, and with more than the average natural facilities for drainage and water supply, has become transformed into a crowded and filthy manufacturing town, with an amount of mortality higher than any commercial or manufacturing town in the kingdom.[4]

the description of Heman Gwent, a local poet of Rhymney, who wrote in the Gwentian dialect: 'Fe godws o'r gwely, 'i gynws y tân, rhows y tegedl i ferwi; 'i wisgws 'i ddillad, 'i fyttws 'i frecwast, rhows fwyd yn 'i gwdyn, a thê yn 'i jar; 'i danws 'i bib, 'i gerddws i'r gwaith, 'i steddws i gael whiff; 'i dorws 'i lo, 'i lenws 'i ddram, 'i ffraews â Wil, 'i regws, 'i gerddws tua thre, 'i fyttws 'i fwyd, 'i olchws, 'i yfws 'i gwrw, ag fe feddws.'

[1] T. W. Rammell, *Report to the General Board of Health on a preliminary enquiry into the sewerage, drainage, and supply of water, and the sanitary condition of the inhabitants of the town of Merthyr Tydfil, in the County of Glamorgan* (London, 1850), p. 34. [2] Ibid., p. 15. [3] Ibid., p. 18. [4] Ibid., p. 24.

Apart from the greater concentration of population in Merthyr Tydfil, these words would apply to every community in the old ironworks district; the one possible exception was Tredegar where there was an early attempt made at some form of street planning.

Materially, and well into the nineteenth century, these were drab communities in which people had little choice of social contacts apart from the strong family kinship that existed there. A person could be a chapel-goer, less frequently a church-goer, or, at the other extreme, the public house was his only social centre. The regular chapel-goer was the core of Nonconformity, but his numbers were not nearly so high as census Sunday seemed to suggest. Between the two extremes of chapel and public house were the clubs, or benefit societies, which met in the latter: the Iforites (the only Welsh benefit society), Ancient Britons, Odyddion, Antediluvian Buffaloes, West of England Operatives—in all about thirty-five of them whose meeting-place was the public house. It was from this class of benefit society men that Nonconformity drew its large number of 'adherents' (*y gwrandawyr*) who formed an outer shell to Nonconformity statistically far more imposing than the membership itself. These were the people who had a link with the chapels, mainly for family reasons, and who usually attended the Sunday evening service only. They followed the Nonconformist line in theology and politics, and on occasions, such as in 1851, they gave Nonconformity a statistical importance it never possessed in reality in this industrial society, except that any adherent would have described himself as a chapel-man. It would be uncharitable to say that thousands went to chapel in those days because there was nowhere else to go, but such a statement is not devoid of all truth.

How important these adherents were, and what a large force they were on the perimeter of Nonconformity is seen when we recall that in Monmouthshire the Independents' membership went up by only 45 in 20 years, from 1862 to

1882, while the adherents increased from 11,186 to 23,185 in the same period, and the Calvinistic Methodists increased their membership by 1,775 in those years, but the adherents showed double that increase.[1] The Baptists did not include adherents in their statistics until 1905.

This, then, was the kind of society within which Welsh Nonconformity worked in the old ironworks communities in the nineteenth century. Lest the figures of census Sunday should have given the impression that these areas were one big Nonconformist chapel, we would do well to recall Dr. Thomas Jones's description of the immigrants who came to these parts: 'They came as christians and as pagans, thrifty and profligate, clean and dirty; and gradually sorted themselves in their surroundings according to tradition and habit.' Nonconformity had its lean times as well as its moments of triumph in these parts.

At this point the word Nonconformity as a generic term must be examined lest it should be thought that it formed one solid phalanx in these communities. There were times and places where the Nonconformist bodies co-operated in worship: they held joint prayer-meetings and Sunday-schools in Hirwaun at the beginning of the last century, and a house was put at their disposal by Mr. Overton, who was the owner of the local ironworks. Likewise in Rhymney, a works' manager persuaded the Baptists, Independents and Calvinistic Methodists to worship together, and in 1807 a building was opened for that purpose, but as the lease of this building in 1809 revealed that the two trustees were Calvinistic Methodists, the Baptists and Independents reverted to cottage worship until they built their own chapels. In Aber-carn, also, the three denominations with the Wesleyan Methodists worshipped together until the Calvinists and Wesleyans withdrew, and the Baptists and Independents were finally separated as the result of a controversy on baptism. But, generally, denominational differences were acute

[1] Thomas Rees, *History of Protestant Nonconformity in Wales*, pp. 450–1, 461–2.

and separated the chapels from each other as much as their common separation from the Established Church. Welsh Wesleyan Methodism had to fight for its place in a religious community whose theology, up to and beyond the middle of the last century, was high Calvinism. The Welsh Wesleyans were few in number,[1] but their influence was out of all proportion to their numerical strength. Likewise the Calvinistic Methodists, although theologically acceptable, were few in number in Monmouthshire, but stronger in north-east Glamorgan. The Monmouthshire societies formed by the eighteenth-century Methodist revival in Wales were all to be found along the Cardiff–Chepstow road, and it was the industrial revolution which caused the spread of this denomination into north Monmouthshire. Great animosity existed between the two strongest Welsh Nonconformist denominations in this industrial area, the Baptists and the Independents, over the question of baptism, and the controversy, which produced a spate of literature, gave rise to a scene which Monmouthshire will probably never see again.

This was the Rhymney Baptismal Fair (Ffair Fedydd Rhymni), which arose out of a controversy in Rhymney on baptism between the Baptists and the Independents, and which began on 18 October 1844. A public debate was arranged to take place on the following 1 and 2 November, when each denomination was to produce its protagonist: Mr. John Jones, of Llangollen College, for the Independents, and Mr. T. G. Jones, of Haverfordwest College, for the Baptists. On the day appointed the roads leading to Rhymney from Blaenavon, Llanelly (Brecknockshire), Nant-y-glo, Tredegar, Ebbw Vale, Merthyr, Dowlais, and Aberdare were crowded with people, some of whom had come from Brecon, Abergavenny, Newport, and Pontypool. Two stages had been erected, each on a wagon, outside the Clarence Hotel, and, to ensure that the rules were observed, two chairmen were appointed. The rules laid down that baptism only was to

[1] Their membership throughout South Wales in 1882 was 4,431.

be discussed; that each protagonist should speak for seven minutes; that no appeal for support should be made to the crowd, and that good order must be maintained throughout the meeting. The rules were soon broken, and the meeting got out of hand. The wagon of those who upheld infant baptism was attacked and removed, and as many of the crowd as were able adjourned to a nearby chapel, where pandemonium again broke loose. When the proceedings were continued the following day, someone asked if the local correspondent of *Yr Haul* (the Church newspaper) was present, so that due praise should be given to Nonconformity for arranging such a meeting to determine a theological question. When things had become farcical, one of the Nonconformist ministers present demanded that the meeting should end for the honour of Nonconformity, but an afternoon meeting was arranged on the second day in spite of this advice. This meeting became a shambles, with cries of 'Twm Paine', and 'Pull him down, pull him down'. When the Independents came to write their report of these proceedings, they denied the accusation that three of their co-religionists had spat tobacco in the face of the Baptist champion; while the Baptists, in their report, claimed that these proceedings had led to an increase in baptism in Rhymney and they reasserted the charge levelled against the Independents of trying to extinguish Baptist oratory with tobacco juice.[1] The more responsible Nonconformists deplored these performances, declaring that the learning of the debaters was superficial and that such proceedings could only result in bitterness and bad feeling; yet all the Nonconformist churches were in a turmoil in those days over the matter of baptism.[2] Such disputes were endemic in the industrial areas. A controversy broke out in Aberdare in 1857 between Dr. Thomas Price, a well-known and very aggressive Baptist minister, and

[1] J. S. Jones, *Hanes Rhymni a Phontlottyn* (Dinbych, 1904), pp. 135–51. The echoes of this debate reverberated in denominational journals for months.

[2] John Thomas, *Cofiant y Parch. T. Rees, D.D., Abertawy* (Dolgellau, 1888), p. 105.

William Edwards, an Independent minister of the town. Price was the editor of a newspaper, *Y Gwron Cymreig*, and was suspected of using this organ to further his denomination's teaching on baptism and of being reluctant to publish contrary views. The controversy in Aberdare led to two publications, one by each protagonist, and both adopted the same title for his contribution: *Bapto a Baptiso.* Price caused his publication to be advertised in the windows of the 'Bute Arms' in the town, complete with his photograph. Edwards had obviously been provoked, and he charged Price with using 'graceless language'[1] (*ymadroddion di-ras*).

These theological controversies reveal that for the greater part of the last century, with the exception of the time when religious revivals temporarily fused the Independents, Calvinistic and Wesleyan Methodists (but not the Baptists) together, Nonconformist churches lived largely a separate existence from each other, a separateness which was emphasized nearly as much as their separateness from 'the world' by a system of discipline which only slowly relaxed later. Discipline was very strict among the Calvinistic Methodists in Tredegar up to the middle of the last century. Persons could be suspended from membership for working on Sundays, for courting on Sundays, for excessive personal adornment—men were frowned upon for wearing wedding rings; the wearing of feathers in women's hats was discouraged (did they want to fly?), and marriages with persons of another denomination were a matter for censure.[2] Baptist *Circular Letters* reveal that occasionally the number of excommunicated exceeded that of the baptized. In Merthyr Tydfil, those who desired to be received back into the church had to make public penance by standing in the aisle (*sefyll yn yr alley*) during the communion service. Exclusion from the Society (*y gyfeillach*) was the punishment, not only for moral offences,

[1] William Edwards, *Bapto a Baptiso* (Llanelly, 1858), pp. 5–13.

[2] James Llewelyn, *Hanes Eglwys Penuel M.C., Tredegar* (Rhymni, Tredegar a Bargoed, 1913), p. 59.

but also if a member attended another place of worship, went to a funeral on Sunday, married an unbeliever, or wore the badge of a benefit society. But after mid-century these standards were relaxed, and it was said that there was then far less difference between the Church and the world.[1] It remained true, however, that chapels kept very much to themselves, and the inner core of Nonconformists found in them not only their spiritual, but their cultural homes as well. Their lives were largely spent between their work, home, and particular chapel. It is little wonder that Dr. Thomas Jones, of Rhymney, was able to say that he knew himself to be a Methodist much more actively and intensely than he felt himself to be a Welshman;[2] and had he been brought up an Independent or a Baptist the nature of his experience would have been the same.

The outward sign of denominational exclusiveness, rivalry and virility was the proliferation of chapels, 399 of them in Monmouthshire by the beginning of the present century, and of these, 317 were in the industrial areas.[3] The Baptists accounted for 119 of these, and the Independents for 81,[4] which means that a chapel for approximately every 750 of the population had been provided, thus maintaining throughout the century the proportion of the population they had provided for in 1851, viz., 73·8 per cent. This generalization, however, conceals the fact of undue concentration in particular areas: 12 Baptist chapels in the Tredegar area, 6 in Ebbw Vale, 9 in Blaenavon; 7 Independent chapels in Ebbw Vale, 82 chapels in all in the Urban District of Merthyr Tydfil, of which the Baptists and Independents between them provided over one-half.[5] In the Urban District of Aberdare there were 67 chapels, with the same preponderance as in Merthyr Tydfil.[6] The truth is that Nonconformity

[1] R. Griffiths, op. cit., pp. 51–52.

[2] Thomas Jones, *Rhymney Memories*, p. 120.

[3] *Royal Commission on the Church of England and other religious bodies in Wales and Monnmouthshire.* (*Nonconformist County Statistics*) (London, 1910), vi. 376–7.

[4] Ibid., p. 374.
[5] Ibid., p. 175.
[6] Ibid., p. 245.

greatly overbuilt in these areas in the last century, and although tribute must be paid to the self-sacrifice which lay behind these chapels, yet they are monuments, not only to denominational rivalry, but too frequently to a lack of co-operation within each denomination.

Throughout the nineteenth century, and into the first decade of the present century, Welsh Nonconformity in these industrial districts generated a revivalistic atmosphere. Religious revivals were endemic in these parts; sometimes common to the whole of Wales, and sometimes local. Once again, the earliest testimony for the century comes from Benjamin Heath Malkin, who wrote of Merthyr Tydfil: 'Almost all the exclusively Welsh sects among the lower orders of the people have in truth degenerated into habits of the most pitiable lunacy in their devotion . . . but the intelligent and enlightened part of the dissenters . . . are everywhere respected.'[1] Malkin was probably describing scenes he saw among the evangelical Calvinistic Methodists, who are known to have been the centre of a number of religious revivals in the town in 1810, 1815, and 1829, and he contrasted them with the older dissenters who had not yet outlived their eighteenth-century description of 'the dry dissenters' (*y sentars sychion*). Sometimes a revival would be local, and named after its originator, such as 'Diwygiad Shôn Bowen, Rhymni'[2] (revival of John Bowen, Rhymney); while in the Mynydd-islwyn area revivals broke out sporadically over a period of thirty-five years, but they were not all of the same character.[3] Then, in 1831–2, there took place the first of a series of 'cholera revivals', revivals which accompanied an outbreak of cholera which was all too frequent in these industrial communities. This took place in the Tredegar district, and although the number of converts was many, 'when the storm abated, places of worship began to be vacated, and the terrified converts "went their way" '.[4]

[1] B.H. Malkin, op. cit. i. 262.
[2] J. S. Jones, op. cit., p. 114.
[3] Evan Davies, *Revivals in Wales* (London, 1859), p. 50.
[4] Evan Powell, *History of Carmel Baptist Church, Sirhowy* (Cardiff, 1933), p. 30.

But the most powerful of these 'cholera revivals' was that of 1849 which became known as 'diwygiad y colera' ('the cholera revival'). An outbreak of cholera took place in Merthyr Tydfil within a week or so of the inquiry into its sanitary conditions already described, and spread across north Monmouthshire. In that year Thomas Rees came to Beaufort as minister of the Independent church there, and he has given an account of the revival in a letter to *The Christian Witness* on 7 May 1850. He says in the letter that revivals had broken out in Wales in 1829, 1841, 1842 and 1843, due principally to the publication of 'Mr. Finney's Lectures', but 'it will be readily acknowledged that the terrible visitation of the *Cholera* was principally the means of arousing the attention of our hearers to consider seriously the important truths with which they were theoretically acquainted; but who will venture to deny that the Lord had mercifully ordained this awful scourge as the means of accomplishing his gracious purposes of saving thousands.'[1] This high Calvinism was shared by Rees's fellow ministers: 'Cadarnhaodd y *cholera* y grediniaeth am lywodraeth gyffredinol Duw dros y byd, a bod ganddo law weithredol yng ngweinyddiad ceryddon yn gystal â chyfraniad trugareddau. Yr oedd yn agos pawb yn addef fod bys Duw yn y cholera.'[2] Rees gave statistics of the converts who became members in the churches of his own denomination: they amounted to nearly 10,000 in the Independent churches within the old ironworks area, apart from the 'thousands' who joined the Baptists and the 'great numbers' who joined the Calvinistic and Wesleyan Methodists.[3] A Merthyr Tydfil pastor also described this revival in his church. On one Sunday 120 were added to membership,[4] and whereas normally people had to attend the 'society' for one month before being admitted to membership, during the epidemic they were admitted without delay. Thomas Lewis, a noted Baptist minister in his day in

[1] T. Rees, *Miscellaneous Papers*, p. 95.
[2] *Llythyr y ddwy gymmanfa ddeheuol*, p. 4.
[3] T. Rees, *Miscellaneous Papers*, p. 95.
[4] R. Griffiths, op. cit., p. 52.

Monmouthshire, wrote about the revival in his diary: 'This year has been remarkable for cholera epidemic in England and Wales. Thousands have died from the disease, which caused a panic among the people—the mere hearers of the Word. Many hundreds fled for membership, especially in the hills and in the ironworks.'[1] Another great revival which broke out in 1859 affected the whole of Wales, and it is claimed that it added 80,000 to the membership of the chapels, whose influence was greatly increased thereby.[2] But it seems that the 1859 revival had less effect in Monmouthshire than in Glamorgan; and only rarely did the Baptists and the Established Church join with the Independents, Wesleyan Methodists and Calvinistic Methodists.[3]

The last 'cholera revival' broke out in the Tredegar district in 1866. John Thomas, pastor of Zoar chapel in that town, wrote of the 'long night of toil and care in connection with the cause of God on the Monmouthshire Hills', but this was followed by the 'dayspring (or sunrising) from on high'.[4] This was a Welsh Independent church, composed mainly of miners, colliers and firemen, and saddled with a heavy debt. In fairness to the author, it should be said that this church had been praying for a revival for some time, and when it happened 'the pestilence that walketh in darkness' appeared at the same time. The alarm was general, and 'the presence of God's judgement' accounted for the scenes that followed. Thomas himself was not blind to what he called 'the defective management of the movement', bound up with an excess of emotionalism.[5]

No general revival happened between 1859 and the end of the century, except for a powerful revival begun in the

[1] Thomas Lewis, *My Life's Work* (Newport, 1902), p. 42.

[2] Edward Parry, *Llawlyfr ar hanes y diwygiadau crefyddol yn Nghymru* (Corwen, 1898), p. 152.

[3] T. Rees, quoted by Thomas Phillips, *The Welsh Revival: its origin and development* (London, 1860), p. 46.

[4] John Thomas, *Sunshine on the 'Hills', being a narrative of a revival of the Lord's work at Tredegar, during the visitation of the cholera in the year 1866* (London, n.d.), p. 1.

[5] Ibid., p. 5.

Rhondda Valley by the Salvation Army in 1879.[1] A revival affected north Monmouthshire between 1875 and 1877.[2] After this, these revivals were usually restricted to particular chapels, such as broke out in Caersalem chapel, Dowlais, in 1890, after a season of prayer for the hearers, and two years later in the Baptist church in Pontnewydd (Mon.),[3] and this is the last recorded in these parts before the powerful revival of 1904–5.

Whether these visitations did permanent good to Welsh Nonconformity is a matter of opinion. That they greatly increased membership is beyond doubt; and it may be pointed out here that census Sunday in 1851 came on the morrow of the 'cholera revival' when thousands of members were added to the chapels. But there is reason to believe that these revivals, usually, but not always, attended with high emotionalism, became the accepted criterion of spirituality in these industrial districts, so that people either looked back to previous revivals or yearned for the next, the present tending to be the time between two revivals. These intervening periods were often periods of spiritual depression in Nonconformity, a depression caused by the reaction which always followed a revival. Only three years after the 'cholera revival' of 1849 the Welsh Independents' *Circular Letter* said that all the churches in the Association were peaceful, and many of them were sound asleep.[4] When Dr. Thomas Price went to Aberdare as a Baptist minister in 1846, the church there was in a low state, both spiritually and numerically, and Price wrote in his diary at the end of 1868 that the year had been characterized by deadness throughout the country, and that very little religion had been experienced anywhere. He himself had baptized only 16 throughout the year.[5] A

[1] Edward Parry, op. cit., pp. 157–8.

[2] J. Vyrnwy Morgan, *The Welsh Religious Revival* (London, 1909), xviii.

[3] Ibid., pp. 164–5.

[4] *Llythyr y ddwy gymmanfa ddeheuol* (1852), p. 1.

[5] Benjamin Evans, *Bywgraffiad y diweddar Barchedig T. Price, M.A., Ph.D., Aberdar* (Aberdar, 1891), p. 213.

fellow Baptist, Thomas Lewis, whose autobiography has already been drawn upon, revealed in his diary the ebb and flow of chapel life in those days in Monmouthshire. The people of Llanddewi Rhydderch, where Lewis held his first pastorate, were 'as hard as stones and as cold as ice';[1] Raglan was a 'heathen locality',[2] and when he resigned his last pastorate, that of Moriah church, Risca, in 1880, he wrote: 'No co-operation in the church; salary was very low for a long time; the leaders were men of straw, and I had altogether a rather unhappy pastorate, because I insisted on doing what was right.'[3] Before the great revival of 1859, things had fallen into a low state; the years 1855–8 were barren in spiritual results; preaching had largely lost its power; there were bickerings and dissensions in the chapels, and 'the meetings in the week were largely forsaken, and on Sundays the empty pews were more suggestive of a timber yard than of a congregation'.[4] There were chapels in the north of Monmouthshire which reached their maximum membership after the 1849 revival, and thereafter slowly declined. Thomas Rees's church in Beaufort showed an increase of 356 in membership during 1850, to bring the total membership to 520,[5] and in two years it had fallen to 450.[6] Every Welsh Independent church in Monmouthshire which appeared in the Association's report showed a substantial fall in membership by 1852, although most had added to the membership in the current year. The Monmouthshire Baptist Association, meeting in Brynmawr in 1863, painted a gloomy picture of the state of its churches: 'Although the last year has not been altogether unfruitful, yet it is more than doubtful whether we have made any real progress—that we have not lost more by death, defection, and other changes, than we have gained by fresh accession. As it often happens after seasons of revival excitement, several of the

[1] Thomas Lewis, op. cit., p. 44. [2] Ibid., p. 55.
[3] Ibid., p. 145. [4] Evan Price, op. cit., p. 52–53.
[5] *Llythyr y ddwy gymmanfa ddeheuol* (1850), p. 21.
[6] *Llythyr y ddwy gymmanfa ddeheuol* (1852), p. 8.

churches have reason to mourn on account of a grievous reaction, on the spiritual decline of the members, the falling away of many professors, and the increasing hardness of the hearers.'[1]

These outbreaks of revivalism throw light on the nature of the denominations which were affected by them. Hitherto it has been generally believed that this spirit was imparted to the older Dissent in Wales as the result of the evangelical Methodist revival of the eighteenth century, though it should be pointed out that the older Nonconformity showed little signs of this spirit up to and beyond the end of that century. But this type of revival is a recurrent experience in a certain type of church, the church of the poor, the church of the dispossessed. Speaking of the Methodist movement in the eighteenth century a modern writer has said: 'It was the only way religion could become real to the class which composed the movement, it furnished that group with a psychologically effective escape from the drudgeries of an unromantic unaesthetic life.'[2] The denominations which were represented on the 'frontier' of the United States of America in the last century experienced this type of revival, the settlers being 'subject to the feverish phenomena of revivalism',[3] whose manifestations were 'fervent preaching, rich in images, nervous disturbances, spreading from person to person, from town to town, the sudden accessions of peace',[4] a description which would fit a Welsh as aptly as an American revival.

Eighteenth-century Nonconformity in Wales did not experience this type of revival; it was not at that time the church of the poor. It became the church of the working class for a period in the nineteenth century when it was powerful on the Welsh 'frontier'. Dr. Thomas Rees attributed the recurrence of revivals after 1842 to 'Mr. Finney's Lectures', Mr. Finney being an American evangelist; and the

[1] *Monmouthshire Baptist Association Circular Letter* (1863).

[2] Richard Niebuhr, *The social sources of denominationalism* (New York, 1960), p. 62. [3] Ibid., p. 142. [4] Ibid., p. 149.

effect of his lectures, according to Dr. Thomas Rees's biographer, was to change Nonconformist preaching from being a matter of the head to being a matter of the heart.[1] This type of preaching certainly appealed to working-class congregations, and the social character of the congregations and the dismal conditions in which their members lived possibly accounted for the successful recurrence of emotional revivalism. Let it be emphasized that the circumstances in which these experiences came neither validate nor invalidate their reality, but only explain why it was that religious experiences came to this particular society in this way.

But these revivals also emphasized the other-worldly nature of Nonconformity and its strong evangelicalism. They saved converts from 'the world' and they strengthened the characteristic of evangelicalism in its negative attitude to the ills of contemporary society. They marked the triumph of Nonconformist evangelicalism, but they left this industrial society very much as they found it. At the root of this attitude was the antithesis between body and soul. 'The sternest Christian opponents of reform were those who believed most completely that the body and soul were antithetical, and that the duty of a Christian was to reject the world, not to sanctify it.'[2] We shall see later that this criticism was levelled at Welsh Nonconformity in the nineteenth century, and it should be pointed out here that Welsh theology was little affected by those movements in English theology represented by Maurice who sought to emphasize the social implications of the Christian Faith; nor for that matter was the evangelical character of the Established Church in Wales much affected by such movements and ideas.

[1] John Thomas, *Cofiant y Parch. T. Rees, D.D.*, pp. 95–96.

[2] K. S. Inglis, *Churches and the Working Classes in Victorian England* (London, 1963), p. 304. Inglis quotes from a report by the Congregational Union in 1890: 'It was the defect of honoured leaders of the Evangelical Revival, as it has remained the defect of that great movement, that it disparaged and belittled the life on earth, except so far as it was a preparation for the life above' (ibid., p. 306). This passage was omitted before the report was circulated to the churches.

Closely connected with these revivals was the temperance movement: indeed, it was believed at the time that it was those churches which supported the latter that benefited most from the former. The temperance movement prepared the way for religious revival, but it also drove a wedge between the older and younger generation of ministers, especially in Monmouthshire, Glamorgan and Carmarthenshire, the older ministers believing that the younger were going too far in their protest.[1] Before the 1840s, Welsh Nonconformity was by no means allied with teetotalism. It was usual for chapel members to frequent public houses, and there were places where public houses were associated with certain chapels; thus in 1837 the 'Three Cranes' in Pontypool was kept by a Calvinistic Methodist elder. Itinerant preachers were supplied with beer, sometimes kept in a barrel under the pulpit, and later to be replaced by peppermint when the teetotal movement began to take effect.[2] Calvinistic Methodist preachers in Tredegar were given a tobacco and beer allowance in addition to their fee.[3] A Calvinistic Methodist minister, William Rowlands of Blackwood, preached a very powerful sermon against strong drink at the meeting of the Presbytery in Varteg on 24 September 1833, and in its published form this sermon greatly advanced the cause of teetotalism.[4] It came to be believed that the strictly temperance societies (*y cymdeithasau cymedroldeb*) were not successful in dealing with the social problem of drunkenness, and so teetotal societies (*cymdeithasau dirwest*) began in north Wales and spread to the south. One such society was founded in Merthyr in October 1836, and in Hirwaun a month later,[5] and they spread across north Monmouthshire in the following months. Resistance was met with in Tredegar, but in Varteg, the works' proprietors, Kenrick and Bowman, were keen

[1] John Thomas, *Cofiant y Parch. T. Rees*, pp. 99–100.

[2] John Thomas, *Jubili y diwygiad dirwestol yng Nghymru* (Merthyr Tydfil, 1885), p. 36.

[3] James Llewelyn, op. cit., p. 15.

[4] John Thomas, *Jubili y diwygiad dirwestol yng Nghymru*, p. 36.

[5] Ibid., p. 143.

supporters of the movement, and by the summer of 1837 it had reached Pontypool;[1] and in 1845 'The Gwent and Morganwg Temperance Society' was formed. What degree of success attended the work of the teetotal societies is difficult to estimate. Thomas Jones says that it was the Baptists in Rhymney who lagged behind in this matter, and we are told that when William Morris was inducted as pastor of his Baptist church in Treorchy in May 1869, he was the only total abstainer in his church, 'a distinction he held for several years'.[2] A fair conclusion of results would be that the strictly teetotal movement affected the Welsh chapel members, but that the mass of the population was not greatly influenced by it, for much beer was consumed in these areas throughout the century. The Calvinistic Methodist Association in their meeting at Hirwaun in 1871 said that in spite of all the efforts of the past years drunkenness was on the increase. After attending a miners' demonstration in Bargoed in 1904, Thomas Jones went with the executive to a local inn for 'an enormous feast', and passing through the bar,

> the room was crowded, not with men from my audience, but with colliers coming off from some shift. . . . They were all gulping down beer . . . the air reeked of stale beer and was thick with the odour of the coal-pit. I experienced an instantaneous and unforgettable physical revulsion, utterly unworthy of a Christian or a Comrade. . . . The contrast between the serious and sober and thoughtful demeanour of the audience I had just been addressing and these slaves of appetite was not to be explained or justified by the pressure of poverty, of the capitalist system, of chapel-going hypocrisy. Indignation with 'the system' was blunted by the fact that the sheep and the goats dwelt as neighbours in the one community. If religion was the opium of the one, alcohol was the opium of the other.[3]

The temperance movement scored a great success in obtaining Sunday closing for Wales, although Monmouthshire was excluded from this legislation. Agitation for this

1 Ibid., p. 148.
2 E. D. Lewis, *The Rhondda Valleys* (London, 1959), p. 223, n. 6.
3 Thomas Jones, *Welsh Broth* (London, n.d.), p. 37.

measure began about 1869, and was greatly strengthened by a conference convened in Cardiff on 17 December 1871 at which Ollivant, Bishop of Llandaff, presided. A house-to-house canvass in Cardiff in 1880 revealed that 82 per cent. were in favour of closing public houses on Sundays, only 4 per cent. being opposed to it; and generally, throughout south Wales, the publicans were themselves in favour of the proposed measure. Of the petitions sent to M.P.s, that from Merthyr Tydfil contained the signatures of 21,450 in favour, while of 2,138 collier householders in Aberdare, 1,976 approved and 91 opposed Sunday closing. Of artisan householders, 776 were in favour, 34 were against, and 23 were neutral. Even among the publicans themselves, 45 were for the proposed measure, 28 were against, and 12 were neutral.[1] The Welsh Sunday Closing Act was passed on 20 August 1881.

Outwardly the passing of this Act was a triumph for the temperance movement in general and for the chapels in particular, but in reality the campaign revealed a theological and social failure. The question of drink was bound up with the nature and structure of this industrial society: put bluntly, most men went to the pubs because there was no other alternative to the churches and the chapels, and the closing of public houses on Sunday did not touch the real social problem underlying drink. The whole attitude of the temperance workers revealed 'a lack of sensitivity to the secular world' shown by 'the tendency of the churches to reduce complex social problems to a matter of personal morality', and 'inevitably the social habits of the working class . . . were the easiest darts of evangelical moralism'.[2] Too often where Welsh Nonconformity and evangelical churchmanship flourished the good life was largely interpreted in terms of Sunday observance and total abstinence.

In this Welsh Nonconformist society the key figure and the natural leader was the minister. G. T. Clark, a trustee of

[1] E. Beavan, *The history of the Welsh Sunday Closing Act* (Cardiff, 1885), p. 56.
[2] E. R. Wickham, op. cit., p. 194.

the Dowlais Works, giving evidence before the Royal Commission on Trades Unions in 1867, said: 'I believe the Dissenting minister to have more influence with the Welshman than any man living';[1] and to the same Commission, George Elliot, owner of the Dyffryn collieries, Aberdare, testified that when he wanted to persuade his men to adopt a new system of working the coal seams he consulted Bruce Pryce, of Dyffryn, and also 'Dr. Price, who is a great preacher and a very clever man, and has enormous influence amongst the people there, and told him what was inevitable. They both recommended me to take a different course from that which had been generally taken'.[2]

Such a position in these industrial communities came only gradually and with the dominant social and political power ultimately achieved by Nonconformity. For the greater part of the first half of the nineteenth century the Nonconformist ministry was of the same pattern as it had assumed in the preceding century when it was largely a part-time ministry in the sense that a number of ministers followed other occupations: farmers, carpenters, underground agents with the Hanburys of Pontypool, and one was an official interpreter in the Monmouth and Usk courts. This arrangement was necessary because the chapels then were too weak to maintain a full-time pastor. The settled ministry arose gradually, and it was preceded by an itinerant ministry by which it was customary, up to and beyond the middle of the last century, for Nonconformist ministers to go on preaching tours, sometimes in groups. This was a form of education for them; and the spread of Nonconformity during the first half of the last century was attributed partly to this custom. An older generation of ministers regarded this practice as apostolic in its nature and deplored those who condemned it.[3] There

[1] *Fifth Report of the Commissioners appointed to inquire into the organization and rules of Trades Unions and other Associations: together with Minutes of Evidence* (London, 1868), pp. 87–88. [2] *Sixth Report of the Commissioners . . .*, p. 2.

[3] Llewellyn Jenkins a Timothy Thomas, *Cofiant o'r diweddar Barch. Thomas Morris, Casnewydd-ar-Wysg* (Caerdydd, 1847), pp. 12–13.

were others who went on preaching tours to reduce chapel debts. Thomas Morris travelled 474 miles in 1838 to help reduce the debt incurred by the building of Crane Street Baptist chapel, Pontypool.[1] Perhaps the outstanding example of a church which relied entirely on visiting preachers, to the neglect of pastoral work, was the Calvinistic Methodist church in Tredegar which existed for exactly one hundred years before appointing its first pastor in 1899.[2] Those were the days of powerful preaching in Welsh Nonconformity, but there were some who deplored this emphasis because it led to the neglect of pastoral oversight.

When the settled ministry became the rule the ministers were very poorly paid. Evan Jones (Ieuan Gwynedd) a well-known figure in Nonconformity and a pastor of the Welsh Independent church in Tredegar, wrote that he did not know of a single minister in the Principality belonging to the Independents, Baptists or Welsh Methodists, whose salary exceeded £120 per annum, that there were not twenty ministers who received £100, and that £50 per annum was a high average of ministerial salaries.[3] The truth is that the average stipend did not amount to that figure, for even the prominent ministers scarcely reached that level for a long time. When J. P. Davies went to Tredegar as a Baptist minister in 1818 he received £40 a year and a free house,[4] and there were some who believed that ministers should not be paid at all. Two earlier co-pastors of the same church had each been paid 12*s*. 6*d*. per quarter in 1813. One of the most famous of all Nonconformist ministers in Monmouthshire in the last century was Dr. Thomas Rees, who was paid 10*s*. per month in his first pastorate in Craigyfargod in 1836.[5] He married on 12*s*. per month, and to eke this out he opened a shop which proved unsuccessful. He went to Aberdare for

[1] Jenkins and Thomas, op. cit. p. 30. [2] James Llewelyn, op. cit., p. 59.

[3] Evan Jones, *Dissent and Morality in Wales* (London, 1847), p. 47.

[4] E. Thomas, *Crybwyllion hanesiol am Eglwys Silo, Tredegar* (ail argraffiad, Tredegar, 1858), p. 24.

[5] John Thomas, *Cofiant T. Rees*, p. 73.

£3. 10*s.* 0*d.* per month, and this was considered generous, while £5 per month was exceptional, and £7 per month was obtained only in the most flourishing chapels in the industrial areas. The number of members in Rees's church in Aberdare at the time was 150; 1*s.* was the payment for a preaching engagement and, in Merthyr, an extra 2*s.* 6*d.* was added for the preacher who travelled on horseback.[1] When Rees went to Beaufort in 1849 the invitation extended to him did not promise a specified sum—'because of our knowledge of the ironworks'—but it said that his predecessor had received £77. 14*s.* 3*d.* in 1846 and £50. 11*s.* 1*d.* in 1848; 'thus you see that we do not desire to mislead you'.[2] But Rees's salary in Beaufort always exceeded the higher sum mentioned. Likewise when Dr. Thomas Price went to Aberdare in 1848 it was the first time that a fixed stipend had been offered, his predecessors having had to make do with what the congregation could afford.[3] His predecessor, William Lewis, had been a foreman carpenter at the Dowlais Works, and was thus not dependent upon his pastorate. Even in Merthyr in 1852 the pastor of Zoar Independent church was paid £5 a year, raised to £7 at the end of the year and five years later to £8 per year. The chapel historian apologized for these low stipends and said that by his time things had improved.[4] Two years before Thomas Rees came to Beaufort a prominent Baptist minister and Welsh poet, Robert Ellis (Cynddelw), came to Sirhowy from north Wales because of the smallness of the stipend in his former pastorate. He said that north Walians expected strong theological meat, but were not prepared to pay for it: 'Mae nhw eisiau bwyd cryf iawn yn y pulpud, cig rhost a phwdin bob tro fel yna, ond pan mae nhw'n talu, talu tatws a llaeth mae nhw'n wir, ie, tatws a llaeth.'[5]

[1] Ibid., p. 155.
[2] Ibid., p. 284.
[3] Benjamin Evans, op. cit., p. 33.
[4] R. Griffiths, op. cit., p. 22.
[5] Quoted by J. Spinther James, *Cynddelw: Traethawd Bywgraffyddol a Beirniadol* (Caernarfon, 1877). [Trans.: They expect strong fare in the pulpit, roast meat and pudding, but when they come to pay, they pay for milk and potatoes, yes indeed, milk and potatoes.]

D. R. Stephen, a well-known Baptist pastor who came to Aber-carn in 1850 was paid £3 per month.[1]

We are not told how much Robert Ellis was given in Sirhowy, but we can follow the financial fortunes of his co-Baptist, Thomas Lewis. In 1847 he began his ministry in Llanddewi Rhydderch at £37 per annum[2] which was raised to £48. 10*s*. 0*d*. on his marriage, and out of which he had to pay £8. 10*s*. 0*d*. annually for the rent of his cottage, 'so I had £40 for a family of four and a servant'.[3] He received 15*s*. for a Sunday's engagement in Rhymney and thought it very good, but only 4*s*. in Tudor Street, Abergavenny, for one service.[4] From Llanddewi Rhydderch Lewis went in 1856 to Llanelly (Brecknockshire) at £60 per year, and four years later to Rhymney where he was given £78 per annum.[5] From 1863 to 1875 he was a pastor in Carmarthen, and he returned to Monmouthshire, to Risca, at the same salary as he had received in Carmarthen, viz., £96 per annum. But in 1877 trade was so bad that this was reduced to £3 or £4 per month because of the closure of the tin-plate works in Pontymister, and this low stipend persisted until the works were reopened in March 1879.[6] In view of the fortunes of prominent ministers, it is unlikely that Evan Jones's minimum of £50 as the average minister's stipend was realized for a long time in the industrial areas. But it was believed at the time that the Nonconformist churches of industrial Monmouthshire and the adjacent areas of Glamorgan were most generous in their financial treatment of ministers in those days.

It is certain that they were able to attract prominent men, endowed with great natural ability, even though most of them had few early educational opportunities. Dr. Thomas Rees, of Beaufort, was the author of *A history of Protestant Nonconformity in Wales*, and as co-author of *Hanes Eglwysi Annibynol Cymru* was one of the best Welsh denominational

[1] Rex H. Pugh, op. cit., p. 25.
[2] Thomas Lewis, op. cit., p. 38.
[3] Ibid., p. 86.
[4] Ibid., p. 59.
[5] Ibid., p. 100.
[6] Ibid., p. 144.

historians in the nineteenth century. Reference has already been made to Evan Jones (Ieuan Gwynedd), of the same denomination as Rees, who is still remembered for his attack on the findings of the Education Commissioners of 1847: *Brad y Llyfrau Gleision* (The Treachery of the Blue Books). But it was the Baptists, with their preponderance in these parts, who attracted the greatest number of eminent men as pastors. R. H. Stephen, in Aber-carn, co-operated with Augusta Hall in popularizing Welsh literature; Robert Ellis (Cynddelw) was pastor of Carmel church, Sirhowy, from 1847 to 1862 and was a well-known poet, author and eisteddfodwr; William Roberts (Nefydd), pastor of Salem church, Blaina, from 1845 to 1872 was an educationist, Superintendent for South Wales of the British and Foreign Schools' Society, and a noted bibliophile; John Jones (Mathetes), pastor of Penuel church, Rhymney, was the author of a Bible dictionary in Welsh; Dr. Thomas Price, of Aberdare, was one of the civic as well as religious leaders of that community, and Dr. Thomas Thomas was president of the Baptist College, Pontypool. These are only a few of the more prominent Nonconformist ministers who held pastorates in these industrial areas in the last century. These men were not only pastors of churches, but were also a strong cultural influence in their neighbourhood. Dr. Thomas Price organized a literary Society in connexion with his church in Aberdare with a very comprehensive programme which included biblical and theological studies, English, Latin, Greek, Hebrew grammar, composition and philosophy. Price organized this Society because the Mechanics' Institutes were 'in the hands of the world', and because most of the social clubs were in connexion with the public houses.[1] Thomas Lewis, when pastor at Llanddewi Rhydderch, kept school there until apathy discouraged him, but when he moved to Llanelly (Brecknockshire) he took a weekly class in English

[1] J. Rufus Williams, *Hanes athrofeydd y Bedyddwyr yn Sir Fynwy* (Aberdar, 1863), pp. 21–24.

grammar and in music,[1] and of his last pastorate, in Risca, Lewis wrote: 'I worked very hard while at Risca. As Pastor I attended Bible Classes, Singing Schools, Y.M.C.A.s, Temperance Meetings, Political Meetings, and School Board Meetings without number. . . . I wrote several hundred letters to the Education Department, and to other parties. More than £7,000 passed through my hands, and without one shilling error.'[2] These are but very few of the activities which went on in those days in connexion with Welsh chapels. These chapels were not only centres of spiritual influence, but were real cultural centres as well, strongly fortified by the vigorous denominational literature which flourished in those days. The debt of the communities thrown up by the industrial revolution to the Welsh chapels is incalculable.

But by the middle of the nineteenth century Welsh Nonconformity had to face the problem of language. Monmouthshire by that time had a fairly well-defined linguistic line between the Welsh north and the English south. But the Baptists did not wait until the language difficulty was obvious before embarking on an anglicizing policy. In 1807 Micah Thomas, a prominent Monmouthshire Baptist minister, founded a Baptist theological college in Abergavenny primarily to train Welsh Baptist students to preach in the English language,[3] and it was not until 1827 that the authorities of the college decided to pay more attention to the Welsh language.[4] Of the 30 churches and 13 branches which constituted the Monmouthshire Baptist Association in 1832, ten of the churches were English and three were bilingual.[5] The Association contained Welsh and English churches until 1857 when the Monmouthshire English Baptist Association was formed, largely 'to aid the formation of English churches in the destitute parts of the county'.[6] The new Association

[1] Thomas Lewis, op. cit., p. 99. [2] Ibid., p. 146.
[3] Rufus Williams, op. cit., p. 26. [4] Ibid., p. 32.
[5] *Llythyron y Gymmanfa* (Beulah, 1832).
[6] D. J. Thomas, *A short history of the Monmouthshire English Baptist Association* (Newport, 1857), p. 8.

consisted of 11 churches with 610 members at its inception, and by 1907 it had grown to 43 churches with 5,961 members.[1] The Baptists accepted the anglicization of Monmouthshire, and 'no effort is recorded by letter or resolution to stem the on-coming English tide by adopting some measures to ground the young generation in the ancient language. Even Mathetes, as sound a Welshman as ever was, confines himself to advocating the opening of more English causes'.[2] The parent body, the Monmouthshire Baptist Association, did show a mild concern with the language question, but only to encourage the founding of more English churches. In their meeting at Risca in 1873 the Association passed this resolution: 'That as the rapid increase of the English language in this county calls for an effort to establish English churches in several localities . . . further attention will be called to the subject at the commencement of the next Quarterly Meeting's Conference.'[3] Yet, when the Monmouthshire English Baptist Association had been formed in 1857, Baptist strength still lay in the Welsh churches, for while 62 dozen copies of the English *Circular Letter* were ordered in that year, 111 dozen of the Welsh *Circular Letter* were called for.

Not only were the Baptists following an English policy in respect of their language of worship, but their Sunday-schools were largely bilingual from an early date. In Glamorgan they had 58 such schools in 1847, of which 8 were conducted in Welsh, 5 were English, and 45 were bilingual. The Welsh Baptists were easily the most anglicized and anglicizing denomination among the Welsh Nonconformists; thus, in Glamorgan in 1847 the Sunday-school language figures for the other denominations were: the Independents, 99 schools, 52 Welsh, 5 English and 42 bilingual; the Calvinistic Methodists, 90 schools, 65 Welsh, 4 English and 21 bilingual.[4]

[1] Ibid., p. 30.

[2] Thomas Richards (ed.), *Monmouthshire English Baptist Association Circular Letters, 1866–1906* (Newport, 1947), p. 6.

[3] *Monmouthshire Baptist Association Circular Letter* (1873), p. 6.

[4] *Reports of the Commissioners of Inquiry into the state of education in Wales*, i. 106.

If the Baptists were the most anglicized body, the Calvinistic Methodists were the most Welsh.

Among the Welsh Independents it was Dr. Thomas Rees who showed most zeal for opening English churches. He began to preach in English when he went to Aberdare in 1840, although there were few English people in the town at that time.[1] He opened an English church there, one in Llanelly (Carm.) in 1839, and another in Beaufort in 1849. The first English Independent church in Monmouthshire was that at Ebbw Vale, founded in 1843,[2] so that the Independents were a generation later than the Baptists in opening English churches. But Thomas Rees was to organize opinion in his denomination to this end. In a paper read at the autumn meeting of the Congregational Union of England and Wales in Halifax in 1858, Rees said: 'In many districts of the Principality the state of society is just now passing through an important change, by the rapid increase of the English population, and the consequent prevalence of the English language. Nothing will prevent the utter extinction of our interests in these districts but the immediate establishment of efficient English preaching.'[3] Seven years later, addressing the same body in Bristol, he claimed that Welsh Nonconformity had succeeded in bringing the means of grace to every Welshman, but the task which now remained was 'to provide an efficient English ministry, attractive places of worship, schools and other places of religious instruction throughout all those districts where the English language prevails'.[4] He went on to say how the Welsh ministers of Monmouthshire had met at Beaufort (where Rees was a pastor) in 1853, when Thomas Thompson of Bath had undertaken to contribute £150 per year for two or three years to help English churches in Brynmawr, Ebbw Vale and Beaufort. Further conferences were held at

[1] John Thomas, *Cofiant T. Rees*, p. 106.
[2] T. Rees and J. Thomas, *Hanes Eglwysi Annibynol Cymru*, iii. 209.
[3] T. Rees, *Miscellaneous Papers*, p. 82. [4] Ibid., p. 86.

Merthyr, Swansea, Cardiff and Newport, when financial support for the same purposes was given by two brothers from Bristol, Messrs. W. D. and H. O. Wills.[1]

The Independent denomination took the same step as the Baptists had done before them by forming two County Associations, an English and a Welsh. By 1871 the former consisted of 27 churches and the latter 35, but it seems that in the English districts the pioneer work was done by the Welsh.[2] It was by no means uncommon for a group of Welsh-speaking members to leave their own chapel to establish an 'English cause'. Many English chapels were founded by Welsh-speaking members. The Calvinistic Methodists were the last of the three leading Welsh Nonconformist denominations even to consider the problem of language. This was not done until the Association (*Y Sasiwn*) met in Sirhowy in 1876 where it was recognized that the English language was prevailing in Monmouthshire because of English immigration, but, as in the other Nonconformist bodies, the only reaction was to encourage the founding of English churches.[3] The matter was again discussed in Ebbw Vale (Pen-y-cae) in 1880, but no policy resulted.[4] It is interesting that the Association at Sirhowy had said that it was the middle class which was being most affected by this change, but in Ystrad Rhondda, in 1877, it was urged that English chapels should not be opened where there was already a Welsh church under the jurisdiction of the Association.[5] In Newport in 1877 it was decided that the Association's *Circular Letters* should be published in English as well as in Welsh,[6] and in Rhymney in 1900 the Association decided to hold its ordinations in English at the request of the Monmouthshire Presbytery, which reported that many of its ordinands could not speak

[1] Ibid., p. 87.

[2] Rees and Thomas, *Hanes Eglwysi Annibynol Cymru*, i. 228.

[3] *Cylchlythyrau Cymdeithasfaol y Methodistiaid Calfinaidd yn Neheudir Cymru am 1876. Cymdeithasfa Sirhowy*, pp. 2, 4.

[4] Ibid., *Cymdeithasfa Penycae* (1880), p. 5.

[5] Ibid., *Cymdeithasfa Ystrad Rhondda* (1876).

[6] Ibid., *Cymdeithasfa Casnewydd ar Wysg* (1877), p. 2.

Welsh.[1] This reluctance of the Calvinistic Methodists to make language concessions was due to their being an entirely Welsh religious body in their origin in the eighteenth century, and they still had no organic connexion with any English ecclesiastical body, whereas the Independents and Baptists belonged to larger unions which were more English than Welsh in their ramifications.

It may surprise some readers that Welsh Nonconformist leaders in these parts in the last century should have been concerned with the problem of language, but it should not be forgotten that they were prepared to sacrifice the language for the sake of religion. If the choice were as clear as this they did their duty as Christians, but they overlooked the close connexion between Welsh Nonconformity and the Welsh language. Nonconformity in Wales was, and is, one with English Nonconformity in its theology and polity; with the exception of the Calvinistic Methodists (now the Presbyterian Church of Wales) Nonconformity was an importation from England into Wales. But there can be no doubt that it took on a Welsh dress and found its expression through the medium of the Welsh language; it had a homespun quality which made it essentially Welsh in texture. Events were to show by the end of the century that it was losing its distinctive character by the decline of the Welsh language and that, consequently, its hold on the industrial areas was weakening. It might have been expected that the decline in Welsh Nonconformity would have led to a corresponding strengthening of the 'English cause' in the same denomination. But this has not been so: the change in language meant the loss of a distinctive quality from which English Nonconformity in these parts did not ultimately benefit. This difference in texture between English and Welsh Nonconformity also probably accounted for a complaint that Thomas Rees made in an address, already referred to, to the Congregational Union of England and Wales in Bristol in 1865, when

[1] Ibid., *Cymdeithasfa Twyncarno* (1900), p. 5.

he accused English Nonconformists of abandoning their Nonconformity when they came to Wales:

> Numbers of educated persons of the middle class come, year after year, from England to occupy positions of respectability and influence in the Principality. We find that many of these gentlemen were members of Congregational churches in England, but on their arrival in Wales, they, almost without exception, renounce their Nonconformity. After reaching the places of their destination, for a few Sabbaths they will go about and visit the Independent, the Baptist, and the Wesleyan chapels; but, finding neither chapels, ministers, nor congregations, up to their mark in point of respectability, they make their home at the parish church, where the presence of a few country squires, lawyers, and surgeons, will feed their pride.[1]

It would probably be more true to say that the English immigrants found that the change to a Welsh parish church in those days, with its prevailing low-church and evangelical character, and especially to those churches in the industrial areas, was less abrupt than the change from English Nonconformity to Welsh Nonconformity. It is equally probable that these English Nonconformists, with their urban middle-class background, either failed or did not try, to assimilate themselves into churches with a working-class membership. If this was so, then English Congregationalism stood for the norm of middle-class Nonconformity, while Welsh Congregationalism for a time had departed from its middle-class character to revert to it later in the century. But for a long time the transition from English to Welsh Nonconformity was a far greater social and cultural change than it was a theological one. Speaking of the Congregationalism of New England, Richard Niebuhr writes: 'Its characteristics were not those of the religiously naïve, but those of the established and cultured social classes.'[2] The same distinction must have struck the English immigrants between the cultured, urban Nonconformity of England and the religiously naïve character

[1] Thomas Rees, *Miscellaneous Papers*, p. 89.
[2] R. Niebuhr, op. cit., pp. 147–8.

of Welsh Nonconformity with its rural background, before it had undergone the change that awaited it in the second half of the nineteenth century.

It is now time to examine the relationship between the chapels and the industrial society in which they were situated, and to which in many respects they made such a great contribution. To what extent did they show a concern and a responsibility for the welfare of that society as a whole? It might be expected that, as this industrial society contained tens of thousands of workers who were members and attenders of the chapels, the latter would have shown consistent practical sympathy and concern with the problems of these areas and with the efforts made by the workers to improve their lot; in fact, however, some of the denominations were more concerned with the welfare of 'our brethren' abroad than with those on their own doorstep.

It is well known that Welsh Nonconformity was antagonistic to the early workers' unions and benefit societies which played an important part in industrial life in the last century. This attitude was partly due to the oaths of secrecy which the members of such clubs had to take and partly to the fact that they met in public houses.[1] In 1831 a pamphlet was published in Newport which purported to give an account of a conversation between two colliers, Thomas Cadogan and David Nathaniel. The former had some doubts about the oaths he had taken on being initiated into a workers' union, while the latter took the view that, having been taken, the oaths should be kept. While they were discussing the point 'the Preacher' joined them and took part in the discussion. He said that he had previously been 'in Mr. Rhys

[1] An interesting benefit society which was only local in its activity was a craftsmen's union called 'Cymdeithas Unol y Blaenau': the United Blaenau Society, which was connected with the Nant-y-glo ironworks and met in the 'Greyhound' (*Gwestfa y Milgi*). The members were sworn to secrecy, held an annual dinner, and on the same occasion attended divine service. This club was registered in Quarter Sessions in 1830. The rules and proceedings were in Welsh, and the benefits to the members in case of sickness and death were carefully graded. (*Rheolau Cymdeithas Unol y Blaenau* (Y Fenni, 1844).)

the Lawyer's office' where he had been introduced to Coke's *Institutes* which satisfied him that the oaths were illegal, while the third commandment taught him that they were immoral. Both Cadogan and Nathaniel resolved to have no more to do with these oaths.[1] The Baptists attacked their members who belonged to the Oddfellows because of 'the concealment of their tenets and their secret signs and symbols',[2] and the Calvinistic Methodists in their Association in Tredegar in 1833 did likewise in regard to union membership; and it will be recalled that one of the grounds of excommunication from chapel membership was the wearing of the badge of a benefit society.

Another attack on the workers' unions came from Thomas Revel Guest, the Methodist brother of the Dowlais industrialist. In a letter addressed to members of all Christian churches he asked his readers to consider if membership of these lodges was conducive to peace or whether it was not calculated to destroy that spirituality of mind that St. Paul referred to in Romans viii. 6.[3] Moreover, the oaths which had to be taken on joining the unions were contrary to Biblical teaching, 'swear not at all', and there were many who had regretted taking them. As for the plea that these unions were for the good of the workers and their families, Guest warned them of covetousness, and of infringing upon the providential order of God. These union societies 'completely oppose one branch of that commandment on which hangs all the law and the prophets, viz., thou shalt love thy neighbour as thyself'. Finally, membership of these unions took workers to places where they should not be found, viz., to public houses: 'are the frequenters of the publick House the most suitable companions for those that love God?', asked

[1] *On the oaths taken in the Union Club* (Newport, 1831).

[2] *Monmouthshire Merlin*, 13 July 1833. It is important to note that a year later (July 1834), the shop of the Reverend Thomas Rees in Craigyfargod was sacked by members of the 'Scotch Cattle' movement because Rees denounced the men for combining against their employers.

[3] 'For to be carnally minded, is death; but to be spiritually minded, is life and peace.'

Guest.[1] Comment on this is superfluous, but it is an indictment of the Christianity of the industrial revolution in these parts that it could have been written at all, and, apparently, in all sincerity. In view of the antagonism of the chapels to these early workers' unions it is easy to understand the following judgement on the collapse of the Friendly Society of Coalmining in 1831: 'Among factors peculiar to South Wales, one obvious reason for the union's collapse was the opposition of the nonconformist religious groups. . . . These religious groups generally declined to interfere in industrial matters, despite the vast influence they possessed.'[2]

It will be readily believed that there was a general antagonism to Chartism on the part both of the Established Church and of Nonconformity. Chartism shook many congregations in industrial Monmouthshire to their foundations. The democratic spirit, characteristic of Independency, was carried to excess, to the detriment of law and order. The movement brought to the fore a type of leader who disturbed the peace of congregations and in some places strained the relationship between pastors and their flocks.[3] When the Chartists assembled in north Monmouthshire and marched on Newport on Sunday night, 3 November 1839, and the early hours of the following morning, John Ridge, pastor of the Independent church at Beaufort, spent the night under the pulpit stairs, and Richard Jones, his counterpart in Sirhowy, spent the night up to his chin in water in the works' feeder.[4] On the following Sunday evening Jones preached a sermon, 'suitable to the occasion', to his flock in which he 'gravely expostulated with every member of his church, male and female, that he had any reason to believe to have any connexion with those outlaws, and excommunicated some known Chartists'.[5]

[1] Thomas Revel Guest, *A Plain Address to such Members of the Union Lodges as are in connection with Christian churches.* (In manuscript).

[2] E. W. Evans, *The miners of South Wales* (Cardiff, 1961), p. 45.

[3] T. Rees and J. Thomas, op. cit. i. 230–1.

[4] John Thomas, *Cofiant T. Rees*, p. 90.

[5] *Monmouthshire Merlin*, 16 November 1839.

The following year the church was split over this matter of excommunication and discipline, a section declaring that such action had not expressed the will of the majority of the church,[1] but it is clear that an antagonism had arisen between the pastor and his people. On the other hand, there were chapels and pastors who were sympathetic to Chartism. Benjamin Byron, pastor of Hope Independent church, Newport, was one of these. John Frost, the Chartist leader, occasionally attended this church, and some members of his family were members there.[2] Another exception to the general rule was David John, a Unitarian minister of Merthyr Tydfil, but he divided his church on social and political issues.

With these few exceptions Nonconformist leaders condemned Chartism and were anxious to dissociate Nonconformity from it. Thomas Thomas, principal of the Baptist College, Pontypool, wrote an article in the *Standard* in which he hoped to counteract the falsehood of those who believed that the late outbreak could be traced to the principles of civil and religious liberty as maintained by Nonconformists, whereas, in truth, thousands had been deterred from participation in the rising through the influence of Nonconformity. Investigation had shown that not more than fifty dissenters had joined the march on Newport and that the majority of the rioters were but 'the neglected population of the Parliamentary Church'.[3]

Thomas's fellow Baptist, Thomas Morris, pastor of the Baptist church at the Tabernacle, Pontypool, preached on the Chartist rising on 24 December 1839. He condemned some of the aims and all the methods of the Chartists, and claimed that the trouble had been caused by English

[1] *Llythyr, yn rhoddi hanes yr ymraniad a gymerodd le yn ddiweddar yn eglwys yr Anymddibynwyr a arferai ymgynull yn Ebenezer, Sirhowy, o dan ofal y Parch. R. Jones* (Crughywel, 1841).

[2] T. Rees and J. Thomas, op. cit., i. 118.

[3] Quoted by J. Vyrnwy Morgan, *Welsh religious leaders in the Victorian Era* (London, 1905), pp. 149–50. It was also claimed at the time that only one Roman Catholic joined the Chartists.

agitators, of whom he said that it were better had they been drowned in the Severn than come to Wales. Obedience to law and recourse to constitutional forms were a Christian duty. It was true that there were Nonconformists who took part in the rising; and there were many Chartists who were earning between five and ten pounds per month who would be better employed in reforming themselves than attempting to reform the government. But the majority of those who took part in the rising were members of the Established Church (if membership could be claimed for those who had been baptized in infancy). The local Chartist leaders were deists and, in one case, an atheist. But Thomas Morris traced the trouble to the bad example shown by the upper classes and by local industrialists. He was at pains to emphasize that Nonconformity was not a revolutionary force: Nonconformists were loyal supporters of the government, and although they acknowledged Christ as their Head, yet, in things temporal, the Queen had no more faithful subjects than they.[1]

Morris was not the only person who believed that English agitators were the cause of social unrest in the industrial areas. R. W. Lingen reported of Merthyr Tydfil: 'Political agitation seldom originates at Merthyr: it is excited by delegates from the English mining districts';[2] and Dr. Thomas Rees believed that one of the weaknesses of the Welsh worker was his readiness to become the dupe of English agitators. The impression Rees gives is that the Welsh worker was a rather docile fellow.[3]

There was no difference between church and chapel in their attitude to Chartism. J. R. Taylor, curate of St. Woolos, Newport, was actually asked to repeat a sermon he gave on the events of 4 November 1839,[4] and James Francis,

[1] Thomas Morris, *Cynghor da mewn amser drwg* (Caerdydd, 1840).

[2] *Reports of the Commissioners of Inquiry into the state of education in Wales*, i. 116.

[3] T. Rees, *Miscellaneous Papers*, pp. 19–20.

[4] *Monmouthshire Merlin*, 16 November 1839.

incumbent of the newly built St. Paul's church in the town had preached a sermon on Chartism on the preceding 21 April. He had little to say in it except that, although there might not be anything sinful in the objects of Chartism, yet the means proposed to achieve them might be sinful; and he struck a more prophetic note than he suspected when he warned his hearers that 'those who have wealth would soon find the means of defence against your assaults, or of removal beyond the reach of your violence'.[1]

Although Merthyr Tydfil had been and was to remain the centre of radicalism for this new industrial area, the physical force school of Chartists had little following there, so that this area was not involved in the events of 3–4 November 1839. On 5 November a service was held in the parish church 'according to the special provision for this memorable day in the Book of Common Prayer', when the attendance was small on account of the excited state of the town,[2] but a little later Evan Jenkins, rector of Dowlais, preached a sermon which was printed and published and went into sixteen editions in one year.[3] In his sermon Jenkins had no difficulty in showing that rebellion is inconsistent with the teaching of the Church Catechism. He believed that a doctrine of equality was unscriptural and that God is alike the author of poverty and riches; and he seems to have satisfied himself that universal suffrage (one of the demands of the Chartists) would only lead to universal confusion, 'universal setting of workmen against each other, Dowlais against Penydarren, Cyfarthfa against Plymouth, Tredegar against Sirhowy, Beaufort against Ebbw Vale, Nant-y-glo against Varteg, etc.'[4] Nor did he trust Chartist leaders, for they were atheists and scoundrels: 'Would you, reader, like to live under the dynasty of king Twist? of king Williams? of king Vincent? of king

[1] James Francis, *A sermon to the working classes* (Newport, 1839), p. 22.

[2] *The Glamorgan, Monmouth and Brecon Gazette, and Merthyr Guardian*, 9 November 1839.

[3] Evan Jenkins, *Chartism Unmasked* (Merthyr Tydfil, 1840). It is quite possible that copies were distributed free.

[4] Ibid., p. 11.

Frost?'[1] As befitted the incumbent of a church built by the ironmaster J. J. Guest, Jenkins reminded his hearers and readers that riches carry great responsibility: 'No wonder the honest tradesman is not able to sleep!! Again, look at what you call the rich Iron Masters:—do not the countenances of many of them tell a tale? What care, what anxiety, what labour and toil must they be subject to, who have such a large stake in trade.'[2] But Jenkins did not forget to mention that not all was well in his parish, and he instanced bad housing, beer shops and truck shops.

We have seen that Welsh Nonconformity did not become involved in working-class movements in this industrial society; it was concerned almost exclusively with its own struggle to achieve legal equality with the Established Church. As far as the Baptists were concerned the main issues were promulgated at a meeting held on 26 December 1833 at the Frogmore Street Baptist chapel, Abergavenny, at which Micah Thomas presided, and an all-out attack was made on church rates, burial rights, tithes, marriage rights in chapels, and the non-admission of Nonconformists to Oxford and Cambridge;[3] the only issue omitted was that of disestablishment. With the exception of this last demand, which became persistent after the disestablishment of the Church in Ireland in 1869, all these rights were won in the nineteenth century: the right to solemnize marriages in chapels in the presence of a registrar in 1836; the right of Nonconformist ministers to officiate at funerals in public burial grounds in 1852 and in churchyards in 1880; the abolition of the church rate in 1868, and the right of admission for Nonconformists to Oxford and Cambridge in 1871, though they were not then eligible for fellowships, professorial chairs or degrees in theology.

The resolutions adopted by the Welsh Baptists in their County Association meetings in Monmouthshire show the

[1] Evan Jenkins, *Chartism Unmasked*, p. 12. [2] Ibid., p. 15.
[3] *Monmouthshire Merlin*, 28 December 1833.

social and political issues which concerned that denomination *in its official capacity* in the nineteenth century, and they reveal an indifference to those social problems which affected thousands of their members in this industrial society.[1] In Nant-y-glo (1834) the Association rejoiced that the Act for the abolition of Negro slavery would soon come into operation, and when the Association met at Llanwenarth in 1840 no reference was made to the Chartist movement and its manifestations in the county six months previously. In Sirhowy (1847) a resolution was adopted expressing thanks to Sir Benjamin Hall 'for his faithful conduct in Parliament in opposing the Government Plan of National Education', and the *Circular Letter* of that year stated:

> To all who have duly considered the subject, it must be obvious that our freedom and prosperity as Dissenting and Baptist Churches are seriously threatened by the course of policy recently pursued by the leading parties in the state, under the active influence of the state priesthood. That policy is not indeed carried out by means of fines, imprisonment, and death, usually resorted to by more honest persecutors of olden times: but by means of oppressive taxation; the multiplication of Bishops, Priests, and Churches; the corrupting of Presbyterian, Independent, and Baptist Ministers with the foul Regium Donum;[2] the bringing of every sect under the direct patronage, and its ministers into the pay, of Government; the general establishment, with the aid of public money, of Day-schools to be placed under clerical influence, and the supervision of Government agents,

with the result that such policies would consolidate the power of the aristocracy in Church and State. The *Circular Letter* went on to say that the Baptists must defend themselves against the encroachment of the 'State-Church principle', and beware of its financial blandishments, whether in the

[1] The account of the resolutions accepted by the Monmouthshire Baptist Association is taken in each case from the *Circular Letter* published by the Association.

[2] Regium Donum: payments made to Nonconformist ministers from public funds from the beginning of the eighteenth century to the middle of the last century.

guise of the Regium Donum or educational grants. Hitherto, Baptists had been content to defend themselves from the aggression of the Church Establishment, but 'henceforth let our policy be reversed, and the triumph of truth, righteousness, and liberty is certain'. Above all, the brethren should be resolute and faithful in the approaching parliamentary election, for it were better to keep away entirely from the polls than give support to any candidate, were he ever so estimable in private life, unless he was qualified to represent Baptist principles 'as perhaps the chief defenders of Christian liberty'.

On the eve of the important general election of 1868 the County Association met in Blaenau Gwent, where it supported the proposal for the disestablishment of the Church in Ireland and called upon all members of Baptist churches, as well as all other Liberals, to enter their names in the list of voters as soon as possible, so 'that all lovers of liberty may be ready and strong for the inevitable struggle so soon to take place'. More than any other denomination in these industrial areas the Baptists did not hesitate to reveal clearly their allegiance to the Liberal party. In 1875, in Llanhiddel, the County Association rejoiced in the Liberal victory in Brecon at the previous election 'and strongly disapprove of those Baptists who publicly supported the Conservative Candidate'. The same note was struck in Blaenavon in 1891 when it was resolved 'that in the County Council and parliamentary elections we trust the members of Churches will not be so unfaithful to their principles as to support or vote for Conservative Candidates', but in Cross Keys (1894) at an Association meeting attended by Mr. Lloyd George it was resolved that the time had come for the formation of a Welsh National party with a policy independent of, but not necessarily hostile to, that of the Liberal party. Throughout these County Association meetings the Baptists supported every motion for the disestablishment of the Church in Wales, legislation on education, international arbitration, and in

Pontypool (1885) for the appointment of more Nonconformist magistrates in Monmouthshire.

Throughout the period from 1832 to 1900 the Monmouthshire Welsh Baptist Association did not once discuss the social conditions of industrial Monmouthshire, with the exception of the problems of temperance and Sunday closing.

The same issues were submitted to and discussed by the Monmouthshire English Baptist Association which was founded in 1857. At the meeting of the Association in Pontypool in 1867 the Reform Bill of that year was welcomed, and in Abergavenny the following year those who voted for candidates who opposed the disestablishment of the Church in Ireland, and those candidates themselves who opposed this measure in the election of 1868, were censured; while in Caer-went in 1880 thanks were given 'to Almighty God [for] the return of so large a majority of Liberals in the recent parliamentary election'. In Maesycymer (1884) the Association approved of the three Liberal candidates for the newly reorganized Monmouthshire constituencies and pledged itself to its utmost to secure their return to Parliament; while resolutions in support of motions for the disestablishment of the Church in Wales were passed as they were required, i.e., as frequently as motions and Bills were introduced into the House of Commons. Such motions and resolutions, together with those concerned with education, temperance, the extension to Monmouthshire of the Sunday Closing Act and an attack on Tory magistrates, were the usual run with the English as with the Welsh Monmouthshire Baptist Association.

But whereas the latter never discussed a single resolution dealing with the social needs of the industrial areas of Monmouthshire, there were two exceptions in the case of the former. In its meeting in Abergavenny in 1883 the English Association passed the following resolution: 'That this Association desires to express its fervent sympathies with the families in the mining districts in which starvation holds so many families in its iron grip, commends the claim of the women and children to the practical assistance of the churches, and earnestly hopes that the present disastrous industrial war may reach a speedy and satisfactory settlement.' The Association met in Blackwood in 1898, a year which saw a disastrous strike of coal-miners in South Wales, and it passed a resolution deploring the continuation of the strike and earnestly hoped 'that grounds of agreement, in harmony with principles of righteousness and equity, will quickly be found, in the interest of starving women and children, the employers and the employed, and the whole community', and again in Newport in 1905 the churches were urged by the Association to show practical sympathy with the unemployed. There may be some significance in the fact that it was the English and not the Welsh Baptist Association which first showed awareness of local social problems, and it will be seen in a later chapter that social protest at the end of the nineteenth century was more closely connected in these parts with English than with Welsh names. Were the English 'causes' as socially conservative as their Welsh Nonconformist parent bodies?

Contrary to expectation the Association meetings of the Welsh Independents were not nearly so concerned with political matters as those of the Baptists, but they had no deeper interest in the local scene. Their problems were the same as those of the Baptists, and were the common concern of Nonconformity, both English and Welsh: marriage, burials, church rate, tithe, and the non-recognition of their registers as equal evidence with those of church registers.[1] At the root of these objections was the ecclesiastical Establishment, which the Independents maintained violated the essentially voluntary nature of the Christian religion. The Association of the South East met in Neath in 1840, but had nothing to

[1] *Llythyr oddiwrth Gymmanfa o Weinidogion yr Anymddibynwyr a gynnaliwyd yn Mhenygraig, swydd Gaerfyrddin, ar ddydd Mercher a dydd Iau, y 4ydd a'r 5med o Fehefin, 1834, at yr amrywiol Eglwysi y perthynant iddynt* (Caerfyrddin, 1834), p. 7.

say on Chartism or the late events in Monmouthshire, but in Sirhowy in the following year reference was made in veiled terms to certain unfortunate events that had happened in the previous year, and the hope was expressed that the spirit of love and peace would possess the churches,[1] a reference, not to the Chartists' riots, but rather to their effect on the Independent church in Sirhowy which has already been described. In Beaufort in 1867 the chairman took as his address, 'The message of the age to the Church', and in the course of it he said that the concern of the Church with the age was moral and religious, and that the age had a claim on the sympathy and service of the Church. The speaker ranged from Britain to Van Diemen's Land, and gave a general account of the progress of religion in the world. He rejoiced that a revival had broken out in Turkey, but regretted that the outlook was dark in Austria where the Emperor Francis Joseph ruled through oppression. But obviously the new society which had evolved in Beaufort in the past half-century had no message for the Church.

Preparation for the celebration of the bicentenary of the Act of Uniformity (1662) was made by the Welsh Independents in Dowlais and Aberdare, and on 1 January 1862 at a conference attended by 100 ministers and 30 laymen in Soar chapel, Neath. The proceedings were largely of a historical nature, and the same ground was covered by many speakers. It was a time when the desire for greater unity in the denomination throughout Wales was being felt, and contacts with their co-religionists in England were becoming closer. Independency was thinking of itself as a corporate denomination and not only as a collection of churches, and it was fitting that Dr. Thomas Rees should propose that all historical materials and records pertaining to the Welsh Independents should be preserved and published in the way thought best. The result, in due course, was the denomination's history, *Hanes Eglwysi Annibynol Cymru*, by Thomas Rees

[1] *Llythyr y Ddwy Gymmanfa Ddeheuol* (Llanelli, 1841), p. 7.

and John Thomas, one of the best ecclesiastical histories to be written in the Welsh language in the last century. The bicentenary of the Act of 1662 did much to nurture a sense of unity among the Independent churches and it was natural that their already strong sense of history should be given permanent expression. Altogether the Neath proceedings of 1862 were dignified and restrained; there were political overtones, but they by no means dominated the conference.[1]

This was more than could be said about the general Nonconformist celebration of the Act of Uniformity which was held in Swansea on 23 and 24 September 1862. This conference was attended by the leaders of the Liberationist Society, and it was the Baptists rather than the Independents who stole the political thunder in the persons of two local leaders and ministers, Thomas Thomas, of Pontypool, and Thomas Price, of Aberdare. The latter pointed out that Wales was not represented at Westminster. He could recall the effort made in 1826 to 'rescue the little pocket borough of Tredegar' [*sic*] from the grasp of the Morgan family, but later the county fell into the hands of the Baileys. Price said that Nonconformity could not produce men of sufficient standing to become M.P.s, and so they had to accept the best available, 'but I very much question whether we could find two better men than Mr. Dillwyn and [H. A.] Bruce. I would not exchange these two men for any other two men I know in Wales.'[2] This was one of the few occasions when Price was in a moderate mood, but his fellow Baptist, Dr. Thomas Thomas, gave the conference a fine exhibition of demagogy in a paper he read on 'The importance of developing the power of Welsh Nonconformity for the liberation of religion from State patronage and control', in which the following was a purple passage to illustrate the evils of the ecclesiastical Establishment: 'It adds to the crimes of past ages a dogged

[1] *Coffawdwriaeth Ddau Can Mlwyddol 1662–1862. Adroddiad cynadleddau Castell-nedd a Dinbych* (Llanelli, 1862), pp. 9–31.

[2] *The Established Church and Nonconformity in Wales. Proceedings of the Conference at Swansea, September 23rd and 24th, 1862* (London n.d.), p. 38.

resistance to the reforming spirit of the present time; fills the highest offices in the Establishment with nominees of Government; monopolises charitable trusts; insists on the indelibility of "holy orders"; upholds intolerant laws, not excepting the iniquitous and ensnaring Act of Uniformity; and clings to ecclesiastical abuses of every kind.'[1] Thomas went on to declare that the ecclesiastical Establishment seized national property to the tune of four or five million pounds per year ('while thousands of useful labourers have barely the necessities of life'), and this money was lavished upon church dignitaries and episcopal palaces. He attacked government education grants (of which he was a strong opponent), church-rates and Easter-offerings.

Independency was largely free of this kind of sentiment and language in these parts; in fact, it rarely made pronouncements of a political nature in its County Association meetings, which were concerned very largely with denominational matters and questions of personal religion. These were the predominant notes in the proceedings of the East Glamorgan Association which was formed in 1868.[2] The subjects of the annual presidential addresses are recorded, and they dealt almost exclusively with abstruse theological matters or problems of personal piety, but rarely with general political matters, and never with local social concerns. Even general elections could come and go: unlike the Baptists, the Independents in their County Association made no comments and gave no directions. Even when the breach between Welsh Nonconformity and the working classes was beginning to show itself in the late 1890s, and the statistics of this East Glamorgan Association were to reveal this fact, the Association itself showed no cognizance of this development. Nothing better illustrates the charge brought against Welsh Nonconformity that it was pre-occupied with the issue of personal salvation to the exclusion of social justice than the reading

[1] Ibid., p. 22.

[2] Unfortunately its annual reports are not available until 1890.

of the reports of the East Glamorgan [Congregational] Association.

The organization of the Calvinistic Methodists was on a regional basis, for their highest court was, and is, the Association (*Y Gymdeithasfa: Sasiwn*) for south and north Wales, while the Presbytery (*Yr Henaduriaeth*) was on a county or part-county basis. Consequently the South Wales Association, which met quarterly, visited every county in the area and only visited the industrial areas, and especially those of Monmouthshire (where Calvinistic Methodism was not strong) at intermittent periods. But a reading of the reports of this South Wales Association from 1846 to 1910 shows that the concerns of this body were similar to those of the other Nonconformist bodies (except that the Calvinistic Methodists did not refer to themselves as Nonconformists until the Association meeting at Hirwaun in 1871), namely, denominational matters, the state of the churches, Sunday observance, temperance, education and, of course, disestablishment. It was proper that there should be communication with Government on legislation affecting Nonconformity, but the local problem did not seem to worry the Association. In September 1852 it met in Monmouthshire, at Ebbw Vale, and its members were urged not to use the trains on Sundays; while in Brynmawr, in 1870, the Association condemned the practice of courting on Sundays (obviously overlooking the truth that in those days there was little time left after long working hours for this important activity). The Calvinistic Methodists were not so politically minded as the Baptists, but the political temperature rose somewhat after 1870. In that year Mr. Gladstone was congratulated on his Education Act, and he was urged to set up school boards forthwith; then came the well-known issues of Sunday closing, parish burials measure, support for a bill to enforce landowners to sell land for the building of chapels and schoolrooms; and in 1898 at the Pontycymer Association, held during the disastrous coal strike of that year, this resolution was passed: 'That this Association judges that the present state of affairs, both at home and abroad, calls upon us to emphasise God's governance of the world, and it urges the churches and pastors to give this truth prominence in their prayers and sermons.'

Such were the social and political concerns of the leading Welsh Nonconformist denominations in this industrial society. The religious bodies which virtually formed the ecclesiastical, social and political Establishment in these parts were almost completely indifferent to the social problems which affected thousands of their members and tens of thousands of their adherents. This does not mean that individual consciences were not sometimes stirred (although there is little evidence of that before the opening of the present century), but that Nonconformity in its official pronouncements revealed little or no concern with local problems. The one mild exception, the Monmouthshire English Baptist Association, may justify the further conclusion that, of the two, Welsh Nonconformity was more conservative in these matters than English Nonconformity. The explanation of this attitude to an industrial society on the part of Welsh Nonconformity is not immediately obvious, for it contrasts with its radical attitude in rural Wales. Both in rural and in industrial Wales the Welsh religious bodies were in a clear majority, but with this difference: in the industrial areas their majority brought with it local political and social power because there was no resistance; they inherited virgin territory, and largely formed a new society where the Established Church, landlordism and Toryism had not much mattered. There was nothing in the new society, as there was in the old, to put Welsh Nonconformity on its mettle: the new society offered no resistances to it: Nonconformists built their chapels at will, and within the existing political framework their members were able to exercise liberty of conscience. There were no evictions by landlords, ironmasters or coal-owners following general elections in these areas—the problem here was the economic problem of intermittent unemployment and the social problem of bad housing, and doubtless Welsh Nonconformists, like many others in those days, believed that little could be done about these things. For the first time Welsh Nonconformity was given the opportunity of creating a new society, and of necessity it was created in Nonconformity's image. Hitherto the chapels had had to fit into a milieu which was ecclesiastically wholly antagonistic, and socially largely antagonistic, to them. But the industrial revolution gave the chapels the opportunity of creating their own society, that is, as far as it lay in their power to do so. Thus it was that the new industrial society revealed both the strength and weakness of Welsh Nonconformity.

It is hoped that full justice has been done to the contribution of Nonconformity to the new industrial society. The chapels made life bearable and meaningful to thousands of people both through their means of grace and their character as social and cultural centres. In their own way they affected the outlook and conduct of thousands who never entered them, and brought home to very many the experiences of evangelical religion. They could have done more for education before 1870 had the religious denominations been more at unity among themselves, but in the Sunday-schools they provided the greatest popular educational movement of the nineteenth century, a movement which provided not only education for children, but adult education as well. Through the greater part of the nineteenth century these areas were religiously, socially and culturally, for better or for worse, what Welsh Nonconformity had made them.

It was inevitable therefore that the weakness should be revealed as clearly as the strength. The complete triumph of Welsh Nonconformity was realized in industrial areas, but its origins were in the countryside, and it never completely lost its rural character. But equally important was the fact that Nonconformity began as the 'gathered church' and within two centuries became, in everything but in name, an industrial religious Establishment. Although it was the theological protest of the 'gathered church' which was uppermost in the minds of the early Puritans, its sociological character is equally important. The basis of historic Nonconformity was a theological and a social withdrawal from the parish and its theological Establishment. The new religious groups came into being when the 'worthiest' entered into a covenant with God, for it was the 'worthiest' who would best further the Kingdom of God rather than the generality who were brought into the Established Church and organized on a parish basis. As the result of what they believed to be the true New Testament doctrine, their conception of the Church was opposed to that of the Established Church, and this necessitated the setting up of new religious organizations. Individualism was necessarily the hall-mark of Nonconformity, for it was only the individual who could judge whether to remain in the Established Church or to enter another church on a covenantal basis. This conception and experience was common to the historic Nonconformists, the Independents and Baptists, but whereas the former were prepared to extend the covenant relationship with God to a new generation by and through infant baptism, the Baptists took this doctrine to its logical conclusion by insisting upon believers' baptism only. It was not an accident that the Baptists became the most radical religious group in these new industrial areas, for the emphasis upon, and implications of, personal decision and commitment were brought home to each successive generation. Religious belief and practice gave the individual a heightened sense of responsibility, and it was inevitable that this should find an outlet in politics.

There was thus a theological withdrawal from the Established Church, and this was of necessity partly sociological, if only because other centres of worship were set up in an increasing number of parishes. In course of time the chapels developed their own concerns and social patterns, and their individualism was reflected not only in the religious experience of their members, but also by their separation from each other as religious groups. Consequently, when the time came for Nonconformity to triumph in a new kind of society, its contribution was through the denominational groups it set up. It was still a collection of 'gathered' churches in a society where the majority belonged to it and not to the officially Established Church. But it never lost the attitude of the 'gathered church' to its contemporary society, for its purpose all along was to call people out of the 'world' into the church; and, in any case, the individualism of the Nonconformist member was reinforced by the individualism of the group to which he belonged, which did not always get on with its brethren, to say nothing of those of another group. Hence Welsh Nonconformity, when it had largely succeeded in dominating an industrial society, never became responsible for that society as a whole, partly because such a responsibility was not in its tradition, and partly because it was too divided within itself to exercise it, had it sought to do so.

Underlying this concept of the 'gathered church', and acting as a theological foundation for it, was Calvinism. John Calvin is the theological father of British Nonconformity, even though many Nonconformist denominations have rejected the polity of Geneva. Welsh Nonconformity was thoroughly Calvinistic in theology for two centuries, and it was only as the nineteenth century ran its course that this system of theology loosened its hold on the Welsh chapels. Each successive number of the *Circular Letter* issued by the Monmouthshire Baptist Association proclaimed its articles of faith:

> Believing in the scriptural doctrines of three co-equal Persons in the God-head; the proper Deity and real humanity of our Lord Jesus Christ; eternal and personal election; original sin; particular redemption; free justification through the imputed righteousness of Christ; effectual grace in regeneration; the law as a rule to all believers; baptism of believers in water according

to the New Testament, and that those only are to partake of the Lord's Supper; final perseverance; the resurrection of the dead; the last judgment; the everlasting happiness of the righteous; the endless punishment of the wicked; together with the whole system and discipline of the New Testament Church.

The Independents did not depart from this confession, except in regard to infant baptism, for in the words of Dr. Thomas Rees, what they preached was 'the total depravity of man by the fall; the atoning sacrifice of Christ as the Sinner's sole ground of hope; the necessity of the Holy Spirit's work to change the depraved heart, with a holy conduct as the evidence of that inward work; the eternal condemnation of all the impenitent, and the eternal salvation of every believer.'[1] Here was the pabulum of Welsh Nonconformist preaching and teaching for the better part of the nineteenth century, except that its rigid Calvinistic features became more and more modified as time went on. These statements emphasize the almost exclusively individualistic note of nineteenth-century Nonconformity, and in their strong emphasis, indeed exclusive emphasis, upon the Godward side of salvation, they brought home to thousands of people an overwhelming sense of divine sovereignty which was one of the characteristics of the Calvinistic outlook. It will be recalled that Thomas Rees did not hesitate to attribute a cholera epidemic to the workings of the Almighty and as part of His gracious purposes. But these great themes invested the life of thousands of ironworkers and coal-miners with an awful significance: they were individuals who profoundly mattered in the scheme of things; human life was the setting for eternal decisions, the ordinary worker was called upon to make the most far-reaching choices which gave his life a dignity and an importance which his drab surroundings could not destroy. It is much too glib to refer to this evangel as 'opium of the people', and other catchwords, for the truth is that there were thousands in this

[1] T. Rees, *Miscellaneous Papers*, p. 24.

society who believed that the world was well lost. But it also meant that the world was of secondary importance in comparison with the scheme of salvation, and this may account for the ugliness and drabness which were too readily accepted, while the sense of divine sovereignty tended to induce a belief that the order of things was of divine ordinance and that one manifestation of the religious spirit was to accept things as they were. Too many things were attributed in those days to the will of God, and no doubt much religion was largely of a compensatory nature; but the deepest and most abiding happiness of thousands in these industrial communities was to be found in it.

III

THE ESTABLISHED CHURCH IN A WELSH INDUSTRIAL SOCIETY

WHEN Dr. Thomas Rees said that Welsh Nonconformity had completed its task of bringing the means of grace to all its adherents he made a claim that could not possibly have been made by the Established Church as far as this new society was concerned. Nor was the outlook promising: Nonconformity had become so entrenched that the prospects for the Church to regain its children seemed remote, for many of them had by now two or three generations of Nonconformist tradition and habit behind them. It is true that by 1850 it was better equipped than ever for its task: its financial resources were better distributed, its administration had been overhauled and, what was most important of all, on the death of Bishop Copleston in 1849 the old diocese of Llandaff was to be given, for the first time for a century and a half, a bishop who resided permanently in his diocese and was not obliged to take an ecclesiastical post in England. Never before had there been such speculation about the appointment of a bishop to Llandaff and so many recriminations made when it was announced that Alfred Ollivant, Professor of Divinity and Fellow of Trinity College, Cambridge, had been appointed. He had served as Vice-Principal of St. David's College, Lampeter, and it was there that he learned Welsh and had begun to preach in that language. Ollivant was enthroned in what remained of Llandaff Cathedral on 1 June 1850, and thus began the episcopal career of a man who must be judged one of the greatest of all the bishops of Llandaff. Unlike his predecessor, Ollivant had a clear insight into the needs of his diocese, and this may have been due to a difference in the background of the two men, for whereas Copleston was a Devonian, Ollivant had been born in Manchester into the kind of society his predecessor had never understood. He was long suspected of being an ambitious man, and his outstanding characteristic was his strength of will. One of his clergy wrote of him: 'His horizon seemed bounded by the Ten Commandments. They were the end as well as the rule of his life.'[1] He was essentially a man of action; and although his visitation charges are still worth reading for their theology and learning, he had no originality of thought, and probably was suspicious of speculation in theological matters. No better insight into the new bishop can be obtained than the self-revelation in the concluding sentences of his first visitation charge:

> If, in the remarks which I have thought it my duty to address to you, I have abstained from matters of doubtful disputation and confined myself to questions of practical interest, the reason for my doing so will readily have suggested itself to your own reflections. The condition of the diocese is such as peculiarly to call for practical exertion. The difficulties with which we have to contend are not speculations, but realities; not nice distinctions of doctrine, but deficiencies in the resources and agency of the Church. Around us and in the midst of us are thousands and tens of thousands entirely without, or inadequately provided with, the means of grace.[2]

He was later to say that the task of the Church differed from that of Dissent, for the latter, being dependent upon a voluntary system for its support, had to 'pitch its tent where it can find not only a field of labour, but also the green pasture and the running stream', and so neglected the 'isolated positions' in the diocese.[3] Having set his hand to a formidable task in 1850, although he mellowed with time and became a little less forbidding in his personal relations, Ollivant's

[1] John Morgan, *Four Biographical Sketches* (London, 1892), p. 40.
[2] Alfred Ollivant, *Primary Visitation Charge* (London, 1851), p. 55.
[3] Alfred Ollivant, *Seventh Visitation Charge* (London, 1869), p. 43.

strong sense of duty did not fail him throughout the thirty-four years of his episcopate. He and his successor, Bishop Richard Lewis, are the founders of the modern diocese of Llandaff (and this includes the daughter diocese of Monmouth).

In confronting this new industrial society with its firmly entrenched Welsh Nonconformity and its popular democratic institutions the Established Church suffered from marked disadvantages. Its primary and fundamental problem arose from its own nature. Over the centuries it had developed in a very different environment from the one it was now called upon to permeate, and consequently its characteristics were not easily adaptable to an industrial society. Nonconformity in England had produced a middle-class, *bourgeois* ethos because it had developed in an urban setting, but Welsh Nonconformity became more democratic in the ironworks areas, although it was to revert to its middle-class ethos later. But the Established Church was essentially the Church of the landed gentry and their dependants, and this social factor had deeply influenced it throughout the ages. Speaking of this religion, Niebuhr has said that it is

> agricultural or military, while the bourgeois religion is commercial and industrial in symbolism and attitude. The one kind of organization is paternal and institutional, the other democratic; the best ethics of the one class is the ethics of *noblesse oblige*, that of the other the morality of strict self-discipline without much regard for the neighbour; the doctrine of the one centres in a magic conception of salvation and of the means of grace, that of the other in the teaching of salvation in and by character. Hence the religion of the bourgeoisie seeks separate organization not only on account of the economic conflicts of the class with aristocracy above and the proletariat below but also because of the divergent attitudes and desires which arise out of these class differences.[1]

The ministry of the Established Church had developed in a rural setting and was, consequently, more pastoral than

[1] H. R. Niebuhr, op. cit., p. 89.

evangelistic, and it had accepted the social gradations of an agricultural society which did not apply in an industrial society. When this latter society produced its own social hierarchy it was Nonconformity which benefited from it, especially in the period of the deep-coal-mining age which began after the middle of the last century. The popular democracy which Welsh Nonconformity assumed in this new society made its chapels virtually self-governing ecclesiastical republics with a large variety and range of opportunity to its laity with which the Established Church could not compete. This truth was grasped by Lord Aberdare when he said at the Church Congress held in Swansea in 1879: 'The Dissenters are men strong in their convictions; they believe that in coming back to the church they would lose a great deal of liberty in the religious life which they enjoyed in their own denomination'[1] The speaker might well have added that, had the Nonconformists then returned to the Church, they would have returned to a body which had not yet discovered the rightful place for the laity.

When the emotional nature of popular religion in the industrial districts is contrasted with the sober piety of the Book of Common Prayer, and the sociological background of the Church compared with that of Dissent, it will be seen that the problem which confronted the former was not only, nor indeed primarily, one of buildings, but rather of so adapting itself as to get under the skin of a society which was new to it. Most interested observers in 1850 no doubt accepted the necessity of more buildings and clergy, but it was only very gradually that the problem of the laity was grasped, and a century's experience has shown that the provision of church buildings, and even the supply of clergy, were more satisfactorily solved in the last century than the problem of lay co-operation.

Within five months or so of his enthronement, Bishop Ollivant took a step that should have been taken at least a

[1] F. W. Edmondes (ed.), *Report of the Swansea Church Congress* (1879), p. 365.

generation earlier, when he made an appeal to the diocese as a whole. But before he did so he had been primed in the needs of his diocese by Thomas Williams, archdeacon (later dean) of Llandaff, in a letter published in the autumn of 1850.[1] Most, if not all, of the ground covered by the archdeacon will by now be familiar to the reader: the unprecedented increase in the population of the diocese, unparalleled elsewhere, an exceptionally high rate of immigration, especially into the Monmouthshire valleys; the loss to the clergy of nearly half of the tithe rent-charge; the very inadequate provision of church accommodation made worse by the language problem which called for two churches in parishes rather than for bilingual services, and the necessity of creating new parishes from the old, medieval, upland parishes, now already transformed or about to be transformed by industry. 'This accession to our numbers mainly gravitates to the point, and is confined to one particular district—one, too, formerly a mere mountain wilderness, where a few lonely dwellers tended their flocks upon the bleak hill side, or wrung a scanty livelihood from an ungenial soil; unprovided, therefore, beyond any other, with the machinery of the church, and least prepared to receive this crowded band of settlers.'[2] The problem in 1850 still lay in those areas which form the core of this study, viz., the old ironworks districts, but soon it was to spread to other areas affected by the development of deep-coal-mining.

Williams's pamphlet formed the basis of the discussions which took place at two public meetings held in Bridgend and Newport on 29 and 31 October 1850 respectively. The purpose of the meetings was to set up a society to further church work in the diocese, a 'Society for providing additional pastoral superintendence and church accommodation within the diocese of Llandaff'. In the Bridgend meeting Bishop Ollivant said that the primary need was for more

[1] Thomas Williams, *A letter to the Lord Bishop of Llandaff on the peculiar condition and wants of his diocese* (London, n.d.).
[2] Ibid., p. 4.

pastors, due not only to the greatly increased population but also to the need of a ministry in two languages. He did not disguise his own belief that one language would be preferable, but 'we have to deal with matters as they are; and so long as the Welsh language is the language of the people, so long must it be absolutely necessary that our Church, if it would be a national Church, should provide for the instruction of the people in the tongue not only in which they speak, but in which they think and feel'.[1] When John Nicholl, M.P., came to move the first resolution, 'That a society be now formed, whose special object shall be, the increase in the number of pastors, and of church accommodation in the diocese of Llandaff', he said that his father had once told him that he recalled the time when there were only eight cottages in Merthyr Tydfil when Anthony Bacon built his first furnace there; and H. A. Bruce, in moving the fourth resolution calling for contributions to the new Society said: 'In the future history of Wales, the names of Guest and Crawshay, Hill and Thompson, Bailey and Fothergill, will for ever be associated with the most extraordinary development of wealth and population in this country of progress. It remains for them to decide whether these mighty operations shall be to their country a blessing or a curse.'[2]

In the Newport meeting, held two days later, the principal speakers were Richard Blackmore, M.P., William Addams-Williams, of Llangibby, and, of course, that great layman Sir Thomas Phillips. The emphasis in this meeting was largely on the Monmouthshire scene. Phillips, who had been mayor of the town, spoke about Newport itself: 'I speak in the presence of those who remember when the church of St. Paul was erected over against the spot in which we are now assembled. Had any opponent of that work counted the

[1] *Substance of speeches delivered at Bridgend and Newport on the 29th and 31st October, 1850, at meetings called by the Lord Bishop of Llandaff, and in support of resolutions for establishing a society for providing additional superintendence and church accommodation within the diocese of Llandaff* (London, 1850), p. 6.

[2] Ibid., p. 18.

congregation of the mother church [St. Woolos], he would have found room unoccupied in that building; and yet a large congregation now assembles for public worship within the walls of St. Paul's church, whilst the attendance at the parish church has not been lessened.'[1] But he went on to remind his audience that no extra permanent church accommodation had yet been provided in Aberdare, Mynyddislwyn, or Aberystruth. Aberdare would soon 'cease to be a by-word and a reproach among the parishes'; in Dowlais much had been done, and Merthyr was at last bestirring itself. But the core of the problem still remained, and was revealed by the bishop when he said that in the new industrial areas, with a population of 164,000, there was church accommodation for only 13,808, and 32 clergy.

The result of these two public meetings was the setting up of the Llandaff Diocesan Church Extension Society with the following objects:

1. To maintain, or contribute to the maintenance of, curates in populous districts.
2. To contribute toward the erection of churches and licensed places of worship.
3. To contribute to miscellaneous objects bearing on the welfare and progress of the Church.
4. To endeavour to stimulate the supply of educated Welsh clergymen.

This Society, until it was wound up in 1911, was the organ through which the diocese tackled the problem of the industrial areas. Like all such ventures it fluctuated greatly in its fortunes. In the first year of its existence its income amounted to £5,112. 18*s*. 2*d*. with a further £2,036. 10*s*. 0*d*. promised,[2] but there came a time when the annual donations fell as low as £13. In 1862 parliament authorized the Ecclesiastical Commissioners to give additional grants to those parishes

[1] Ibid., p. 26.

[2] *First Annual Report of the Llandaff Diocesan Church Extension Society* (Cardiff, 1852), p. 5.

which did not receive more than £50 per annum from the Society for the maintenance of the curates, so that while the Society contributed £750 per annum for this purpose, the Commissioners added £1,020 to this sum.[1] By 1873 the complaint was that the income of the Society was not commensurate with its needs or with the wealth of the diocese, and the bishop reminded his diocese that the population was still growing at a greater rate than that of any other in the province of Canterbury and that it was obvious that a new drive for funds would have to be made.

The 1879 meeting of the Society was the most important held since its inception in 1850. It was presided over by Lord Aberdare, who reported that since 1851 the total receipts had amounted to £40,675, of which £20,359 had been spent on pastoral provision for the new areas (in addition to the £20,284 provided by the Ecclesiastical Commissioners for the same purpose); £6,152 had been granted towards the building of new churches, £1,883 on licensed rooms, and £575 on new parsonages.[2] Between 1840 and 1877, £359,000 had been spent on new churches, and this had already made an appreciable difference to the fortunes of the Church in such parishes as Aberdare and Gelligaer. But the increase of population still outstripped the provision made for extra accommodation: as soon as the situation was eased in the older industrial parishes, new areas, particularly those of the Rhondda valleys and Cardiff, were developing rapidly and presented new problems. In spite of the appeal made for fresh money in 1879 the response was not nearly so favourable as the appeals of 1850 and 1862.

It would be impossible in this present study to give details of church building in the industrial areas. Bishop Ollivant did not repeat the mistake of his predecessors, viz., to wait until a complete church was built in a given area before

1 *Twelfth Annual Report of the Llandaff Diocesan Church Extension Society* (Cardiff, 1864), p. 6.

2 *Twenty-seventh Annual Report of the Llandaff Diocesan Church Extension Society* (Cardiff, 1879), p. 8.

beginning services there. His Register[1] shows how many temporary buildings were licensed for worship, especially schoolrooms, and the type of building which appears so frequently in the Register and is described as the 'iron structure' is obviously the forerunner of many of the stone churches in our industrial parishes. It is not an exaggeration to say that, after 1852, not a month passed by during the whole of Ollivant's episcopate without at least one building being licensed for divine worship, and, as time went on, the rate of building increased. To attempt to be more precise is not easy, for it is not always possible to ascertain from his Register whether Ollivant had licensed a schoolroom or consecrated a temporary building, an unfinished permanent building, or a completed permanent church. But it would do far less than justice to his great work if he were credited today only with those permanent buildings begun or completed during his episcopate; it is true to say that he sowed more widely than he reaped, and the full harvest was gathered by his successors, Bishops Lewis and Hughes.

Bishop Lewis's Registers[2] show the same pattern as those of Ollivant. Lewis's episcopate (1883–1905) coincided with the great development in deep-coal-mining and the opening up of new areas in mid-Glamorgan. The same policy was followed in most cases: the temporary building, followed by a permanent building which, in some cases, even today remains unfinished. But by the time Richard Lewis began his episcopate in 1883 the funds of the Llandaff Diocesan Church Extension Society were well-nigh exhausted, and one of the first acts of the new bishop was to inaugurate the 'Bishop of Llandaff's Fund' with an appeal for £50,000 'for the erection of inexpensive Churches in the most populous districts and toward the stipends of Additional Curates'. Within ten years £38,022 of this sum had been received or promised, and during this same decade 126 building projects were

[1] LL/BR/2. This Register extends from 1852 to 1883.
[2] LL/BR/3; LL/BR/4.

partly financed by the Fund at a total cost of £168,000, of which the Fund contributed £21,452; and by the end of Lewis's episcopate in 1905, 201 projects, involving an expenditure of £362,817, had been inaugurated by grants from the Fund amounting to £30,570. At the turn of the century, Bishop Lewis had made another appeal which he called a 'Million Shilling Thank Offering Fund'. This, however, was not a success, only one-tenth of that sum being raised.

It will have been noted that only a small proportion of the money spent on new buildings came from the Llandaff Diocesan Church Extension Society, much of it being raised locally in the parishes.[1] It is clear that the industrial areas were ready to respond when the responsibility was placed upon them for providing their own places of worship, and this marked a very great advance since the days when such places had no churches to worship in until they were provided by a local industrialist. This is an important piece of evidence which shows that such areas were coming to life as far as the Established Church was concerned. At the same time, industrialists proved to be more generous in the second half of the century than they had been in the first half, especially in the Glamorgan industrial districts. Monmouthshire had fared better from the ironmasters than Glamorgan, and this was to continue: the Ebbw Vale Company provided that parish with the finest church in industrial Monmouthshire. But the coal-owners did more for Glamorgan than they did for Monmouthshire. In the Annual Report of the Llandaff Diocesan Church Extension Society for 1859 it was said that 'a spirit of benevolence has been increasingly diffused, and private liberality is now displaying fruits in daily rising Churches, almost as abundant as in ancient times'.[2] In the same Report there appeared the names of Anthony

[1] Bishop Lewis estimated that nine-tenths of this money was raised locally in large and small gifts.

[2] *Eighth Annual Report of the Llandaff Diocesan Church Extension Society* (Cardiff, 1859), pp. 10–11.

Hill, of Pentre-bach, the Maesteg Company, the Dowlais Company, H. J. Grant, of Melincryddan, the Earl of Jersey, Bruce Pryce of Mountain Ash, and others. Mention should also be made of the Wayne family of Aberdare, of Howel Gwyn, who largely defrayed the cost of Dyffryn church, the Llewellyn family of Baglan Hall who were generous in the building of churches in their own parish and in the Rhondda valley, of Crawshay Bailey's work in Ton Pentre and Nant-y-glo, Lady Windsor's at St. Fagans (Aberdare), and Penarth; Sir George Elliot's in Aberaman, and the Bute family's in Treherbert. To go beyond Ollivant's episcopate into that of Richard Lewis, mention should be made of G. T. Clark's generosity at Talygarn, the Earl of Plymouth in Grangetown, and, without doubt the most generous benefactors of all, the Talbot family of Margam. No doubt names have been omitted through ignorance, and the names of those who contributed greatly to the restoration (in some cases amounting virtually to a rebuilding) of many country churches have not been included in this study.

The industrialists were more generous after 1850 than they had been earlier in the century, but the class most castigated for their lack of generosity were the landlords who profited from coal royalties. In the first Diocesan Conference (1884) William Lewis, vicar of Ystradyfodwg,[1] a parish from which most of the Rhondda parishes were later to be carved, said: 'I imagine that the sight of a clergyman makes some landowners exceedingly uncomfortable';[2] and eight years later he told the same body that since he had become vicar of the parish the landowners, most of them churchmen, had taken about £500,000 in royalties from his parish without contributing one penny toward church building. 'Not a penny has ever been given toward Church endowment, and the great bulk of that money has gone to

[1] For a description of William Lewis's work in church building in the Rhondda valley, see T. J. Jones, *William Lewis diweddar Ficer Ystradyfodwg* (Dolgellau, n.d.).

[2] *Report of the Llandaff Diocesan Conference*, (Cardiff 1884), p. 52.

Churchmen.'[1] Exception was taken to this statement, but those who objected confused the royalty owners with the industrialists.

The ratio between money raised by the parishes themselves and grants from diocesan funds can be gathered from a passage from Bishop Lewis's last presidential address to the Llandaff Diocesan Conference a few months before his death, when he described the transformation which had taken place in the Rhondda valley during his episcopate. When he came to the diocese in 1884 those areas contained 7 churches and 10 mission rooms served by 14 clergy, and by 1904 these figures had risen to 20 churches and 26 mission rooms, with 43 clergy. The bishop went on to say:

> The above picture which I have drawn of the Church's growth and progress in the Rhondda Valley represents to a very large extent what has been going on throughout the whole diocese, in which 150 new Churches and Mission Rooms have been erected and twenty three enlarged. In addition to the above, through the munificence of private individuals, seven new churches have been erected at a total cost of £60,000. The £50,000 for which I appealed has been raised; it has fulfilled my anticipations and brought forth £300,000 from other sources and provided accommodation for 70,000 church worshippers.[2]

In the same address, Bishop Lewis paid tribute to the zeal 'of our Nonconformist brethren' for their chapel building in the Rhondda valley.

The degree of success in providing churches for the newly developing industrial areas can be measured by the statistics prepared for presentation to the Welsh Church Commission in 1906 for the following rural deaneries. The sum represented what had been spent from 1840 to 1906 on (*a*) church buildings and furnishings (not including expenses of less than £500), (*b*) on parochial buildings, churchyards and day-schools.

[1] *Report of the Llandaff Diocesan Conference* (Cardiff, 1892), p. 79.
[2] *Report of the Llandaff Diocesan Conference* (1904), pp. 9–10.

		£	s.	d.	Total £	s.	d.
Deanery of Aberdare[1]	(a)	51,490	12	3			
	(b)	14,769	5	3			
					66,259	17	6
Deanery of Merthyr Tydfil[2]	(a)	49,560	1	0			
	(b)	17,197	17	4			
					66,757	18	4
Deanery of the Rhondda[3]	(a)	103,127	14	0			
	(b)	23,930	0	9			
					127,057	14	9
Deanery of Blaenau Gwent[4]	(a)	74,375	11	0			
	(b)	25,520	14	3½			
					99,896	5	3½
Deanery of Bedwellty[5]	(a)	32,340	11	4			
	(b)	7,833	10	0			
					40,174	1	4
Total for the archdeaconry of Llandaff					1,041,719	0	1
Total for the archdeaconry of Monmouth					522,796	17	6½
Total for the old diocese of Llandaff[6]					1,564,515	17	7½

The extent to which the efforts of church building had satisfied the needs of a rapidly growing diocese since 1850 can be gauged by the report of the archdeacon of Llandaff to Committee No. 5 of the Llandaff Diocesan Board of

[1] Aberdare, Aberaman, St. Fagans, Mountain Ash, Hirwaun, Penrhiwceiber.

[2] Merthyr Tydfil, Cyfarthfa, Dowlais, Pentre-bach, Penydarren, Treharris.

[3] Cwm-parc, Cymer and Porth, Dinas and Pen-y-graig, Ferndale, Glyntaff, Llanwonno, Llwynypia, Pontypridd, Treherbert, Tylorstown, Ynys-hir, Ystradyfodwg.

[4] Aberystruth, Abersychan, Abertillery, Beaufort, Nant-y-glo, Blaenavon, Ebbw Vale, Cwm, Llanhiledd, Trevethin, Pontypool, Pontnewynydd, Newtown and Willowtown.

[5] Bedwellty, Fleur de Lis, Rhymney, Tredegar, New Tredegar, Mynyddislwyn, Pen-main.

[6] LL/WCC/319.

Finance in 1918 on the need for new churches in the archdeaconry. The report estimated that twenty-two new and enlarged churches were needed, at a cost of £90,000.[1]

The new churches were built, and in too many cases the old mistakes were repeated of introducing into an industrial society those social gradations which were symbolized in rural communities by the appropriated pew. This institution has a long history behind it,[2] and it provided an outward ecclesiastical sign of class distinction between those who sat in the appropriated pews on the one hand, and on the other those who sat on the benches. 'The gentry and wealthy yeomanry were permitted to build themselves wainscot pews in the chancel or in the east end of the nave, while those lower down on the social scale sat on benches. The poorest parishioners had to make do with deal forms at the west end, placed in the darkest and draughtiest corners of the church.'[3] The appropriated pew was a 'status symbol', accepted for a long time in the country districts, but which even there gave rise to much bickering and litigation by those who nursed social pretensions. In industrial areas, however, this division of the seating accommodation of the church between those who sat in appropriated pews, for which they paid an annual rent, and those who were provided with free, but less desirable, seats, became a major issue in the last century. 'This situation was a danger to the Church, and was a major factor in the growth of Dissent.'[4] Where the institution of the appropriated pew had been accepted in those towns which later expanded and changed their character in the industrial revolution, doubtless a transitional phase was necessary

[1] *Llandaff Diocesan Magazine*, x. 6. This is the list: Abercwmboi, Hengoed, Gelligaer, Cathays, Grangetown, Docks, Pen-lan Hill (Cardiff); Pen-coed, Lewistown, Port Talbot, Aberpergwn, Jersey Marine, Tonyrefail, Beddau, Merthyr Vale, Abercynon, Pontypridd, Llanddewi Mission, for new churches; and enlargements at Cwmbach, Barry Dock, Mardy, and Pwll-gwaun.

[2] W. T. Morgan, 'Disputes concerning seats in church before the Consistory Court of St. David's', *Journal of the Historical Society of the Church in Wales*, xi. 65–89.

[3] Ibid., p. 68.

[4] Ibid., p. 85.

before the complete disappearance of such an institution, but it showed a lack of imagination to introduce the system into an industrial society where a spirit of egalitarianism was for a long time characteristic of its democracy.

This, however, is what happened. Churches built with the aid of grants from the Church Building Commissioners in the industrial areas from 1830 to the early 1850's were divided into 'pews' and 'free'. Thus, St. Thomas's, Abersychan (1831–2) was divided into 60 and 493 respectively; St. George's, Tredegar (1835–6), had 614 pews and 394 'free'; St. Fagans', Trecynon (1851–2), 17 and 658 respectively; St. Elvan's, Aberdare (1852–3), 240 pews and 560 'free'; Nant-y-glo Church (1852–4) had 216 pews and 319 'free'.[1] The religious census of 1851 showed that the majority of churches had their seating accommodation thus divided, and in proportion to numbers there were as many churches as chapels where the seats were free. The only instance of a church which had no free seats was Aberdare parish church, whereas, on the other hand, Mynyddislwyn was 'all free', as was also Ystradyfodwg.

An increasing volume of protest came from the Established Church against this system of appropriated pews. John Coke Fowler, who became stipendiary magistrate for Merthyr Tydfil in 1852, wrote: 'In populous areas it has become painfully obvious, that the Church is grievously hampered in this reception of her flock by the system of closed pews . . . they are in fact most injurious to the business and interests of the church.'[2] This protest was more clearly heard after 1884 when the institution of the Diocesan Conference in the old diocese of Llandaff gave a platform for views which had hitherto not been voiced in the diocese. In the first Diocesan Conference a speaker said: 'I feel that the Church will never be the Church of the people until the pews are swept out.'[3]

[1] M. H. Port, *Six hundred new churches* (London, 1961), pp. 172–3.

[2] John Coke Fowler, *Church Pews, their origin and legal incidents* (London, 1844), pp. 4–5.

[3] *Report of the Llandaff Diocesan Conference* (1884), p. 50.

It is to be regretted that such pronouncements were not voiced earlier, and heeded.

Reference has been made to a system of pew-rents in chapels. Nonconformity adopted this method of raising money and it is only very recently that it has disappeared in the industrial areas. But all chapel members paid for their seating accommodation, and no distinction was made between rich and poor; while the hearers were accommodated free in the chapel gallery. Dr. Thomas Rees defended this system: 'Separate services, free sittings, and a distinct class of teachers for the working class, would never have succeeded to win them in Wales, and they will never succeed anywhere else. The Welsh churches do not raise their ministers' salaries by pew-rents, and therefore they can afford to let the sittings at such a moderate rate, which every working man who is not a pauper can pay, and working men always had rather pay than occupy a free sitting.'[1] Although one or two of these arguments may be specious, yet it is true that the pew-rent system of Nonconformity was not nearly as objectionable and distasteful as the appropriated pew of the Established Church.

Together with the building of new churches the large parishes were gradually subdivided into smaller units. In this matter the diocese was greatly helped by the Ecclesiastical Commissioners, who alone had the authority to create new ecclesiastical districts and provide for their incumbents. This work had already begun in the days of Bishop Copleston,[2] and no doubt would have gone on more rapidly were it not that a minimum number of 4,000 population was necessary before a new ecclesiastical district could be created. Geographical considerations made this difficult, for, as we have seen earlier, many of the older parishes consisted of a series of lateral valleys which made them difficult to subdivide into convenient new districts,[3] and their income was

[1] T. Rees, *Miscellaneous Papers*, p. 29.

[2] Dowlais (1837), Rhymney (1839), Tredegar (1840), Pen-main (1845), Cyfarthfa (1846), Nant-y-glo (1846), Beaufort (1846).

[3] This factor was not borne in mind by those writers of the last century who

quite inadequate for their needs, even if much of it had not been appropriated elsewhere. Bishop Ollivant described the financial difficulties when he said: 'When we build a new church, it is not by appropriating the income of a wealthy benefice that we can hope to provide for a stipend for a clergyman; neither can it be expected, even if it were desirable, that a church built in the midst of Miners and Colliers can be maintained by pew-rents.'[1]

But gradually the creation of new parishes went ahead, and, as with the church buildings themselves, the new ecclesiastical districts began with a humbler status; Ollivant's registers contain more frequent references, as his episcopate went on, to 'district chapelry assigned', 'Consolidated chapelry', and so on to the status of parish, the Ecclesiastical Commissioners contributing generously to the stipend of the incumbent. In this way the large mountain parishes in the new industrial areas were subdivided into the smaller parishes we know today, and it can be claimed that the spread of industry from valley to valley in Monmouthshire and Glamorgan can be traced by the building of churches and the creation of parishes. The first area was that of the old ironworks industry which was beginning to be reorganized before the middle of the century, and it was the remainder of these areas which called for reorganization in the 1860s and 1870s.[2] But the Rhondda valleys and the other new deep-coal-mining areas were soon calling for attention, so that after 1870 the reorganization of ecclesiastical districts in the industrial areas was largely concentrated in the Rhondda valleys and their approaches, together with the deep-coal-mining

accused the Ecclesiastical Commissioners of having neglected the old diocese of Llandaff and who pointed to the very different treatment meted to the diocese of Ripon. But this latter diocese included Leeds whose subdivision into smaller parishes was a straightforward matter compared with the industrial areas of South Wales.

[1] A. Ollivant, *Fifth Visitation Charge* (London, 1863), p. 52.

[2] St. Fagans, Aberdare (1856), Pentre-bach (1860), Blaenavon (1860) Mountain Ash (1870), Pontlotyn (1870), Ebbw Vale (1870), Penydarren (1871).

areas of Monmouthshire.[1] During the episcopate of Richard Lewis (1883–1905) which saw the heyday of the deep-coal industry and the decline of the old iron industry, 25 new districts were created, most of them in the industrial valleys. In 1911 Bishop Joshua Hughes said that a further 25 districts in the diocese, with populations varying from 4,000 to 9,000, and now forming part of larger parishes, ought to be formed into new ecclesiastical districts, and between 1911 and 1913 6 Conventional Districts and 7 new parishes were formed.[2]

This increase in the number of ecclesiastical districts necessitated a change in the number and structure of rural deaneries. On 11 May 1895 Bishop Lewis signed and sealed the scheme for the reorganization of the deaneries, and the scheme was promulgated by an Order in Council, dated 29 June 1895. Henceforth, and until disestablishment, the old diocese consisted of the following deaneries:

The archdeaconry of Llandaff: Aberdare, Barry, Caerphilly, Cardiff, Groneath Lower (Eastern Division), Groneath Lower (Western Division), Groneath Upper (Eastern Division), Groneath Upper (Western Division), Llandaff, Merthyr Tydfil, Penarth.

The archdeaconry of Monmouth: Abergavenny, Bedwellty, Blaenau Gwent, Caerleon, Chepstow, Monmouth, Netherwent, Newport, Raglan, Usk.

Between 1850 and 1910 the old diocese of Llandaff underwent a complete transformation: a resident bishop, churches

[1] Glyntaff (1848), Caerphilly (1853), Abertillery (1876), Llwynypia (1879), Pontypridd (1884), Hirwaun (1886), Tylorstown with Ferndale (1887), Ynyshir (1887), Aberaman (1888), Ystradmynach (1890), Treherbert (1893), Cymer and Porth (1894), Fleur de lis (1896), Penrhiwceiber (1897), Cwm-parc (1898), Griffithstown (1898), Garw Valley (1899), Cwm (Mon) (1900), Ferndale (1900), Treharris (1900), Dinas and Pen-y-graig (1901), Llanbradach (1904), St. James's Tredegar (1904), Bargoed (1904). This list does not include the new parishes created in Cardiff during the episcopate of Richard Lewis.

[2] Garndiffaith and Varteg (Mon), Blackwood, Abercarn, Cilfynydd, Mardy, Tonyrefail, Gilfach, Bedlinog, Llansawel (Giant's Grave), Caerau, Crynant, and Seven Sisters (Joshua Prichard Hughes, *Third Visitation Charge*, Cardiff, 1913, pp. 10–11). This list deals only with the industrial parishes.

built in all the industrial areas, an administrative reform; the problem of the large urban towns such as Cardiff, Newport, Barry, Port Talbot was tackled, together with the extensive restoration of country churches; the provision of the new parishes with parsonage houses, and the replacement of almost all the rural parsonage houses by the familiar and easily recognized vicarages or rectories which are now being replaced by more modern houses. Never before, in the whole of its long history, had such a change been effected in anything like so short a time. Without doubt, this was the heroic age of the old diocese of Llandaff.

The provision of competent clergy to man the new churches and parishes was the second problem confronting the old diocese of Llandaff in the second half of the nineteenth century, and the problem was bound up with the question of language. It was the problem of Nonconformity in reverse, for whereas the latter had to make provision for an anglicized population, the Established Church had to find clergy to serve the Welsh population of the new parishes. The question of numbers did not arise in those days, for this was the economic heyday of the Anglican parson, and, in any case, the new industrial areas were served by clergy who came from the Welsh rural areas; and in this respect both Nonconformity and the Church drew from the overplus of clergy and ministers of Welsh-speaking Wales. It was not the quantity but the quality of Welsh clergy which most concerned the Church in those days.

The problem of staffing parishes with Welsh-speaking clergy had not been entirely absent in the eighteenth century, but it arose in a far more acute form during the episcopate of Edward Copleston. At the beginning of his episcopate, in 1828, there were 33 churches in Glamorgan and nine in Monmouthshire where the services were in Welsh; 27 churches in the former county and 104 in the latter where English services only were conducted, and 47 churches in Glamorgan and 14 in Monmouthshire where they were bilingual.[1] The pressure on Copleston to remedy this state of affairs came from two quarters, one beyond his diocese, and the other within. The former came from the Association of Welsh Clergy in the West Riding of Yorkshire which was founded in 1821 to 'expose the many corruptions which have crept in the Church of Wales from time to time and to seek their removal in a kind but earnest spirit by memorializing our gracious Queen and by petitioning both houses of legislature'.[2] The other pressure came from Llanover where Benjamin and Augusta Hall lived;[3] and of these two pressures it was the one from what Copleston described as 'my aristocratic radical neighbour' which proved irksome to him.

The Association of Welsh Clergy in the West Riding of Yorkshire petitioned the government of Sir Robert Peel in 1835 against the evil effects of English appointments in the Welsh Church, with the result that a clause was added to the Pluralities and Non-Residence Bill that no person without a thorough knowledge of the Welsh language should be appointed to a bishopric or living in Wales, but this clause was amended by the House of Lords to apply to livings only. But a few years later a Bill was passed to ensure that 'within the several dioceses of St. Asaph, Bangor, Llandaff, and St. David's it shall and may be lawful for the bishop, if he shall think fit, to refuse institution or licence to any spiritual person who, after due examination and enquiry, shall be found unable to preach, administer the sacraments, perform the pastoral duties, and converse in the Welsh language';[4] and an appeal from an adverse verdict lay to the archbishop of Canterbury, who was frequently too ready to grant it.

Before this legislation had been passed, Bishop Copleston wrote on 16 July 1832 that he had intended to be more strict than his predecessors in this matter of language

[1] C. R. Sumner, op. cit., p. 25.

[2] *Report of the proceedings of the Association of Welsh Clergy in the West Riding of Yorkshire* (Carnarvon, 1852), p. 6.

[3] Sir Benjamin and Lady Hall after 1838; Lord and Lady Llanover after 1859.

[4] 1 & 2 Vict. c. 106, s. 104.

qualification, but added that he had been informed that the learning of Welsh by book, without colloquial use of the language, was useless in the Church.[1] Copleston believed that many communicants had been lost to the Church because of the neglect of ministration in Welsh, but whereas in a 'mixed parish' the clergyman should be able to speak Welsh, the only solution in such parishes as Merthyr Tydfil and Dowlais was the provision of a Welsh church. He later wrote about the difficulties of the problem: 'You have no idea of the plague which these mixed cases bring upon me. There is a party spirit, easily put in activity by lovers of discord, & the dormant national prejudices are quickly excited. They have no thought of the difficulties & of the absolute necessity of a compromise, or in many cases of consulting the good of the greater part, where we cannot comply with the inclinations of each individual.'[2] His own patronage was severely limited, and there were factors beyond his control. On 19 May 1848 he criticized in the House of Lords the way in which Crown patronage in Wales was dispensed, complaining that clergy were appointed to Welsh livings without a knowledge of the Welsh language,[3] and on 18 April 1849, a few months before his death, he wrote to the Home Secretary: 'The only complete remedy . . . would be to have two places of worship and two clergymen for each parish. The Welsh attach themselves to that place of worship, whether Church or sectarian, in which their own language alone is used, and the English even, when a minority, often complain that they have not had an English service regularly at one part of the day.' Copleston was confronted by a problem for which there was no ideal solution, and there is no doubt that, within his very straitened circumstances, he did his best in his appointments to bilingual parishes, even when he had to withstand pressures, English and Welsh, from some of the

[1] Letter to J. M. Traherne, 16 July 1832.
[2] Same to same, 2 April 1844.
[3] *The Times*, 20 May 1848.

leading clergy and laity in his diocese. At the same time, it cannot be denied that Copleston's predilections were decidedly English and he had little sympathy with things Welsh; and for the efforts of Lady Hall to revive the Welsh language in Monmouthshire he had nothing but scorn: 'I wonder they are not tired of this barren nonsense.'[1]

Copleston's successor, Ollivant, inherited this problem, for the building of churches and the creation of parishes in Welsh industrial areas for a long time taxed the capacity of the Church to provide them with competent Welsh-speaking clergy. Ollivant made a few public statements on this problem, which he attributed to the nature of the Welsh social structure. He said in his first visitation charge in 1851 that there was no lack of candidates for the ministry, but they were too straitened in circumstances to bear the expenses of education and this, in turn, was bound up with the Welsh social system which, unlike that of England, had not that 'imperceptible gradation', so that there were 'no intermediate links between the two [social] extremes'. Preferments in Wales were not calculated to induce the higher classes to educate their sons for the ministry, while the Welsh peasantry had not the means to do so.[2] A year later the report of the Llandaff Diocesan Church Extension Society referred to the difficulty of supplying Welsh parishes with suitable clergy, and it concluded that if the choice lay between the appointment of a competent Englishman or an ill-educated Welshman to a Welsh parish, the former should be chosen as likely to have the least injurious consequences. In private, to his rural deans whom he called into conference annually, Ollivant was frank and outspoken on the quality of the clergy, and especially the Welsh clergy, and in the visitation charge of 1869 he said: 'The complaints that reach me in reference to the inefficiency of the younger Welsh clergy are, I assure you, neither few in number, nor expressed in

[1] Letter to W. Bruce Knight, 8 October 1843.

[2] A. Ollivant, *First Visitation Charge* (1851), p. 46.

gentle terms.'[1] The laity, likewise, were equally frank in their criticism of the clergy, except that these criticisms were not voiced until the situation had considerably improved. The essence of the problem lay in the provision made for clerical education. Since the eighteenth century most of the candidates for Holy Orders had gone either to Oxford or Cambridge, or to divinity schools attached to the old grammar schools at Usk, Abergavenny and Cowbridge; and later it became popular to undergo a two-year course in St. Bees College, Cumberland. Ollivant said that this scheme was inadequate, as was also the provision made by St. David's College, Lampeter, in the case of ordinands who were given a three-year course without a grammar-school training. Ollivant insisted more and more on a pre-college training for the less academically minded, to be followed by residence in St. David's College, Lampeter, and it was by these means that the standard of the Welsh clergy was raised, so that by the days of Bishop Lewis, although responsible laymen were free to talk of the bad old days of low clerical conduct, it was generally recognized that they had now passed.

But they left one legacy: in the days when pulpit oratory mattered more than anything else in a successful ministry the Church was unable to meet Nonconformity on its own ground. Although some of the industrial parishes were served by excellent parish priests, it is true to say that it was Nonconformity that stole the oratorical thunder, with the result that, even in its most successful parishes, the Church ministered to a minority only of the large Welsh population. The Welsh churches of the new industrial parishes were not nearly so powerful or as influential as the Welsh chapels. Ollivant, however, realized that this condition would change, for he judged that industrialism brought with it a social revolution

[1] A. Ollivant, *Seventh Visitation Charge* (1869), p. 15. Such difficulties and criticisms were not confined to diocesan appointments; the task of finding a competent Welsh-speaking cleric to occupy an episcopal office in Wales was one of Mr. Gladstone's headaches (Kenneth O. Morgan, *Wales in British Politics 1868–1922*, pp. 32–33, 60–61).

and that one consequence of this revolution would be more widespread education. Hitherto the Welsh people had depended for their instruction largely on the pulpit, and it was pulpit oratory, 'addressed to an uneducated and excitable people', which had accounted for the success of Welsh Methodism.[1] The spread of education was leading to a wider use of the English language, and already Dissent had to take account of this. Ollivant, in his second visitation charge (1854) quoted from an article in the Calvinistic Methodist periodical, *Drysorfa*, for August 1852, in which the writer said that it was already becoming increasingly difficult to sell Welsh books of good quality, although there was a market for trash. Likewise *Y Traethodydd* foresaw the rising power of the press and the decline in the power of the pulpit: 'we are at present as a nation, one great ear, that is never satisfied with hearing', and many who would give one shilling to listen to a lecture would not spend threepence on a book. The Welshman had got from his chapel what the Englishman had sought for in the playhouse; and *Y Traethodydd* went on to say: 'The fact of our going to chapel for excitement in the place of instruction, has an effect upon our teachers, and causes them often to aim more at exciting the congregation than instructing them.'[2] In the same charge, Ollivant went on to quote from the Independent *Diwygiwr* for 24 April 1854, which deplored the low standard of many Welsh books: 'If all the books, pamphlets, songs, etc., *that have been sold from the pulpit* in the course of the last twenty years were collected together in one heap, what a spectacle of degeneracy would be seen. True there would be some wheat in it, but how much of it would be made of chaff.'[3]

However, the day when instruction through reading was to replace that through hearing was still in the future as far as these Welsh industrial communities were concerned.

[1] A. Ollivant, *Second Visitation Charge* (1854), p. 9.
[2] Quoted by Ibid., pp. 58–59.
[3] Ibid., p. 60.

Seymour Tremenheere in his report on education in the industrial areas already referred to, had noted the very limited demand for periodical literature. In the parishes of Merthyr Tydfil and Bedwellty there were seven booksellers, all of whom stated that they could not live by their book trade only. They fared better with the sale of English than of Welsh periodicals, but admitted that the greater part of the sale of the latter went through the hands of 'ministers and other zealous individuals'. Tremenheere examined 720 titles in three Welsh catalogues and found that all the titles, except 114, were on religious subjects; and of the Welsh periodicals circulating in those parts he said that they were few in number, 'and the information they contained on passing events, or on the science and the literature of the day [was] scanty and incomplete. The demand for the London newspapers among the working classes was also said to be very slight.'[1] Up to the middle of the last century the Welsh section of the industrial population does not seem to have been as literate and as well instructed as the rural population of Wales is traditionally thought to have been. They lived in a closed intellectual community, the mental pabulum being Welsh denominational literature, and when, toward the end of the century, the more inquisitive spirits began to look over the linguistic and denominational fence, they turned, not to the English counterpart of denominational literature, but rather to Blatchford's *Merrie England*. But until this happened, Welsh denominational literature exercised a great influence in arousing a political consciousness among its readers, although we shall see that its triumph in the industrial areas was short lived.

Ollivant might have been too optimistic in 1854 of the effects of a more widespread education in the industrial parts of his diocese, but he was certainly aware that he was living in a revolution. He urged the clergy to pursue their studies more diligently, for the social revolution would make more

[1] *Report of Committee of Council on Education* (1840), pp. 161–2.

demands on them. 'Should the shrewd and keen sighted mechanic find his clergyman deficient in ordinary information, less intelligent and instructed than other members of society, it is very unlikely that he will listen to his instruction with deference and respect. . . . It is my heart's desire and prayer that our clergy may be a class of well-educated and intelligent men, full of the Holy Ghost and wisdom.'[1] They should master the art of simple teaching, for it was the absence of it that was one of the causes of the Dissent that existed in South Wales. Ollivant was to learn that it was easier to build churches than to staff them with competent clergy.

An innovation introduced by Ollivant was an extra-parochial ministry for evangelization in the industrial areas. He first broached the question of what he described as 'itinerant ministrations' in his first visitation charge in 1851 and returned to it in his two following visitation charges of 1854 and 1857. In 1860 he made another plea for such a missionary agency: 'Is the Church so rigid and inelastic that the people are to be estranged from her communion, too often, it may be said, abandoned to a practical heathenism—and she to be a merely indolent spectator of so great a calamity?' A missionary clergyman 'might preach to the colliers in the open air, or follow them into their pits, or gather together the sheep who are scattered abroad over our hills and valleys, or living in the remote corners of our large Parishes, which the overwhelming occupations of the Parochial Clergyman will rarely permit him to visit'.[2] These parish priests would be prepared to receive the missionary into their parishes as fellow workers to 'cultivate that portion of their vineyard which it would be hopeless for them to attempt to cultivate themselves'. He had in mind a regular and permanent force of six clergy for this purpose, but he would be content to begin with one or two.

[1] A. Ollivant, *Second Visitation Charge*, (1852), p. 16.

[2] A. Ollivant, *A proposal for establishing a Missionary Agency for the purpose of promoting the spiritual welfare of the mining population of his Diocese* (n.d.), p. 3.

In his charge on the occasion of his visitation in 1863 he reported on this venture by quoting from the Journal of one of the missioners for June of that year:

Cwm Bargoed Pits: These belong to the Dowlais Company, and are in the District of Dowlais. They are about . . . three miles from the parish church. The inhabitants are not many, but as they have no services of any kind, except on very rare occasions, I thought it a proper place for the attendance of the Home Missionary; the people were very glad that I had come among them.

Pont y Waun: This place is situated on the mountains, among the coal and mine tips, midway between Rhymney and Dowlais; including Twyn y Waun, Blaen Carno, and a few other cottages near it [and] its population must be upward of two hundred. It has hitherto been sadly neglected, and its Sundays are spent a good deal in drinking. A very few are Baptists; the rest, almost without exception, are careless. I found a schoolroom here built by the Baptists, where a Sunday School is held in the afternoon. These also have occasional preaching, and on Sunday evenings, if no sermon, a prayer meeting is held. While visiting, and again after the service, I took an opportunity of stating that I was a Clergyman sent by the Bishop to preach to them, and if any were ill, to read and pray with them. I was very well received, and a very great number attended the service in the evening.[1]

This is the only direct account we have of the work of this particular mission agency which was put on a more permanent basis later. The Diocesan Conference of 1887 set up a Diocesan Committee on Mission Work and this presented its first report at the Diocesan Conference the following year by Canon William Evans, vicar of Rhymney. He emphasized that such missioners should have a satisfactory knowledge of the people among whom they worked, for 'if some of the missions have failed to produce good results I believe it to be because the Missioners have been strangers to the idiosyncrasies of the Welsh people'.[2] This agency

[1] Quoted by A. Ollivant, *Fifth Visitation Charge* (1863), p. 52, n. 4.
[2] *Report of the Llandaff Diocesan Conference* (1888), p. 22.

continued, and reports were submitted to successive diocesan conferences until the creation of new parishes and ecclesiastical districts presumably made them unnecessary as all parts of smaller parishes could be served by the parish priest.

The third great problem which confronted the old diocese of Llandaff after 1850 was to enlist the co-operation of the laity in the work and witness of the Church, and this proved to be the most difficult task of all. Centuries of custom and canon law had given the laity a very minor role in the affairs of the Church. For centuries parishes had been administered by the incumbent and two churchwardens, and the latter had frequently regarded their obligations more in the nature of a necessity than a privilege. Until the middle of the century the Established Church was very largely a clerically administered body, and even until disestablishment it was not obligatory to set up representative councils in the parishes, although incumbents were encouraged to do so on a voluntary basis, if only to meet the financial demands that were being made on the parishes by the diocesan authorities in the decade or so preceding 1919. Before the middle of the last century the laity had been enrolled on diocesan committees for such purposes as education, but the democratic procedures of elected bodies such as Nonconformity was accustomed to were completely absent from the Church.[1] It was therefore a foregone conclusion that the earliest lay co-operation should come from county families and business men in the towns, both because these were the only vocal section of Church laity and also because Nonconformity had captured the working class and rising middle class in the industrial areas. Consequently, in the higher councils of the diocese, the rural voice and interest preponderated over

1 'The Church of England gives the working man nothing to do. He feels he forms no integral part of her, that he is in no vital connection with her, that he is not built into her structure, but is left a loose stone lying about for anyone to tumble over.' K. S. Inglis, *Churches and the Working Classes in Victorian England* (London, 1963), p. 60, quoting J. Foxley, *A Sermon on Church Reform* (1895), p. 6.

the industrial; or, to put it in another way, the rural south, and the urban areas such as Cardiff and Newport, were much more evident in the diocesan picture than the industrial north.

Bishop Ollivant was alive to this challenge in the industrial parishes. He urged the clergy to set up working men's clubs, night schools and libraries in their parishes so that the laity could be brought into the work of the Church. He urged the laity to take a deeper interest in the evangelizing work of the parishes: 'The conviction has forced itself upon us, and upon Churchmen universally, that we must get rid of the old-fashioned and injurious notion that the Clergy alone constitute the Church. It is to the Laity that we must look for help, not merely for their money, which many are ready to bestow, but for personal co-operation with us in our actual work.'[1]

There were three specific issues which affected the position of the laity in the Church at that time. The first, already mentioned, was the closer co-operation with the clergy on the parish level through the setting up of church councils. This step was advocated by Ollivant in his last visitation in 1881: 'Let me recommend every Incumbent to form in his parish an Association of the lay members of the Church who may make it their business to interest others in all matters that concern its welfare.' Above all, 'We have not yet dug into the deep mine of the hearts and affections of the middle classes as we might. The givers are many of them liberal, but in numbers they are not what they should be.'[2]

The second issue bore upon the teaching function of the laity in the Church, and this involved the recognition of lay readers to correspond to the lay preachers upon whom Nonconformity had depended so largely. Ollivant was wary of this step, and he told his annual conference of rural deans in 1867 that it would be most undesirable in a Welsh diocese

[1] A. Ollivant, *Seventh Visitation Charge* (1869), p. 43.

[2] A. Ollivant, *Eleventh Visitation Charge* (1881), pp. 43–45.

to give a lay reader's commission to a class of men who, in point of education and social condition, would not be in the popular mind distinguishable from dissenting ministers.[1] But in his visitation charge of 1869 he said that he was prepared to license those who had a vocation to teach as lay readers, subject to certain safeguards and upon the understanding 'that the Commission so given was not to be regarded as a passport to Ordination'.[2] The step was taken on 27 April of the following year, when the first lay readers for the diocese were licensed by the bishop in his private chapel at Llandaff. In his address on this occasion Ollivant stressed that the laity were part of the 'royal priesthood' of the New Testament. The reader would not be a paid agent, but a voluntary worker. 'He will systematically appropriate such a portion of his time as his worldly calling enables him to give up—whether it be an hour every day or an hour every week —in short, whatever he can, only by some fixed rate and standard, not of necessity, but of a ready mind, to such good works as his clergyman may be willing to commit to him, and as may be included in the terms of the bishop's commission.'[3] On this occasion six lay readers were commissioned, one to the parish of Dowlais and five to that of Gelligaer. With the exception of Sunday-school teachers this was the first break-through to enlist the co-operation of the laity in the teaching work of the Church, and it is significant that all the readers came from industrial parishes, whence the majority of lay readers have since come.

When the diocesan voice was heard for the first time at the first Diocesan Conference in 1884 a motion was presented to it that 'the circumstances of the times urgently call for the organized services of qualified laymen in the ministration of the Church', and in the debate that followed, it was clear that the members did not share Ollivant's misgivings on

[1] LL/Ch/31.
[2] A. Ollivant, *Seventh Visitation Charge* (1869), p. 53.
[3] A. Ollivant, *Address of the Bishop of Llandaff on the first appointment of Lay Readers for his diocese, delivered in his chapel, April 27, 1870* (Cardiff, n.d.).

this matter. There were some who believed that a Lay Readership was an irregular ministry which should be replaced by a settled Lay Diaconate; while others objected to this limitation. Bishop Perry, formerly of Melbourne, who had come to live in Llandaff, said that the kind of person who came forward as a lay reader was often the best to minister as a priest in the new industrial areas and should be encouraged to do so. Others advocated the division of lay readers into paid and voluntary, and that they should be admitted after examination and not only upon the recommendation of an incumbent. But in regard to the principle itself, the Conference was unanimous in accepting the motion which represented a great advance in the recognition of the laity in and by the Church.[1]

Ollivant was equally reluctant to take the next step, that of setting up a consultative conference for the diocese. Diocesan conferences had been formed in every diocese in the Church with the exception of Worcester, but Ollivant had expressed hesitation on this matter, for he doubted the capacity of such a body to discuss doctrinal questions. Something, however, could be said for a consultative body, but 'the experiment of such meetings will be made elsewhere, and the issue of them may determine whether it will be well to adopt them generally as a permanent Institution'.[2] In any case, Ollivant was now drawing to the end of a long and very arduous episcopate, and he might well have believed that this further step of providing the diocese with larger constitutional forms and extended lay co-operation was better left to his successor whose advent could not be far distant.

His successor, Bishop Richard Lewis, inaugurated the Diocesan Conference in 1884, within a year of the beginning of his episcopate. The purpose of the Conference was explained by the Bishop in his presidential address to the first

[1] *Report of the Llandaff Diocesan Conference* (1884), pp. 56–70.
[2] A. Ollivant, *Eleventh Visitation Charge* (1881), pp. 43–45.

meeting: 'to gather up the opinions of the clergy and laity of the diocese upon important questions affecting the interests of the Church in general for the information of Convocation, and with a view, as far as possible, to influence the course of Church legislation in Parliament'.[1] This original purpose of the Conference became widened as time went on, and it can be claimed that it was the establishment of this body which provided the first platform for the expression of the views and opinions of the diocese as a whole.

But the original composition of the Diocesan Conference mirrored the authoritative and paternal nature of the Established Church in those days. Ex-officio members composed a high proportion of its membership: the bishop, as president, the dean and chapter of Llandaff, rural deans, the bishop's chaplains, the diocesan inspector of schools, the clerical secretary and treasurer of the Conference, the secretaries and treasurers of the Llandaff Church Extension Society, the Society for Church Building, Boards of Education, and Home Missions. The lay ex-officio members were the lords-lieutenants of Glamorgan and Monmouthshire, all peers of the realm residing in the diocese, all M.P.s having constituencies in the diocese, the diocesan chancellor, the bishop's secretary, the lay secretaries of diocesan societies, and twelve laymen nominated by the bishop. The elected members were 84 laymen and 64 clergy representing the rural deaneries in proportion to population. It was soon felt that the elected representatives did not form a sufficiently high proportion of the members of Conference, and in 1890 their numbers were increased to 168 and 148 respectively, and by 1910 these had grown to 250 and 228. Not the least significant sign of the feeling of the Conference was this progressive increase in its representative character. Bishop Joshua Hughes was later to complain that insufficient care was being taken to ensure that the laity were adequately represented by the best men; he was anxious that they should take their rightful

[1] *Report of the Llandaff Diocesan Conference* (1884), p. 3.

place in the councils of the Church, for the seat of authority lay with the whole Church, both clergy and laity.[1] The laity of the diocese were given an increasing part in the councils of the Church, but a reading of the proceedings of these conferences shows clearly that lay leadership remained where it had been for the past 50 years, viz., in the rural areas, and that the voice of the layman from the industrial areas was rarely heard.

Although the primary purpose of the Diocesan Conference was to make representations to the Convocation of Canterbury on issues which were to be the subject of parliamentary legislation, it soon extended its scope to discuss other matters: how best to deal with the bilingual problem (1887), housing needs (1893), divorce and remarriage, and biblical criticism (1896), art and the Church (1899); the duty of the Church toward the 'Welsh National Awakening' (1904), support for the National Insurance Bill (1911), the Church and Socialism (1912), are only a few of the matters of general interest discussed by the Conference during these years. In the course of some of these debates there was some plain speaking, especially by the clergy from the industrial parishes. In the first Conference, that of 1884, the problem of the industrial areas was discussed, and it was said that the parochial system was overweighted, for in spite of dissenters and Roman Catholics, there remained a vast body of people with no connexion with church or chapel. Nor had the Church succeeded in obtaining the active co-operation of working men: 'The organization of dissenting bodies gives them great facilities for increasing their numbers, and if the Church is not only to hold her own, but regain the lost ground in these districts, she must make the population sharers in Church management.'[2] Churches must be made free and appropriated pews abolished so that poor people could attend church. One speaker said: 'I feel that the Church will never

[1] J. P. Hughes, *Second Visitation Charge* (Cardiff, 1910), p. 22.
[2] *Report of the Llandaff Diocesan Conference* (1884), p. 49.

be the Church of the people until the pews are swept out';[1] and the vicar of Aberdare said: 'The co-operation of the so-called working class is neither solicited nor obtained. Our Nonconformist brethren are far ahead of us in this matter. In the Chapels much help and large sums of money are often given by those of a class that is, for some reason or other, generally considered exempt from us.'[2] In the Conference of the following year (1885) C. J. Vaughan, dean of Llandaff, urged parish priests to set up consultative councils in their parishes; they would have no statutory authority, but they would be none the worse for that.

If lay leadership was conservative in its tone, not in a positive, but in the negative sense that the laity generally eschewed the discussion of social issues in the Conference, this was by no means true of the clergy, and particularly of those from the industrial parishes. There was more social criticism to be heard in the Llandaff Diocesan Conference than in the contemporary councils of Nonconformity in these parts.[3] In the Conference of 1893, T. Jesse Jones, rector of Gelli-gaer, said that the greatest difficulty facing the clergy in Wales was that the cause of the Church was linked with Toryism, 'as we find that Toryism finding expression in Wales'. He said that he had recently tried to build a church in the Rhymney valley, and

> I have appealed far and wide, and appealed with no effect whatsoever to those who are concerned in the mines. I had occasion to write to one of them the other day, and to say 'In the Rhymney valley, as far as I know, there is not as much as one brass farthing's worth of philanthropy—not even as much for a little scoop for a dog to lick water out of to quench his thirst; and I ask you, how do you expect to retain your property, or have things to go well with you, or for the working men to have

[1] *Report of the Llandaff Diocesan Conference* (1884), p. 50.

[2] Ibid., p. 54.

[3] This was true of the whole country. As the century drew to its close Methodism receded more and more from its traditional working-class supporters while the Established Church became more and more conscious of this class (see K. S. Inglis, op. cit., Int., p. 9).

good feelings toward you, when you do nothing for them, and when you are not known to them, except by name and except as receiving things from these parishes.'[1]

In the same Conference there was a discussion on the problem of poverty in which it was stated that philanthropy and charity were not the answer to bad conditions. There was too much of the *laissez-faire* attitude in the letting of land and houses, and the condition of country cottages in the diocese was becoming worse. Daniel Lewis, rector of Merthyr Tydfil, said that the necessary legislation was available but was not being implemented. 'First of all, we have on the Boards of Health, whose duty it is to carry out the law, men who are largely interested in cottage rents. Secondly, you have employers of labour who are also interested in cottages. Thirdly, you have certain gentlemen called appointed officers under the Board. They are absolutely under their control, they dare not say anything but what the Board fully approves of.'[2] In the same debate another speaker said that he hoped the clergy would do all they could toward promoting a feeling of discontent against bad sanitary conditions.

In 1901 the housing problem was once more debated in the Diocesan Conference, and it was initiated by Llewelyn Williams, rector of Dowlais. He described how these communities had grown: 'The story of the planting and growth of these huge areas of population within this area is almost identical in every instance. Coal is struck at a certain point, and a pit is sunk: with mushroom-like growth a village or town suddenly springs up, and people crowd into the new district heedless of the dangers that lie in the fact that housing accommodation is insufficient, and that overcrowding with all its broods of physical and moral poison must follow.'[3] Overcrowding, the worst enemy of health, decency, morality, and religion, was rampant. The Church should urge District Councils to do their duty, but 'unhappily much indifference

[1] *Report of the Llandaff Diocesan Conference* (1893), pp. 55–56.
[2] Ibid., p. 90.
[3] Ibid. (1901), p. 92.

exists, and in many instances positive opposition. Vested interests drown, with their clamour, the moan of the sufferers.'[1] Another speaker, (a Cardiff layman this time) said that he knew the Dowlais area very well, and 'in no part of this diocese can you find such miserable hovels in which people are expected to live respectably. And yet millions of money have been dragged out of Dowlais for the aristocracy to build large houses', but, as for the homes of the workers, 'Lord Wimborne would not stable his horses in some of them'.[2] This Conference passed the resolution 'that it was an essential part of the mission of the Church under the present industrial and social conditions to throw the weight of its influence and sympathy in favour of the rigid enforcement of the powers vested by Parliament in sanitary and municipal authorities for the better housing of the poor, and endeavour by such means as it may be able to command, to obtain from the legislature an extension of such powers'.

In 1905 the Conference deplored the length of shop hours and its results, and urged that the local authorities should exercise their powers under the Shop Hours Act. William Lewis, vicar of Ystradyfodwg, who had been prominent for years in debates on social issues, suggested that the scenes in industrial townships on Saturday nights could be ended if colliery-owners could be induced to pay their men on Fridays.

A year later the motion that a sympathetic relationship of the Church with Labour was desirable in the interest of national welfare was accepted by the Conference. During the debate, the incumbent of a parish in the Rhymney valley said that it was obvious that there was an estrangement between the Anglican Church and Labour, due principally to the alliance between the Church and the upper and middle classes; 'and her government as a result has been largely

[1] *Report of the Llandaff Diocesan Conference* (1901), p. 94.

[2] Ibid., p. 101. Lord Wimborne was the local industrialist. He lived in Canford Magna, Dorset.

influenced by an autocratic rather than a democratic spirit'. The class spirit was too marked in her. In the last decade a considerable number of communicants had allied themselves with the Independent Labour Party because they saw in that movement an opportunity of solving their problems. 'With their doing so we have absolutely no fault to find, and they cannot but receive our full sympathy and support.' But, unfortunately, secularism had become a cardinal principle of that movement; however, 'the salvation of the socialist and labour movement lies in the hands of the Church, and not in Dissent with its characteristic individualism'.[1] The Conference returned to this theme in the following year (1907), and one speaker, the vicar of Aberavon, said that the cleavage between the Church and the working class was due to the laity and not to the clergy, and the fact that the churches were sometimes like refrigerating chambers was losing communicants to the I.L.P. and socialist movements.

The founding of the Diocesan Conference gave the clergy and laity an official platform for the expression of ecclesiastical, theological and social views. It was inevitable that many of these questions should be connected with strictly ecclesiastical matters, but it has been shown that a wide variety of subjects was discussed year after year; and the examples given have not included educational matters which were by no means concerned only with church schools but included Welsh intermediate and higher education. It should also be recognized that the fact of the Establishment made it inevitable that the Conference should not be too introspective in its interests, but that its attention should be directed to that society toward which in theory, and to a lesser degree in practice, it had a pastoral responsibility. The Establishment had had many deleterious effects upon the Church, but among its beneficent influences was that it never allowed the Church wholly to forget its responsibilities to society as a whole. But the annual meetings of the Diocesan Conference

[1] *Report of the Llandaff Diocesan Conference* (1906), pp. 109–11.

also revealed that the old and the new in the diocese, the historic rural and the new industrial, had yet to be welded into one; indeed, if a definite mission could have been attributed to the Church in the old diocese of Llandaff in the nineteenth century, it was just this task of resolving the dichotomy which had been created in the diocese. Two distinct ways of life with their own different expressions and problems had to be welded together in a religious fellowship which should have been concerned as much with material as with spiritual and moral problems. To say that the Church completely failed would be an exaggeration. It should not be forgotten that this was the one body, civil or ecclesiastical, which made the attempt: other religious bodies were sectional in a geographical and linguistic sense; yet the Church would have succeeded to a greater degree if it had been conscious at the time that its primary task was fellowship and not personal salvation. The division lay, not between the clergy, but among the laity. The industrial revolution ultimately produced such vigorous clergy as William Lewis of Ystradyfodwg, T. Jesse Jones, rector of Gelli-gaer, William Evans, vicar of Rhymney, J. D. Jenkins of Aberdare, John Griffith of Aberdare (and later of Merthyr Tydfil), and Daniel Lewis of Merthyr Tydfil, to name only those who figured most prominently in the debates of the Diocesan Conference; and this list does not include the clergy who transformed church life in the towns such as Cardiff and Newport. The division in the Church in the two societies was lay rather than clerical; the clergy spoke the same language, but the gap between the layman of the historic, traditional south on the one hand, and the new industrial north on the other hand, was still unbridged. They just did not speak the same language.

It is difficult to assess the progress made by the Established Church during the second half of the nineteenth century in these older areas of the iron industry. The outlook in 1851 was by no means promising, but the situation as revealed in census Sunday of that year reflected the Church at the very nadir of its fortunes; even when the census was held, its basic reorganization had sufficiently advanced to equip it for its task, but a great deal needed to be done before any marked impression could be made on these strongholds of Welsh Nonconformity. The earliest signs that an impression was being made came when the Established Church began to draw the fire of the Baptists. In his visitation charge of 1863 Bishop Ollivant said: 'Before my Confirmations took place last year I was surprised by the number of applications that reached me on behalf of persons of riper years, who had been nominally attached to Baptist Congregations, and were desirous of being baptized that they might become members of the Church.'[1] He reported that the number of baptisms and confirmations had increased: in Merthyr the numbers were 445 in the last Confirmation and 177 in Aberdare. But the revelation that there were still 98 churches in the diocese where no services were held on Ash Wednesday and 138 where Maundy Thursday was not observed, showed that the Church had yet a very long way to go before its house was put in order. Gradually things improved, and this was particularly true of the quality of the Welsh-speaking clergy, an improvement which resulted in a steady but not spectacular progress in the industrial areas. Although there was enough to do without encroaching upon Nonconformity, it was inevitable that a scene which was largely the result of local social and ecclesiastical conditions should become fluid to a certain degree. Individual conversions from Dissent, although not perhaps significant in the aggregate, became a feature of Church life as the century wore on. At their quarterly meeting in Blaenavon in November 1891 the Monmouthshire

[1] A. Ollivant, *Fifth Visitation Charge*, p. 36. It was on this occasion that Ollivant suggested that the new churches which were being built should be provided with baptisteries to make it clear that the Church had no objection to baptism by immersion. This was done in a number of cases. Ollivant quoted Gelli-gaer and Trevethin among the older churches, and Ebbw Vale among the newer.

Baptist Association deemed it necessary to pass the following Resolution: 'That we are glad to understand that after listening to statements made after full investigation by the Baptist Ministers of Blaenavon, and others, the account that has appeared in some papers that 43 Ex-Baptists were confirmed at Blaenavon, is grossly erroneous.'[1]

However, Bishop Lewis consistently claimed that a considerable percentage of adult confirmation candidates came from the ranks of Nonconformity, but that only a small number were Welsh candidates. Out of 5,709 confirmed by him in 1883, 341 were Welsh candidates,[2] but during the years 1885–7 he confirmed 10,359 candidates, a figure 'due in great measure to the remarkable increase in the number of those who during the past few years have been gathered into the Church from the ranks of Nonconformity. At some of the centres I visited last year, considerably more than half of the number confirmed were persons of this class.'[3] The total number of candidates from 1888–90 rose to 12,247, and the number of adult candidates was 'unusually large, sometimes as high as one-third of the whole, the majority of these being converts from Nonconformity',[4] which Bishop Lewis attributed to the improvement in the quality of the clergy and to 'the substitution of political for religious teaching in many [Nonconformist] pulpits, and in the utilization of the press for the encouragement of lawlessness, dishonesty, and fraud'. He went on to quote from such periodicals as the *Cambrian News*, *Y Faner*, and the London *Echo*, all of which stated that there was a decline in Nonconformity and an increase in the influence of the Church.[5]

There is sufficient evidence to show that, if the Established Church had touched the lowest point in its fortunes by the middle of the century, Welsh Nonconformity reached its

1 *Monmouthshire Baptist Association Circular Letter* (1891), p. 8.
2 Richard Lewis, *Primary Visitation Charge* (1885), p. 6.
3 Richard Lewis, *Second Visitation Charge* (1888), p. 8.
4 Richard Lewis, *Third Visitation Charge* (1891), p. 14.
5 Ibid., pp. 15–16.

zenith in the industrial areas in the 1880s, and that thereafter it retained its position for a generation or so before it began its period of decline. The situation of the Established Church in the same areas was greatly improved by the end of the century, but this was due to its progress among the English-speaking population and the anglicized Welsh. It failed to regain the allegiance of the Welsh-speaking people in these areas. This was brought out clearly in the evidence given to the 'Royal Commission on the Church of England in Wales and other religious bodies in Wales and Monmouthshire' during 1906 and 1907. It was one of the objects of the Nonconformist members on this Welsh Church Commission to reveal and emphasize that the Established Church did not possess the support of the majority of Welsh-speaking Welshmen, and there is no doubt that, with the exception of one parish in these industrial areas, they succeeded in doing so.

If one parish had to be marked out as having shown the greatest progress in the second half of the nineteenth century, it would be that of Aberdare, which was probably the most backward in 1850. This was due to such incumbents as John Griffith (later rector of Merthyr Tydfil), Canon J. D. Jenkins, who played a leading part in the civic life of Aberdare and was President of the Amalgamated Society of Railway Servants, and C. A. H. Green, who, with others, built up one of the best 'church' parishes in the old diocese of Llandaff. The incidence of Welsh-speaking people in Aberdare in 1906 was 74·5 per cent., and for this proportion of the population there were four and a half services per Sunday while there were six services per Sunday for the remaining 25 per cent.[1] Green said that a great many Welsh-speaking people attended the English church in Aberdare and the Welsh church was by no means full. In the Rhondda Valley the monoglot

[1] *Royal Commission on the Church and other Religious Bodies in Wales, Minutes of Evidence* (ii. 254). There was one Welsh service on alternate Sundays in the parish church of St. John; hence the 'half service' referred to in the text.

English amounted to 35·5 per cent. of the population, while the monoglot Welsh and bilinguals made up the remainder.[1] The vicar of Ystradyfodwg (William Lewis) did not reply to the charge made by a Nonconformist member of the Commission, Sir John Williams: 'you have 420 sittings for the monoglot Welsh, who amount to 11 per cent. of the population, something under 12,000, and for the monoglot English you have 1,900 for 35 per cent. of the population'.[2] This pattern of small Welsh congregations was repeated, with one exception, throughout north Monmouthshire and the Aberdare–Merthyr Tydfil area, and it reveals that the Established Church had done little to breach Welsh Nonconformity. But it revealed another significant fact: that because of this defect in language, the Established Church failed to enter fully into the life of these communities and partake of the popular Welsh culture which was characteristic of them while the native language reigned. Even where, as in Aberdare, the Church itself was transformed beyond recognition within fifty years, yet it remained apart from the general life of a Welsh community. 'It kept very much to itself.'

The obverse of the picture is, however, that the Church did not suffer nearly as much as Nonconformity from the decline of the Welsh language.

The exception referred to above is the parish of Rhymney. Of all the parishes in the old ironworks belt, it was Rhymney which proved to be the most successful on the Welsh side. The causes for its success are obvious; the Church was established in the new community before Nonconformity had taken almost complete possession. The Rhymney valley was the last of the valleys to be affected by the first phase of the

[1] Whereas the Nonconformist members of the Commission added the bilinguals to the Welsh population, Church witnesses claimed that they could equally validly be added to the English population. But the above figures were not disputed.

[2] *Royal Commission on the Church and other Religious Bodies in Wales, Minutes of Evidence*, ii. 187. On the face of it this was not an unfair apportionment, but the point of the question was to show that no provision was made for the bilingual Welsh.

industrial revolution, and the Rhymney Iron Company provided it with a church in 1843, but before this happened church people had worshipped in cottages on the Nonconformist pattern. There then followed an amazingly successful ministry by the first incumbent, Lodwick Edwards, and this was succeeded by the long ministry of one of the leading clergy in the old diocese of Llandaff, Canon William Evans. Evans was a thorough Welshman of the evangelical school of churchmanship. He edited Welsh Church periodicals, and in his time the Church in Rhymney possessed a strong Welsh congregation which could be compared with any Welsh Nonconformist denomination in the parish. Moreover, both Evans and the laity entered fully into the flourishing cultural life of the community. It was not an accident that this parish became the best nursery for ordinands in Monmouthshire, and this was the result of contact with the grass roots of the local community. The vicar of Rhymney was the one clerical witness from those parts who was able to reply with confidence to the charge always brought by the Nonconformist members of the Royal Commission of 1906 that the church had neglected the Welsh-speaking parishioners. In the other industrial parishes there is little doubt that the figure of the churchman who was also a thorough Welshman was a rarity among his felllows.

The following statistics will illustrate the progress made by the Established Church in these areas with which this study began, viz. the old ironworks district, during the second half of the last century, although it must be confessed that they conceal her failures.

RURAL DEANERY OF ABERDARE: a rise in population from 14,999 in 1837 to 65,949 in 1901. An increase from 3 to 27 churches; from 2 to 25 clergy, and from 5 Sunday services in 1848 to 61 in 1906. Communicants 4,129.

RURAL DEANERY OF MERTHYR TYDFIL: a population increase from 46,378 to 70,999 from 1851 to 1901. An increase from 4 to 24 churches, from 4 to 22 clergy, and from 11 Sunday services in 1848 to 53 in 1906. Communicants: 4,175.

RURAL DEANERY OF BEDWELLTY: a rise in population from 32,728 in 1851 to 54,061 in 1901; and an increase from 5 to 25 churches, from 9 to 23 clergy, and from 10 to 54 services between 1848 and 1906. Communicants: 4,302.

RURAL DEANERY OF BLAENAU GWENT: a population increase of 35,195 to 91,490 from 1851 to 1901; and an increase from 9 to 32 churches, from 8 to 29 clergy, and from 16 to 70 Sunday services between 1848 and 1906. Communicants, 4,372.[1]

[1] LL/WCC/320,323.

IV

SOCIAL AND RELIGIOUS CHANGES

THE society created by the industrial revolution in the old ironworks district was one in which Welsh Nonconformity predominated and it could fairly be described as a religious society in the sense that an appreciably higher percentage of its inhabitants than the national average had some connexion or other with places of worship and religious observances. But it was also a society in which, because of its great lack of social variety and amenities, the contrast between the church and 'the world' was very marked. There was no middle way for those who did not want the church or chapel on the one hand or the public house on the other, for these were the only social centres available to the majority of the inhabitants of these industrial districts. H. A. Bruce (later Lord Aberdare) dealt with this lack of social amenities in a lecture in Merthyr on 20 March 1850, in the course of which he said:

> To me the simplest, most natural, most efficacious, instrument of redemption seems to be, to provide, or to assist the working class to provide, those means of innocent pleasure, of social enjoyment, at which moral and mental improvement rather insinuate themselves than are enforced—where recreation may lead on insensibly to refinement, and pursuits commenced for the mere purpose of amusement and relaxation, may gradually improve the manners, elevate the tone, and expand the intellect of those who little suspect the transformation they are undergoing.[1]

[1] H. A. Bruce, *On Amusements, as the means of continuing and extending the education of the working classes* (Cardiff, 1850), p. 4.

The work of education should go on in the playground as well as in the schoolroom; innocent pleasures should be made the handmaidens of education; temperance societies should be conjoined with horticultural societies; playing-fields should be provided for the young, and village libraries should be opened. In these matters, said Bruce, Great Britain lagged far behind other countries:

> Of all the leading people of Europe, I grieve to say, those worst provided with the means of rational and manly amusements are the Inhabitants of the British Isles. I will undertake to say that there is not a modest little town of 4,000 or 5,000 Inhabitants in France or Germany, which is not furnished with more means of instruction—more appliances for amusement for its adult inhabitants, than our great English Towns of the second class, with wealth twentyfold as great, and everything but the will to do good, in proportionate abundance.[1]

Whether this policy of doing good by stealth underlay the provision of social amenities in these industrial districts during the second half of the nineteenth century is doubtful, but there is no doubt that social life became more varied, albeit very slowly, as the century wore on. The societies which existed in the first half of the century had had a very limited range of amenities. Malkin, writing of Merthyr Tydfil in 1807, says that it had a printing office, several book societies, and a Philosophical Society. It was the Unitarians who were foremost in the intellectual life of the town, and later there were 'many of the inhabitants who apply themselves to the study of mineralogy, chymistry, and other branches of natural knowledge, in a regular train of scientific initiation'.[2] But this Philosophical Society did not last long. A Mechanics' Institute was established in Dowlais in 1829, and the same town had a society where Welsh literature and history were studied. There was a theatre in the district, and races were also held, 'but, from the

[1] H. A. Bruce, op. cit., p. 12.
[2] B. H. Malkin, op. cit. i. 275.

depressed state of the iron trade within the past few years, both these sources of amusement have been discontinued'.[1] Merthyr Tydfil got its library in 1846, and three years later both Ebbw Vale and Tredegar embarked on ventures which were independent of the chapels, although both relied on chapel support. On 5 November 1849 the Ebbw Vale Mutual Improvement Society was founded and was later held in the vestry of the old Penuel chapel. The society changed its name in 1852 to the Ebbw Vale Literary and Scientific Institute. Progress was slow; the society relied for years on social gatherings and light entertainment, and it was not until after the passing of the Education Act of 1870 that its educational work was emphasized.[2] In 1849, also, a library was formed by the leading citizens of Tredegar. A reading-room followed, but did not flourish. A hall was provided in 1861 for 'entertainment, instruction, and for the propagation of temperance' largely by the subscription of the local workers who, however, soon tired of it 'when the first intoxication of temperance was over', and left its amenities to be enjoyed largely by the middle class.[3] In 1850 a Literary and Scientific Institution was formed in Rhymney, and was housed later in the National School built in 1858 by the Rhymney Iron Company. This Institution was managed by the leading officials of the Company and the local ministers of religion, and the workmen paid 1*s*. per quarter subscription. But the great mass of the workers remained untouched by this venture, and it was not until 1894, when elementary education was made free, that they undertook to make regular contributions to the Institution.[4] Likewise the early attempts to supply Aberdare with a public library failed. Its promoters were John Griffith, the vicar, and Dr. Thomas Price, the Baptist minister.

[1] Samuel Lewis, *A Topography of Wales*, ii. 216.

[2] *Ebbw Vale Literary and Scientific Institute. The History of a hundred years, 1849–1949.*

[3] *Tredegar Workmen's Hall . . .*, p. 23.

[4] T. Jones, *Rhymney Memories*, p. 25.

The attempts to supply these areas with public libraries were characteristic of the 1850s and after,[1] and during this period most of these industrial townships were supplied with libraries: Dowlais (1852), New Tredegar (1873), Merthyr Vale (1880), Blaina (1884), Blaenavon (1883), Cwmtillery (1884), Abercarn (1888), Tredegar (1890), and Risca and Cross Keys (1894). But it was later that the full significance of these ventures became apparent, when the workers themselves elected to pay a poundage toward their maintenance and extension, so that the Miners' Institutes, often imposing structures, became well-established institutions in the iron and coal districts. They became real social centres for the workers, and, in one case at least, were supplied with accommodation for women also. Before the end of the century, and until recent times, they were flourishing social clubs for the workers, providing entertainment and recreation as well as cultural activities in the form of library facilities and public lectures. But they were also counter-attractions to the chapels which, nevertheless, continued with their concerts, eisteddfodau and penny-readings in addition to their other activities.

Mention must also be made of the development of local government in these parts, a development made necessary largely by the concern for public health. The state of affairs existing in Merthyr Tydfil shows the extent to which the problems of local government had outstripped the provisions.

The Poor Law Amendment Act (1834) resulted in local boards of guardians, and the necessities of public health led to the formation of local government boards for such matters as burial grounds, water supplies and street cleansing. The Education Act of 1870 saw the rise of local school boards to which members were elected often after a hotly contested campaign which had far less to do with primary education than with the church *v.* chapel issue. It is not too much to

[1] John H. Phillips, *An Essay on the advantages of Free Libraries* (Cardiff, 1867); John Coke Fowler, *On Public Libraries* (Swansea, 1871).

say that one important purpose of these elections was to see that the vicar did not get on the board. The culmination of this movement in local government was the formation of county councils in 1888 and district councils, both urban and rural, in 1894. It would be difficult to exaggerate the importance of these developments in the second half of the last century as they affected the older industrial areas, for they offered greatly increased opportunities for civic leadership. Little by little the control and destiny of these communities came more and more into local hands. At first the representatives were largely from the middle, trading classes and Nonconformist ministers, and to a lesser degree the clergy of the Established Church played a leading part in these developments. Local government bodies up to the end of the last century, and into the present century, mirrored the prevailing state of society which, in spite of ominous changes which were beginning to make themselves felt in certain quarters, was still middle class, trading, Nonconformist and Liberal, as far as its leaders were concerned. As with so many other aspects of local and national life, in this respect also the nineteenth century did not come to an end until 1914, although there were unmistakable signs that radical changes were taking place in this industrial society.

As leadership came largely from the middle class, that of Nonconformist ministers, shopkeepers and colliery officials, the hold of Nonconformity on this society was temporarily strengthened by the development of local government. Nonconformist ministers added the power of local politics to their status, and some managed not to abandon their positions when the balance of power shifted from the middle class to the working class. This was especially true of Glamorgan, where a kind of political, radical succession among Baptist ministers survived the swing from Liberalism to Labour. Most of these ministers were to be found in the Liberal party until the shift in political allegiance in their own congregations after 1918 made a change desirable, if not necessary.

Another institution which indirectly strengthened Nonconformity were the schools set up under the Welsh Intermediate Act (1889), schools known generally, and for a long time, as 'Intermediate Schools' and 'County Schools'. These were the schools which brought a liberalized grammar-school education into the society of the industrial revolution. Schools such as the Intermediate schools at Aberdare, Mountain Ash, Merthyr Tydfil, Tredegar, Ebbw Vale, Abertillery, Pontypool, and Risca were to have a very great influence upon their localities. They produced the first professional class in this new society, a class which consisted for a long time of the children of Nonconformist ministers, tradesmen and colliery officials. These children passed through the schools to become lawyers, doctors and schoolmasters, and although many were to leave the industrial scenes for other pastures, those who stayed at home became prominent in their circles. It was Welsh Nonconformity which largely benefited from this grammar-school education and its social results, for the schools were Welsh in atmosphere and, although unsectarian in religion, their ethos was Nonconformist. The leaders in the schools themselves, head-teachers and staffs, were drawn far more heavily from Nonconformity than from the Established Church, whose members, especially among the clergy, looked to the English and Welsh public schools, rather than to the new Welsh Intermediate schools, for their sons' education.

The social changes which took place, and especially the development of education, gave an opportunity for civic leadership to that middle class which the industrial revolution was then producing in the iron and coal districts. As the workers had been largely of Nonconformist stock, so also was the rising trading class; as the ironworker or collier had been a religious dissenter, so the owner of the one-man business was more a chapel man than a churchman, and this was particularly true if he happened to be an immigrant from rural Wales. The new middle class was far more Nonconformist than Church in its ecclesiastical allegiance.

Thus it was that Nonconformity supplied social and civic leadership in these industrial communities up to and beyond the end of the nineteenth century. The economic basis of this triumph of Nonconformity in the social field was bound up with the transition from iron to coal. The hierarchy of the iron and steel industry strengthened the churches rather than the chapels in north Monmouthshire and north-east Glamorgan, because the managerial and technical staffs for those industries had to be imported, usually from the north of England. There were few parishes in the iron and steel-works belt where the Established Church did not benefit greatly from the families of the officials of these industries; and their names and activities are still easily recalled. In Tredegar the higher ranks of the iron industry were occupied by churchmen, but the colliery official was usually a Nonconformist. In the purely coal-mining areas local social and political power was largely Welsh Nonconformist in its ecclesiastical allegiance, and this allegiance was by no means a mere formality.

To appreciate the change that Welsh industrial Nonconformity underwent in the second half of the nineteenth century, it is necessary to emphasize that its essentially working-class character for the first half of the century in the ironworks districts was itself a departure from the original social character of Welsh Nonconformity. Monmouthshire was the home of Welsh Nonconformity in the seventeenth century, and its leaders were drawn from the lesser gentry and Puritan squires: Walter Cradock of Usk, Henry Walter of Piercefield, the Rogers family of Llanfaches, Henry Rumsey of Sudbrook, Samuel Jones of Magor, William Blethin of Dinham, and Edward Herbert of Undy.[1] The 1715 list of Nonconformist chapels and their membership shows that the social character of Nonconformity was by no means working class. The list gives 3 esquires, 56 gentlemen, 273

[1] See T. Richards, 'Eglwys Llanfaches', *Transactions of the Honourable Society of Cymmrodorion* (London, 1941), pp. 150–84.

yeomen, 238 tradesmen, 218 farmers, 397 labourers, which included 445 county and borough votes,[1] which reveals that the lesser gentry and farmers were the leaders of Nonconformity at the beginning of the eighteenth century. Much of the leadership of the lesser gentry was lost when many of them reverted to the Established Church during the same century, and this left the leadership in the hands of farmers and yeomen. The working-class character of Welsh Nonconformity was the result of the industrial revolution which gave it, for the first time, working-class leadership. But by the end of the nineteenth century Welsh Nonconformity was fast reverting to its middle-class character as the result of economic and social changes.

One reason for this change was because more Welsh capital was invested in the coal-mining industry in south Wales than had been the case in the iron industry, and much of this money came from men who were Nonconformists, and who proved to be very generous to their denominations. The days when congregations built their own chapels unaided were over, for prominent Nonconformists could now come to their aid. When a conference was held in Neath to arrange for the celebration of the bicentenary of the Act of Uniformity of 1662, the expenses of the celebration were met by a Thomas Williams, Esq., of Aberdare, who undertook to give £250 if three others would follow his example; and when the 'Welsh Calvinistic Methodist Assurance Trust, Limited' was registered in 1886, of the 22 lay members of the Trust, 9 were justices of the peace,[1] a less democratic honour then than now. The Davies family, of Llandinam, founders of the Ocean collieries, helped very generously in building Welsh Calvinistic Methodist chapels in those areas where their pits were situated; and D. A. Thomas, M.P. (later Lord Rhondda), who was reputedly agnostic in his religious

[1] T. Rees, *History of Protestant Nonconformity in Wales*, pp. 259–60.

[2] *Cymdeithasfa Chwarterol y Methodistiaid Calfinaidd yn Neheudir Cymru, a gynhaliwyd yn Ceinewydd, Mawrth 23ain, 24ain, 25ain, 1886*, p. 5.

views, gave much financial support to Nonconformity in his Merthyr constituency. With the exception of the landowners and royalty owners (who were ungenerous churchmen) it can be said that the wealth of the coal-mining communities before the days of the great combines was at the disposal of Nonconformity to a greater degree than it had been in the same areas fifty years previously; and this was certainly so with the wealth that came with trade and the professions. Moreover, the new capitalists had a great deal of affinity with their workers: they were Welsh-speaking, and in most cases they themselves had been manual workers. Above all, they were Nonconformist in religion.

Thus it was that Welsh Nonconformity fared better under the coal-owners than under the ironmasters. But the transition from iron to coal meant far more to the Welsh chapels than this: it meant that the local leadership in the coal industry was composed very largely of chapel men. Gradually the Puritan virtues of hard work and thrift had produced an enterprising, self-reliant type of worker in the pits who could, and did, in those days aspire to the more responsible local positions in the industry. In the days when technical training for pit management was neither expected nor provided the way lay open to the intelligent collier, and hundreds of them made the grade. They were the days when the local community threw up its industrial leaders, and these leaders were, for the most part, Welsh Nonconformists. As these hardworking, intelligent, albeit very narrowly puritanical men advanced in the pits, so did their influence grow in the chapels; and the height of personal success to many was symbolized not only by the seat of authority in the local colliery but by a seat (often separate) in the big pew in the chapel. Thus arose a very influential figure in industrial Nonconformity, the colliery-manager–chapel-deacon man who, except in the case of the strongest ministers, successfully challenged the authority of the minister himself. So close was the connexion between pit and chapel through the figure of the deacon-manager and the other members of the colliery hierarchy that in some areas particular pits were associated with particular chapels: there were pits where the good Calvinistic Methodist, for example, would get a job because the manager was a deacon in the local Calvinistic Methodist chapel. Welsh Nonconformity attained its greatest influence in the industrial areas of south Wales in the coal age.

These social, industrial and political changes affected the chapels profoundly: they converted Welsh Nonconformity from a working-class to a middle-class movement as far as leadership was concerned, and this change is reflected in many ways. One of the most valuable insights into this borderland between society and religion would be a detailed analysis of the composition of the 'big pews' of the chapels, and especially the Welsh chapels, in the iron districts and coalfields at the end of the last century. The 'big seat' was expressive of local chapel leadership and also of the social composition of that leadership in a society slowly changing. The heroic days of Welsh Nonconformity were those when it had been essentially a working-class movement, but by the end of the century the composition of the 'set fawr' was made up largely of the local trading community and the hierarchy of the mining industry in the locality. The collier might get in on the strength of his personal piety, but he did not carry the influence of the prosperous grocer or the under-manager who might sit next to him on Sunday. No doubt it was a disappointed candidate for the diaconate in the Calvinistic Methodist church at Ebbw Vale who said publicly after the election: 'Do you not think that it is a pity that we did not elect just one deacon to represent, not bricks and mortar and rent books at all, but Him who went about not collecting rents, but doing good, a homeless wanderer in his own world.'[1]

The outward sign of this change in Welsh Nonconformity

[1] Evan Price, op. cit., pp. 59–60.

was seen in the neo-Gothic and neo-classical style of the chapels built in the second half of the nineteenth century.[1] These buildings were not a sign that Nonconformity was shedding its narrow Puritanism, but rather that such Puritanism had become a little more opulent and succumbed to the temptation of a false architectural image. The truth was that the heroic age of Welsh Nonconformity in the industrial areas was over.

But the deep sign of the change could be seen only over a number of years, and it lay in the relationship of the 'hearers' to the chapels. The political strength of the Welsh chapels lay in their contact with this outer fringe. The core of membership was never so great as was claimed at the time, but the strength of the chapel was its ability to influence a large section of non-members who were still not entirely of 'the world'. It was these 'hearers' who were the direct object of the evangelistic efforts of Welsh Nonconformity; the chapel member and the 'hearer' were intimately connected with each other through many social ties; they spoke the same language; there was even a common religious and theological language which the members and the hearers would understand if not accept to the same degree, for both were products of the Sunday-school; and most important of all, and in consequence of the other factors, it was from the ranks of the hearers that the chapels gained their converts at the time of religious revival. While the core of members did not fluctuate greatly throughout the century, the fortunes of Nonconformity fluctuated in accordance with its relationship with the hearers. The members themselves remained faithful and constant but the hearers gradually became fewer. Thomas Rees claimed that five-sixths of the working classes of Wales were frequent attenders at places of religious worship, 'and that in this respect they afforded a startling contrast with the corresponding class in England'.[2]

[1] See Anthony Jones, *Chapel architecture in Merthyr Tydfil* (1962).
[2] T. Rees, *Miscellaneous Papers*, p. 18.

The doubtful word here is 'frequent'. A contemporary observer, *c.* 1860–5, noted in Rhymney that when work was plentiful the public houses were full and the chapels were full when work was slack.[1] We have seen that the Welsh chapels went through some difficult times during the second half of the nineteenth century; and in any case, the figures for census Sunday 1851 do not bear out Rees's estimate, for even if they represent separate persons (which it is certain they do not), 48 per cent. of the population of Monmouthshire did not attend church or chapel even on that day, but this figure was appreciably lower for the industrial areas. If we take denominational figures for 1881 we find that the total membership of the three leading Welsh Nonconformist denominations came to 21,267, being slightly more than ten per cent. of the population of the county, and if we double this figure to account for adherents, the total strength of Welsh Nonconformity, members and adherents, did not exceed 30 per cent. of a population of 211,267. A further addition of twenty per cent. would easily account for the members and communicants of all the other religious bodies taking the county as a whole, thus leaving at least half of the population outside church or chapel but with a lower percentage of this latter class in the industrial areas, as in 1851. By 1880 Welsh Nonconformity had reached its peak in these parts, and its hold on an industrial community was maintained until at least the end of the first decade of the present century, but with a decline in the proportion of adherents to members.

Another factor which greatly influenced the change that was to take place was the decline in the Welsh language. It has been pointed out that there is a close connexion between Welsh Nonconformity and the Welsh language, and that the latter has given the former such a unique character that the decline of the language has confronted Welsh chapels with what is probably their greatest problem. This language

[1] O. Parry, op. cit., p. 57.

problem was bound up with population changes, and these, in turn, were due to the development of the deep-coal-mining industry after 1860. The population of Glamorgan increased from 317,752 in 1861 to 1,120,910 in 1911, an increase of 253 per cent. as compared with an increase in England and Wales of 80 per cent. during the same period.[1] This increase was due partly to migration into the coal-mining areas, and in the decade 1861–71 the migrants into Glamorgan came largely from the adjoining Welsh counties, including Monmouthshire; but during the next decade, when the number of migrants increased three and a half times, only 38 per cent. of them came from these adjoining Welsh areas.[2] At the same time there was a migration from the older iron-works districts to the newer coal-mining area: 'During 1871–81, the Census returns show that the Registration District of Merthyr Tydfil lost 18,800 people by migration and that of Bedwellty (adjoining it in Monmouthshire), 5,051.' During the decade 1881–91 the immigration into Glamorgan went on, with an increasing number of people coming from the non-border (i.e., English) counties; of the net absorption during these ten years of 76,200, 63 per cent. came from the non-border counties, and this percentage was to be increased during 1901–11. Monmouthshire continued to attract from the same English border counties, but it lost on an increasing scale by migration to Glamorgan, the estimated migration from the former to the latter county from 1901 to 1911 being 11,600.[3] It is important to emphasize the nature of these migrations into the Glamorgan industrial areas and to recall that after 1881 the English migrants always substantially, and often overwhelmingly, outnumbered the Welsh migrants. The bearing of these changes upon religion will not be obvious unless it is realized that the society in which Welsh Nonconformity flourished was slowly being changed at that point where the Welsh chapels were most

[1] Brinley Thomas, 'The Migration of Labour into the Glamorganshire Coalfield 1861–1911', *Economica*, x (1930), p. 277.

[2] Ibid., p. 284.

[3] Ibid., p. 293.

vulnerable, that of language. It will be shown later how suspicious the chapels were of the 'English ideas' and customs which came with the migrants. And while this migration into Glamorgan slowly changed the character of the eastern part of the county, so also did that into Monmouthshire profoundly affect the north of this county. Gradually Welsh migrants into north Monmouthshire became fewer and fewer, and ultimately ceased. The census of 1911 showed that, of a population in the administrative County of Monmouth and the Borough of Newport of 395,719, 215,969 had been born there, while, of those who had migrated to these parts, 45,796 came from a Welsh county (27,370 from Glamorgan), and 98,954 had come from the English counties.[1]

The consequence of this change in the pattern of migration into the industrial areas of Glamorgan and Monmouthshire was a decline in the number of those who spoke the Welsh language. This showed itself in north-east Glamorgan, not in a net decrease in the number of Welsh-speaking people, but in a decrease in proportion to the increase in population, as

Local Authority	*Population (1901)*	*Welsh-speaking (1901)*	*Population (1911)*	*Welsh-speaking (1911)*
Aberdare R.D.C.	39,932	23,067 (59%)	46,844	26,894 (55%)
Merthyr Tydfil C.B.	63,861	31,763 (49%)	74,597	34,826 (46%)[2]
Rhymney U.D.	7,246	4,283 (59%)	10,489	5,340 (51%)
Bedwellty U.D.	9,069	2,980 (33%)	20,506	4,141 (20%)
Mynyddislwyn U.D.	3,072	1,179 (38%)	9,014	2,061 (23%)
Risca U.D.	8,820	630 (7%)	12,981	678 (5%)
Blaenavon U.D.	10,010	857 (8%)	11,087	616 (5%)
Ebbw Vale U.D.	19,061	4,108 (21%)	27,857	3,435 (12%)
Nant-y-glo and Blaina U.D.	12,255	2,370 (19%)	14,055	1,544 (11%)
Pontypool U.D.	5,658	256 (5%)	6,021	246 (4%)
Tredegar U.D.	16,889	4,494 (25%)	21,572	4,063 (20%)[3]

[1] Census 1911, County Monmouth, p. 66.
[2] Census 1911, County of Glamorgan, p. 93.
[3] Census 1911, County of Monmouth, p. 67.

the foregoing figures and analysis show. It will be noted, too, that the decrease became a net decrease the further removed these communities were from the Monmouthshire–Glamorgan border.

It had been foreseen earlier in the nineteenth century that the fate of the Welsh language would affect the fortunes of Nonconformity, and this was becoming clear in Monmouthshire twenty years before the end of the century. The Welsh churches belonging to the Independents in rural Monmouthshire were declining even when they had turned to English, and this was true of the Vale of Glamorgan. In the northern part of the county the state of a Welsh chapel depended on the state of the local industry as well as on language, and up to the end of the century there was sufficient Welsh spoken in Tredegar, Sirhowy, Ebbw Vale, and especially in Rhymney, to maintain the chapels in a fairly flourishing state; the language problem had not yet affected the Welsh chapels in the Rhondda Valley, Aberdare and Merthyr Tydfil, although these were to feel the effect of a decline in the speaking of Welsh during the first decade of the twentieth century, and to feel it rather disastrously after 1919. Thus, the Congregational Association of East Glamorgan (Cyfundeb Annibynol Dwyreiniol Morganwg) formed in 1868 to include the Welsh churches of that denomination in the mid-Glamorgan valleys and Cardiff areas, where the language still held its ground, had 70 churches and 10,522 members in 1889, and this had increased to 16,642 members and 85 churches by 1911.[1] The really significant feature of the membership statistics of this Association was at first the progress and later the catastrophic decline in the number of adherents. They rose from 13,055 to 16,921 in the year 1889–1890, and continued to rise until they reached a total of 19,248 in 1897, to be followed in 1898 by a drop to 12,667. This sharp decline is significant, for it corresponded with a

[1] See *Adroddiad(au) Cyfundeb Annibynol Dwyreiniol Morganwg* from 1889 to 1914.

long-drawn-out coal-miners' strike of that year. Two years later this column was omitted from the annual report of the Association. Thus the decline in Welsh Nonconformity was first revealed by a drop in the number of adherents, until the time came, after the First Word War, when this class virtually disappeared. The Congregational Association of North Glamorgan (*Cyfundeb Annibynol Gogledd Morganwg*), consisting of churches of that denomination in the Merthyr–Aberdare district, increased the number of churches from 50 to 56 from 1901 to 1910, but its membership went up only from 12,193 to 13,287 in the same period, and had it not been for an increase of 4,067 in the membership of these churches as the result of the religious revival of 1904–5, the figures would have shown a substantial drop in membership during the first decade of the present century.[1] It was clear that the augmentation of membership to Welsh Nonconformity in these parts was from the families themselves, and this had been so for some time. Dr. Thomas Price, of Aberdare, claimed that the increase in Baptist membership in that area was greater in proportion than the increase in population. The original 91 members of his church had grown to 3,096 in the mother church and its branches by 1862, but thereafter the growth was not so great: between 1846 and 1866 1,090 were received into membership, but this number was reduced to less than one-half, viz. 504, in the following twenty years, 1866–85.[2]

A half-century of slow social change showed a marked acceleration as the century came to its close, and the years 1900–12 were a period of great social and industrial unrest. The society of 1900 was different from that of 1850: it was more varied, had more educational opportunities, through English immigration and the decline of the Welsh language it became more susceptible to English social and political ideas, and these changes resulted in a loosening of the hold of

1 See *Adroddiad(au) Cyfundeb Annibynol Gogledd Morganwg* from 1901 to 1910.
2 Benjamin Evans, op. cit., p. 96.

religion in general, and of Welsh Nonconformity in particular, on the mass of working-class people.

The change which affected Nonconformity has already been described: as far as its leadership was concerned, it became more and more middle-class, and this resulted in a loss of contact between the chapels and their communities, as shown by the loss of the adherents, and even within many of the chapels themselves between the middle-class big pew and the ordinary member. This lack of social leadership was not a new phenomenon, for even in the days when the minister was the unchallenged leader of a working-class congregation, Welsh Nonconformity did not give a lead to the aspirations of the workers. The antagonism of the chapels to the early workers' unions, the benefit clubs and Chartism has been dealt with; and bereft of this leadership the early working-class movements had to rely upon English leadership; and this was suspect. Speaking of the Scotch Cattle movement in the industrial valleys of east Glamorgan and Monmouthshire, a recent writer has said: 'It may be true to say that the Scotch Cattle typified the only lasting type of combination which the Welsh colliers were capable of forming without English leadership.'[1] The indifference of Welsh Nonconformity to labour unions meant that the Welsh workers in these parts had no other leadership to follow except that which came from England. This leadership was suspect, as the sermons preached on Chartism showed; and it can be said that there was a latent anti-English feeling in these Welsh industrial communities throughout the nineteenth century, because most of the initiative for working-class unity came from England. Dr. Thomas Rees said that the Welsh worker was a docile fellow if only he was left alone by English agitators. One of his weaknesses was his readiness to be made the dupe of cunning and designing men, and it was because of such cunning men as Twist and the mob orators who came from England 'that

[1] E. W. Evans, *The South Wales Miner* (Cardiff, 1961), p. 51.

our working men are invariably led to invite in strikes'.[1] Likewise Dr. Thomas Price, of Aberdare, wrote in 1863 against the formation of a national union for the miners because he distrusted its leadership, which came from the north of England, and he urged the miners to postpone the issue for ten years; and a year later he claimed that his views had been justified. It has also been shown that Welsh Nonconformity in these parts took little interest in the social problems which affected the great majority of its members, and the urge toward unity grew among the Welsh miners with little encouragement from the chapels.

It is worth recalling the words of a prominent social worker in Wales on this failure of Nonconformity:

Why the voluntary collectivism of co-operation has not taken deeper root in Wales is a question not easily answered. One might have expected that the training which Nonconformity has furnished the Welsh people would have prepared and predisposed them for so democratic a form of industrial organization as the Co-operative System. Of course, it cannot for a moment be disputed that Nonconformity has rendered incalculable services to the cause of personal freedom and popular rights. At the same time, it may be worth considering whether the Calvinist view of Salvation, as essentially individualistic rather than social, may have tended to produce a type of character which has adopted as its motto 'each by himself' rather than 'each for all and all for each'. Another fact of importance is that the rise and progress of Nonconformity have been practically contemporaneous with the development of modern commerce and the growth of the middle class. Now, speaking generally, the middle class is largely dominated by the commercial and competitive spirit; and it is to the middle class that the adherents of Nonconformity mainly belong. The very poor, the unskilled labourer, and the man who cannot rise above the living wage, are, even in Wales, more especially in the towns, largely outside the pale of Nonconformity; while, on the other hand, the professional class is but thinly

[1] T. Rees, *Miscellaneous Papers*, p. 21. This is not the only testimony to the docility of Welsh industrial workers in those days. A witness at the Royal Commission on Truck Shops testified to the same characteristic.

represented in its ranks, and the aristocracy not at all. The middle-class character of the Free Churches may therefore account to some extent for the fact that, though democratic as to their form of government, they often lack a corresponding sympathy with labour.[1]

Certainly the prevailing theology in Nonconformity throughout the century was Calvinism, and the passion for personal salvation produced the self-reliant character rather than one which had a passion for social righteousness, but the writer of this passage should have made it clear that Nonconformity in the industrial areas had once been a thoroughly working-class movement.

That Nonconformity made for political freedom is not disputed, and this freedom was bound up with its own struggle for religious rights. These rights had been largely, if not completely, won by the end of the last century, but then came the demand for disestablishment. It is possible that if Nonconformity in the industrial areas had paid more attention to the problems of an industrial society and less to what must have appeared to be the academic question of disestablishment, it might well have retained its hold on the industrial areas. While Nonconformity in the Welsh rural areas was no doubt a radical influence, in the industrial areas it was socially conservative. This effect of the chapels has persisted to our generation. An observer of a group of mining villages in Monmouthshire in the 1930s had this to say: 'In his attitudes and behaviour he [that is, the miner] exhibits certain individualistic values inherent in a capitalist society. His trade union and his chapel have tried to provide him with the discipline which would enable him to secure some of its potentialities. While there has been a revolutionary aspect to these institutions as well, this role has been secondary to the fundamental one of securing the best adjustment within the framework of the existing society.'[2] The chapels

[1] D. Lleufer Thomas, *Labour unions in Wales: their early struggle for existence* (Swansea, 1901), pp. 8–9.

[2] G. H. Armbraster, 'The Social Determinant of Ideologies' (unpublished

had much to conserve in the society of the second half of the last century, for its lay leaders had assured positions in the hierarchy of the coal-mining industry and its tradesmen-leaders depended directly on the pits. There was a certain incongruity in the concern of industrial Nonconformity for the problems of rural Wales, and, from the standpoint of its hold on the mining communities it retained the rural image too long. This image was kept bright, not only by the immigrants from rural Wales but more especially by the pastors who came from the same parts; for the chapels, like the parishes, had to rely on rural Wales for their pastors.

The political wing of Welsh Nonconformity became more and more clamant during and after the 1880's, and their programme became less and less relevant to the problems of an industrial society. By the end of the century the workers had concluded that they could best achieve their aspirations through their own industrial and political organizations, and they ceased to look to the chapels as their political allies.

The year 1898 may be accepted as a dividing line. For twenty years before that date the miners' unions were weak. This was the period which, politically, can be called the 'Lib-Lab' period in politics and the 'sliding scale' period in industrial relationships. It was the period of co-operation between the owners and the workers. 'The Rhondda and Aberdare [Miners'] Associations were specifically devoted to encouraging mutual understanding between employer and workman, and the other district organizations pursued the same policy.'[1] It was the period in which most miners' leaders came from the ranks of Welsh Nonconformity, and William Abraham (Mabon), a prominent Calvinistic Methodist from the Rhondda, is the key figure. Those were the days when miners' meetings and demonstrations were addressed by Liberal M.P.s (even if they were coal-owners like D. A.

Ph.D. thesis, pp. 58 and 59) quoted by T. Brennan, E. W. Cooney, and H. Pollins in *Social change in South-west Wales* (London, 1954), p. 115.

[1] E. W. Evans, op. cit., p. 137.

Thomas), largely in the Welsh language, and to the accompaniment of Welsh hymns. 'Political nonconformity and industrial paternalism were still the most important factors in the political structure of the valleys.'[1] But the bitter and long-drawn-out strike of 1898 brought this phase to a close; thereafter the struggle was for the minimum wage, and the immediate result of the strike was the creation of the South Wales Miners' Federation which was the first union to represent the entire South Wales coalfield. New voices were heard in the coalfield. Keir Hardie, and not Mabon, became the new symbol, and he, with Robert Smillie, Tom Mann, Ben Tillet, Bruce Glaiser and even George Bernard Shaw, was addressing meetings in the Merthyr constituency. The new local leaders had English names: William Brace, A. J. Cook, Vernon Hartshorn, Frank Hodges, James Winstone, to name only a few. They were originally chapel men, mainly Baptists and Primitive Methodists, the two most politically radical denominations. These men were the product of the chapels and their Sunday-schools, and although most of them left the chapels, their early training left an indelible impression upon them. Socialism and class warfare were the keynotes of the new industrial gospel.

As the Welsh miners developed their own organization the politics of Welsh Nonconformity became more and more irrelevant to them. The main plank in the Nonconformist platform, that of the disestablishment of the Welsh Church, had no place in the workers' politics, and even Liberal candidates had to mute this issue. This was progressively true of all the general elections following the reorganization of the Monmouthshire constituencies in 1884 into the Monmouth Boroughs, Northern, Southern, and Western Divisions. With the increasing anglicization of the county it was to be expected that the Liberal programme, as understood in rural Wales, would make less appeal to the electors; in any case,

[1] Kenneth O. Morgan, *Wales in British Politics 1868–1922* (Cardiff, 1963), p. 39.

'Liberalism was always transcendent in Wales, while Monmouthshire, west Gloucestershire, and Herefordshire were always supposed to be leavened with Conservative ideas'.[1] These two factors, the growth in working-class organizations and the spread of the English language, minimized the appeal of Welsh Nonconformist politics to the people of these parts. The former especially affected the Merthyr Tydfil constituency, while the latter affected the whole of Monmouthshire.

This was true of Monmouthshire in the general election of 1885. For the Northern Division, which included the industrial communities of Pontypool and Blaenavon, the Liberal candidate was T. P. Price, son of the vicar of Llanarth; and at his adoption meeting in Pontypool on 19 November he placed disestablishment last on his programme, and at the end of his speech he said 'a word about disestablishment'.[2] His election address contained the following passage: 'No public question has been more fully discussed, and none has met with greater unanimity of opinion, on the part of the vast majority of the people of the Principality, than that of the Disestablishment and Disendowment of the Established Church in Wales; I consider the matter is now ripe for settlement, and measures for carrying into effect and settling this great question, upon an equitable basis, would have my support.'[3] But during an eve-of-poll meeting in Pontypool in support of Price, although the chairman made reference to disestablishment, the candidate himself did not mention the matter.[4] In the Western Division, C. M. Warmington emphasized the question, and so did Henry Richard and C. H. James, the two Liberal candidates for Merthyr Tydfil.[5] This election, which resulted in a sweeping victory for the Liberal party in Wales, was fought mainly on the land question,[6]

[1] *The Monmouthshire Merlin and South Wales Advertiser*, 4 December 1885.

[2] Ibid., 20 November 1885.

[3] *Pontypool Free Press*, 20 November 1885.

[4] Ibid., 6 December 1885.

[5] *The Merthyr Express*, 14 November 1885.

[6] Kenneth O. Morgan, op. cit., p. 57.

but even this issue was not relevant to the industrial areas of north Glamorgan and north Monmouthshire. In the election of 1886 T. P. Price did not refer to disestablishment either in his address or his speeches.[1] This election was overshadowed by the question of Irish home rule.

In the election of 1892 the Liberal candidate for the Monmouth Boroughs Division (which included the town of Newport), was Albert Spicer, a Nonconformist of conviction who became Chairman of the Congregational Union of England and Wales. In this election one of the Monmouthshire representatives on the Welsh Disestablishment Campaign Committee urged all the Nonconformist ministers 'to exert during the next few days all the influence at your command to secure the return to Parliament of those candidates only who are known to favour the passing of a Disestablishment Bill for Wales, including Monmouthshire'.[2] But it was Irish home rule which dominated the election in Monmouthshire. T. P. Price included disestablishment in his election address,[3] but said that it was of secondary importance as compared with the Irish Question, and he paid little attention to it in his election speeches, and W. Pritchard Morgan, one of the Liberal candidates for Merthyr Tydfil, took the same line, while his colleague, D. A. Thomas, pledged himself to 'absolute religious equality for Wales'.[4]

When the election of 1895 was pending, the leading article of a Monmouthshire paper announced that 'in the Monmouthshire Boroughs and County Divisions the candidates are well known to the electors, and the one cry must be that of Disestablishment'.[5] Liberal meetings were frequently held in the chapels, but there was such disorder in an Aberdare chapel on 8 July of that year that the deacons publicly announced that the building would never again be used for

[1] *Pontypool Free Press*, 2 July 1886.
[2] Ibid., 8 July 1892.
[3] Ibid., 24 June 1892.
[4] *The Merthyr Express*, 2 July 1892.
[5] *South Wales Daily Star*, 26 June 1895.

such a purpose. There were prominent Liberals among the candidates, among them Reginald McKenna for the Northern Division and Sir William Harcourt for the Western Division. The former, like all Liberal candidates in Wales and Monmouthshire, included disestablishment in his election address, but the press reports of his speeches do not indicate that this question figured prominently in the election campaign, although one of Harcourt's speeches was devoted entirely to this subject, and so also was that of Pritchard Morgan in Merthyr on 22 June.[1]

But the importance of this election lay in the fact that the voice of organized Labour was heard for the first time, and it revealed that the working-class movement was not concerned with disestablishment. The Trades Council of the Monmouth Boroughs Division addressed a questionnaire to Albert Spicer, the Liberal candidate, in which disestablishment was not mentioned, and Allan Upward, an Independent with Labour sympathies and a candidate for the Merthyr Tydfil constituency, struck a prophetic note in his election address when he said: 'My sympathies with the great question of Welsh freedom and Irish freedom are as firm as ever. But still greater is the question of the freedom of Labour from the fetters laid upon it by capitalists and landlords.'[2]

The political scene was changing rapidly.

In the course of seven years, the political pattern of industrial Wales had become transformed. The traditional struggles—disestablishment, education, land reform, temperance—were class struggles of a kind, representing the uprising of nonconformity against social inferiority. In origin, they derived from the social structure of the Welsh country-side, where the 'unholy Trinity' of the bishop, the brewer, and the squire, had long formed the entrenched opposition. But to the problems of an industrial community—the low living standards and the purchasing power of the industrial workers, the bitter conflict of capital and labour,

[1] *The Merthyr Express*, 29 June 1895.
[2] Ibid., 16 July 1895.

the rootless society of a vast proletariat—to such issues as these, the old Liberal platform had no solution and its Welsh national character little relevance.[1]

The Labour candidate, Keir Hardie, won a seat in Merthyr Tydfil in 1900, although the Liberal, D. A. Thomas, headed the poll. It was radical Merthyr which first breached the Liberal strongholds, but Monmouthshire remained Liberal for another generation. On 14 June 1903 the miners of Abersychan opposed running a Labour candidate in opposition to Reginald McKenna, and a vote of confidence in him was carried unanimously.[2] But the price of the workers' support was a greater emphasis on social reform and a muting of the issues which had hitherto concerned Liberalism and Welsh Nonconformity. Lewis Haslam, the successor to Albert Spicer in the Monmouth Boroughs Division, made no reference to disestablishment in his election address in the 1906 general election;[3] similarly, Colonel Ivor Herbert of Llanover, who described himself thus: 'I am a Roman Catholic Nonconformist, but a Nonconformist all the same', and who was the successful Liberal candidate for the Southern Division, spoke vaguely throughout the campaign about 'religious liberty', and Reginald McKenna in the Northern Division did not once mention disestablishment in his major speeches in the course of his successful campaign.

How dead this issue had become in the areas of growing socialism in north Glamorgan and in the now largely anglicized Monmouthshire was shown by the first general election of 1910 in the Merthyr Tydfil constituency.

The Federation of Evangelical Free Church Councils in Wales had issued a pamphlet in preparation for an election, in which it urged Nonconformists to secure a pledge from all the candidates 'to maintain the premier position of the Disestablishment Bill in the Government's legislative

[1] Kenneth O. Morgan, op. cit., pp. 210–11.
[2] *Pontypool Free Press*, 19 June 1903.
[3] *South Wales Argus*, 4 January 1906.

programme, so as to secure its enactment into law at the earliest possible opportunity in the next Parliament'.[1] But the Socialist organizations showed no interest in this question. In a questionnaire addressed to the candidates by the Mountain Ash and District Trades Council, not one of the questions related to disestablishment; it was not mentioned in a pamphlet issued by the Church Socialist League; nor was it raised in an address *To the Members of the Miners' Federation and other Trade Unionists*, signed by local Socialist leaders. The Liberal candidates made only a passing reference to disestablishment, declaring among other things that the Socialists regarded it as of 'secondary importance only'. The real issue was Liberalism v. Socialism, with the latter being represented as ungodly, immoral, advocating free love and no marriage bonds. It is true that there were other issues which overshadowed disestablishment in every one of these elections since 1885: the Irish Question, Education, the Budget of 1909, and the power of the House of Lords in December 1910, but in spite of every effort to keep disestablishment in the forefront, it became less and less important as an election issue as time went on. The chapels, as strongholds of political Liberalism, lost their power, and the early Socialist movement grew outside their walls, with a degree of mutual antagonism that has now passed away.

The chapels could not be blamed for their antagonism to much of the Socialist propaganda of those early days, for it was more than tinged with secularism and anti-religious sentiments. One of the Liberal candidates in the first general election of 1910 in Merthyr wooed the Roman Catholic vote by quoting from *The Socialist Standard* for 1 November 1908: 'The Holy Catholic Church may go hang. When we have nothing more important to do it might well be possible to amuse ourselves by crumbling it up.' It is true that prominent clerics and ministers from England appeared on

[1] Papers, Manifestoes, Petitions, &c., relating to the General Election of 1910 in the constituency of Merthyr Tydfil.

Keir Hardie's platform, but this was not enough to allay the fear of the chapels that Socialism was an ungodly movement; and underlying a religious objection to the new propaganda was the latent Welsh suspicion of English ideas which had not been far from the surface of these communities throughout the century. In his address to the Congregational Union of England and Wales in Halifax in 1865 Dr. Thomas Rees had said: 'The country [Wales] is in a state of transition. Englishmen, English capital and enterprise, English customs, and, unhappily, English vices, with very little English virtue and religion, are rushing in upon us, like mighty irresistible torrents, carrying away before them our ancient language, social habits, and even our religious customs and influence over the masses.'[1]

This phase in the life of a Welsh industrial community at a time when it was in the course of social, political and religious change has been well described by an intelligent and sensitive writer who lived through it. He was a Welsh Independent, reared in Aberdare, and the parlour of the cottage where he lived possessed the symbols of the Welsh Nonconformist outlook of that time: on the walls photographs of Mr. Gladstone and of the chapel minister, and on the parlour table the family Bible and *Pilgrim's Progress.* As long as his mother lived he maintained a rather tenuous contact with the chapel, but her early death made it easier for him to loosen these bonds, even though the sister who kept house for him perpetuated the mother's influence in the home. His real education came in the pit, where in the course of discussions he first heard the names of Charles Darwin, Herbert Spencer and Karl Marx. But the decisive moment of his life was his meeting with Keir Hardie, and he went to the meeting with the disapproval of his sister. 'It was a beautiful evening, and when I was ready to leave the house for the Plough Tip, Eliza said, "Are you going to listen to that atheist on the Plough Tip, John? Shame on you, if you

[1] T. Rees, *Miscellaneous Papers*, p. 86.

are. Better if you went back to Saron Chapel as you used to, than listen to that man Keir Hardie. He don't believe in the Bible, or God, and you do." I did not answer her. I did not answer her because I would have had to tell her that I would never go back to Saron Chapel: and that would have broken Eliza's heart.'[1] He never went back, and the symbols in the front parlour were changed: instead of Mr. Gladstone was Karl Marx (Mr. Gladstone having been relegated to the kitchen where Eliza reigned); the parlour table bore, not the family Bible and *Pilgrim's Progress*, but rather the *Communist Manifesto*, *Das Kapital*, and *Origin of Species*. This was the spiritual odyssey of many of the more intelligent young men in the industrial areas in those days, but this particular young man was to discover later in life that the chapel influence had gone much deeper than he had suspected. But he never returned. The same experience befell Thomas Jones of Rhymney who left his home to enter the Welsh Calvinistic Methodist ministry but whose subsequent career turned out to be very different from what he had intended: 'I had moved from evangelicalism to the study of social questions; from Liberalism to Labour; from the theology of the Pauline epistles to the economics of the Kingdom of God. I was earnest and enthusiastic, ascetic and nonconformist. My ambition was to be dedicated to a life of unselfishness in the service of the poor and unprivileged.' These examples were not typical, but the more popular propaganda of *Merrie England*, the *Clarion* and the I.L.P. made great headway in the industrial areas before the First World War, even though the political and social results were not to be seen until after 1919.

It was while the gap between the chapels and the industrial communities was widening that another powerful religious revival broke out in the autumn of 1904 and went on until the summer of 1905, the first large-scale revival for nearly fifty years. It was general in its effect throughout Wales

[1] W. J. Edwards, *From the valley I came* (London, 1956), p. 89.

but its intensity was felt in the industrial areas. There is no doubt about the nature of the revival: it was highly emotional and very frequently hysterical, and produced scenes which are still recalled in these areas and have passed into the folk-legends of industrial south Wales.[1] The movement began in the New Quay district of Cardiganshire and was introduced into Glamorgan by Evan Roberts, a young ministerial student with the Calvinistic Methodists. Roberts was an 'enthusiast' in the original meaning of that word, for he believed (and so did tens of thousands of others), that he was directly inspired by the Holy Spirit; and when he was once asked why he himself did not conduct his meetings in English, he replied that it was because the Spirit had not told him to do so. Yet, although he was the focal point of remarkable scenes which suggest that some psychical force was at work, he himself does not seem to have indulged in the extravagances of his followers. It was frequently sufficient for him to enter a chapel to generate or release energies which soon reduced meetings to a state of pandemonium which went on frequently until the early hours of the morning and occasionally throughout the night. Coal-miners held prayer meetings in pits, public houses lost much of their trade and football clubs cancelled their fixtures. All the Nonconformist bodies were deeply affected by this revival, and although the Established Church remained very much on the fringe, yet it was not altogether detached. Timothy Rees, chaplain of St. Michael's College, Aberdare, and later bishop of Llandaff, conducted missions in Anglican churches and although they were very mild affairs compared with what was going on in the chapels, at least one Anglican congregation was known to sing 'Throw out the life-line'.

[1] The brief account of the revival of 1904–5 is based on the files of the *Western Mail* and *South Wales Daily News* from November 1904 to July 1905. These two newspapers reported the course of the revival very fully, and their columns can be regarded as the primary source for the course of the revival.

There is no doubt that the thousands of converts strengthened the chapels for the time being. The Monmouthshire Baptist Association, at its meeting in Blaina in February 1905, claimed 6,698 converts; the Primitive Methodists, an entirely English denomination, claimed that 3,025 people had been converted in their chapels; the East Glamorgan [Welsh] Congregational Association increased its membership by over 3,000, and, as we have already seen, the North Glamorgan Congregational Association by over 4,000. On 28 January 1905 the *Western Mail* gave the total number of converts up to date as 70,199, the great majority of these being in south Wales, but the claim of the *South Wales Daily News* on 20 February 1905 gave a more modest total of 35,000. A later estimate gave the number of increased membership of Welsh Nonconformity as 80,000.[1]

Although the voices of doubt and criticism would have been drowned in the singing and prayers of the revival, yet they were raised and became more audible as the revival ran its course. A prominent Independent minister in Merthyr Tydfil cast doubts on the genuineness of the movement. In a letter to the *Western Mail* on 31 January 1905 he said that he was sure that a true revival was taking place, but that there was also 'a sham Revival, a mockery, a blasphemous travesty of the real thing', and that the chief figure in the mock revival was the leader himself, Evan Roberts. To the writer of the letter (the Reverend Peter Price), the 'best thing that could happen to the cause of the true religious Revival among us would be for Evan Roberts and his girl-companions to withdraw into their respective homes, and there to examine themselves and learn a little more about the meaning of Christianity. . . . Why, we have scores of young colliers in Dowlais with whom Evan Roberts is not to be compared either in intellectual capacity or spiritual power.' The correspondence which followed this letter showed that

[1] J. Vyrnwy Morgan, *The Welsh Religious Revival 1904–5. A Retrospect and Criticism* (London, 1909), p. 248.

opinion was overwhelmingly against the writer.[1] But it was believed at the time in the Aberdare area that the revival made its appeal largely to non-readers; and, as the movement progressed, its essential weaknesses appeared in the fact that it had no message for the society where it made most of its converts.

Later and more reflective opinion on this revival was more sober and balanced in its judgement than contemporary opinion. There were signs of degeneracy: dry rot was allowed to eat into the gains of the revival. 'It was on the anvil of Welsh superstition that Evan Roberts forged his fame.'[2] 'He [Roberts] had no fundamental doctrine, no system of theology, no distinctive ideal.'[3] As had happened before, the decline set in: within two years there was a decrease of 20,000 in the membership of Welsh Nonconformity, and the workers were more and more listening to the 'socialistic gospel'. 'These working men have recently reverted to the old belief that their salvation is not to come by the way of the pulpit or by the way of churches, but by the way of the Labour Party and Westminster';[4] so that the condition of the churches was worse [in 1909] than it had been in 1904. It is significant that the subject of the presidential address at the quarterly meeting of the East Glamorgan Congregational Association in Aberdare on 12 January 1909 was 'Religious Indifference' (Difaterwch Crefyddol). The real legatees of the revival were the pentecostal groups which hived away from Welsh Nonconformity.

There are certain matters arising out of the revival of 1904–5 which concern this present study. In the first place the very fact of the revival was itself unexpected, for such events are most likely to arise in unsophisticated societies. Writing about the Methodist revival of the eighteenth century, a modern

[1] It was perhaps unfortunate that he added 'B.A. Hons.' after his name in his letter to the press. This strengthened the belief among many chapel people that the academic standard represented by Price was greatly inferior to the 'inspiration' of Evan Roberts.

[2] J. Vyrnwy Morgan, *The Welsh Religious Revival 1904–5. A Retrospect and Criticism* (London, 1909), p. 45. [3] Ibid., p. 55. [4] Ibid., p. 255.

writer has said: 'Religious enthusiasm declined in later days because Methodist Christianity became more literate and rational and because, with increasing wealth and culture, other escapes from the monotony and exhaustion of hard labour became available. The substitution of education for conversion, finally, played its part in making revivalism less important for successive generations.'[1] Another writer wrote: 'This [revival] is an isolated case of mysticism, not likely to occur again, not even in Wales. The Welsh people are already coming out of their cultural isolationism which has provided the fundamental conditions necessary for a popular mystical movement of this kind. Already the Welsh middle and upper classes are becoming enlightened and this enlightenment will soon soak down to the lower classes.'[2] Certainly the society of 1904 was more sophisticated than that of 1849 or 1859, and it is inconceivable that a religious revival should again accompany or follow an epidemic, but the present generation, with its increased knowledge and experience of mass psychology, may hesitate to pronounce that this or any other country has seen the last of this type of revival.

The claim has been made that the revival 'partially restored Nonconformity to a position of leadership in the social and economic life of the Welsh people, that it produced a generation of Nonconformist leaders—both ordained and lay —who were socially and politically conscious and who were able to appraise the new conditions which were affecting the life of the workers'.[3] It is true that as time went on Nonconformist ministers became more outspoken on social issues, but this was due to the pressure of events and to that public opinion which was already affecting the chapels if only by draining from them the new social leaders. The revival itself did nothing to affect this development; indeed,

[1] H. R. Niebuhr, op. cit., p. 63.

[2] J. Rogues de Fursac, *Un Mouvement mystique contemporain* (Paris, 1907), pp. 183–4, quoted by C. R. Williams, 'The Welsh Religious Revival, 1904–5', *The British Journal of Sociology*, iii, 3 (1952), p. 252.

[3] C. R. Williams, op. cit., p. 259.

in so far as it emphasized the factor of personal salvation, it is more true to say that, for the time being, it reinforced the religious individualism characteristic of nineteenth-century Welsh Nonconformity. The fact that increased social protest came from the chapels in the years after the revival cannot be attributed to the revival itself. It would probably have come in any case.

But the problems which accompanied and followed the revival have a definite bearing on the society of those days. On its moral side the revival did nothing to replace the rather crude Puritanism of these industrial areas. The good life was still thought of in such negative terms as total abstinence. It was sad that a newspaper correspondent should rejoice that the conversion of a footballer meant that 'a passion for football' had been abandoned for a 'passion for righteousness', implying that the one excludes the other. The problem soon arose of what to do with the converts, and this meant little more than how they could be kept away from the public houses. How could the chapels deal with them? Could the workmen's halls raise their cultural levels a little to cope with those who for the time being had turned their backs on the pubs? These were the questions which were being asked, but the problem was not solved; the chapels lived in the glow of the revival for some years; and some basked in the emotion and tried to simulate it, with the result that many of the converts fell away. It was the advent of the cinema to these industrial areas which bridged the gap between the chapels and churches on the one hand and the public houses on the other.

It was fortunate for Welsh Nonconformity that it enjoyed this Indian summer just at a time when it was called upon to show itself to its best advantage, thus repeating its good luck of 1851 when another enumeration had followed hard on the heels of a religious revival. Upon the return of a Liberal government in the election of 1906 a Royal Commission was appointed 'to inquire into the origin, nature, amount, and application of the temporalities, endowments, and other properties of the Church of England in Wales and Monmouthshire; and into the provisions made, and the work done, by the Churches of all Denominations in Wales and Monmouthshire for the spiritual welfare of the people, and the extent to which people avail themselves of such provision, and to report thereon'.[1] This 'Royal Commission on the Church of England in Wales and other religious bodies in Wales and Monmouthshire' was set up on 21 June 1906, and issued its report in 1910. It was popularly and semi-officially known as the Welsh Church Commission, the term by which it has been referred to in this book.

It was inevitable that the interpretation of terms such as 'adherent', 'communicant', 'member' which would radically affect the statistics would present the greatest difficulty to the Commission. This proved to be the case, and no satisfactory basis was found for the interpretation of these terms. This was especially so in respect to the 'adherents', that body which played so prominent a part in Welsh Nonconformity in the last century and which inflated its statistics to such a a large degree. The only denomination to give official figures of this class were the Calvinistic Methodists, the other denominations supplying an estimated number only. The Calvinistic Methodists had used the term adherents in an 'all inclusive' sense to include that portion of the total population attached more or less closely to a Nonconformist church. Thus the 'sphere of influence' of Nonconformity would include its members and their children, plus the adherents and their children; and the Calvinistic Methodist case was based on the theory that if the names of all the members and of their children up to a certain age were deducted from the 'all inclusive' number, the remainder, the adherents, could then be ascertained. This was the most important problem to be considered by the Commission's Central Evidence

[1] *Report of the Royal Commission on the Church of England in Wales and other religious bodies in Wales and Monmouthshire*, i. 11.

Committee, but this committee 'failed entirely to provide for anything approaching uniformity in the meaning attached to the word 'adherent' in the county statistics, collected under its direction by the Nonconformist County Committees'.[1] It was discovered that the meanings given to this term differed not only from denomination to denomination, but from district to district within the churches of the same denomination. The Commission reported that its Central Evidence Committee had conspicuously failed in obtaining even an approximate estimate of the number of adherents in Nonconformity, and that, consequently, 'the column of adherents in the [Nonconformist] County Statistics became a hopeless medley of figures, which it is useless to add up even for the roughest of estimates'.[2] This conclusion was repeated more than once.

At the same time, a general picture of the incidence and distribution of adherents was arrived at. They were shown to be more numerous in English Nonconformist chapels than in those of the Welsh sector of the denomination; they were also higher in proportion in Welsh chapels in the industrial areas than in rural areas. They were not prominent in Welsh rural areas, where the great majority (5 out of 6 adults) of those who attended chapel did so as members, but in the English chapels this ratio was 4:7. Taking Wales and Monmouthshire as a whole the Commission concluded 'that the ratio of adherents (all inclusive) to full members is 168 to 100 in Welsh chapels, 279 to 100 in English chapels, and 183 to 100 in Welsh and English chapels taken together'.[3] The implication of these conclusions for the industrial areas is clear: that the statistics reveal the maximum ratio of adherents to membership both on account of language and social structure; even Welsh Nonconformity showed a larger proportion of adherents to membership in the areas covered by this study, and English Nonconformity in the same areas

[1] Ibid., i. 137.

[2] Ibid., i. 149.

[3] Ibid., *Memorandum by Archdeacon Owen Evans and Lord Hugh Cecil, M.P.* (i. 138).

showed the maximum number of adherents. Unfortunately it is not possible to compare the Welsh and English sectors, as the statistics provided by the Nonconformist County Committees to the Commission did not distinguish between the Welsh and English 'causes'.

As the adherent raised the most difficult problem in the statistics of Welsh Nonconformity, so did the 'communicant' in the statistics of the Established Church. It should be noted that the basis of these latter statistics is the communicant; had it been baptisms, or confirmations, Anglican statistics here would tend to approximate to Roman Catholic statistics for continental countries, statistics which are based on baptism and, in such countries, are virtually equivalent to the birth rate. As it was, the number of communicants approximated to the confirmation figure and the diocesan authorities provided the Commission with the name and address of every communicant in the parishes, i.e. those who were eligible to communicate, while at the same time not resisting the charge that not all who were eligible did communicate, even at Easter. It was estimated that 71·18 per cent. of communicants communicated at Easter in the old diocese of Llandaff,[1] but what proportion of these communicated more regularly could not be statistically assessed.

In view of these difficulties which affected church and chapel, a memorandum written by one of the Nonconformist members of the Commission claimed that no distinction should be drawn between the classes of 'member', 'communicant', 'adherent'. 'It may therefore be premised that the status of the church or chapel-going person is a secondary consideration, and is only of value as it is an index of the extent to which the people of Wales avail themselves of the spiritual provision made for their welfare.'[2] It will be recalled that the terms of the Commission provided that an

[1] *Report of the Royal Commission on the Church of England in Wales and other religious bodies in Wales and Monmouthshire*, i. 142–3.

[2] Ibid., *Memorandum by J. H. Davies on Chapel and Church Statistics*, i. 159.

inquiry should be made 'into the provision made, and the work done, by the Churches of all Denominations in Wales and Monmouthshire for the spiritual welfare of the people, *and the extent to which the people avail themselves of such provision*'.[1] The truth is that the Commission did not carry out this term of reference, for it did not distinguish between the congregational character of Nonconformity on the one hand, and the parochial nature of the ministry of the Established Church on the other, which latter results in an influence and an active ministry which cannot be statistically recorded. The only means of ascertaining the extent of the two types of ministry, their spiritual provision, and the degree to which people availed themselves of those provisions, was by means of a religious census. The first two Nonconformist witnesses to appear before the Commission raised no objection to such a census, 'but after this, for some reason or other, not a single Nonconformist witness approved of it at all'. All the Church witnesses approved of it, and the Welsh bishops expressed a desire for it.[2]

[1] Author's italics.

[2] *Royal Commission on the Church and other religious bodies in Wales, Memorandum by Archdeacon Owen Evans and Lord Hugh Cecil, M.P.* (i. 139–40).

APPENDIX I

AN ANALYSIS OF FIGURES RELEVANT TO THIS STUDY WHICH WERE PRESENTED TO THE WELSH CHURCH COMMISSION

THIS Appendix is an analysis of those figures which were submitted to the Welsh Church Commission by the Established Church and Nonconformity and published by the Commission on a local-government basis. The first four items in each section are those figures supplied by the Commission and the concluding seven items are an analysis of these figures prepared for this book. The term 'communicant' stands for 'church communicant', 'member' means 'chapel member', and 'adherent' means exclusively 'chapel adherent'.

ABERDARE (Aberdare, Aberaman, St. Fagans, Hirwaun)
Population: 44,104
Church communicants: 2,741
Nonconformist membership: 13,942
Nonconformist adherents: 10,744[1]
Percentage of communicants to total number of communicants and members (i.e. church and chapel, excluding adherents): 16·4
Percentage of members to total number of worshippers: 83·5
Percentage of communicants to population: 6·2
Percentage of members to population: 31·6
Percentage of members and communicants to population: 37·8
Percentage of members and adherents to population: 55·6
Percentage of communicants, members and adherents to population: 62·2

MERTHYR TYDFIL (Merthyr Tydfil, Cyfarthfa, Dowlais, Pentrebach, and Penydarren)
Population: 62,109

[1] *Report of the Royal Commission on the Church of England in Wales and other religious bodies in Wales and Monmouthshire. Statistics of the Church of England and Nonconformists in Urban and Rural Areas*, i. 353.

Church communicants: 3,649
Nonconformist membership: 14,662
Nonconformist adherents: 12,351[1]
Percentage of communicants to total number of communicants and members): 20
Percentage of members to total number of worshippers: 80
Percentage of communicants to population: 5·9
Percentage of members to population: 23·6
Percentage of members and communicants to population: 29·5
Percentage of members and adherents to population: 43·5
Percentage of communicants, members and adherents to population: 49·4

RHYMNEY (Llechryd and Rhymney)
Population: 7,915
Church communicants: 844
Nonconformist membership: 2,556
Nonconformist adherents: 4,221
Percentage of communicants to total number of communicants and members: 24·8
Percentage of members to total number of worshippers: 75·2
Percentage of communicants to population: 10·7
Percentage of members to population: 32·3
Percentage of members and communicants to population: 43·0
Percentage of members and adherents to population: 85·6
Percentage of communicants, members and adherents to population: 96·3

TREDEGAR (Dukestown and Tredegar)
Population: 18,497
Church communicants: 962
Nonconformist membership: 4,102
Nonconformist adherents: 6,586
Percentage of communicants to total number of communicants and members: 19·0
Percentage of members to total number of worshippers: 81·0
Percentage of communicants to total population: 5·2
Percentage of members to total population: 22·2
Percentage of members and communicants to population: 27·4
Percentage of members and adherents to population: 57·8

[1] Ibid. i. 354.

Percentage of communicants, members and adherents to population: 63·0

ABERTILLERY (Abertillery and Llanhiledd)

Population: 21,945.
Church communicants: 1,023
Nonconformist membership: 4,302
Nonconformist adherents: 10,144
Percentage of communicants to total number of communicants and members: 19·2
Percentage of members to total number of worshippers: 80·8
Percentage of communicants to population: 4·7
Percentage of communicants and members to population: 24·3
Percentage of members to total population: 19·6
Percentage of members and adherents to total population: 65·8
Percentage of communicants, members and adherents to population: 70·5

ABERSYCHAN (Abersychan, Trevethin, Pontnewynydd)

Population: 17,768
Church communicants: 685
Nonconformist members: 2,881
Nonconformist adherents: 5,814
Percentage of communicants to total number of communicants and members: 19·2
Percentage of members to total number of worshippers: 80·8
Percentage of communicants to population: 3·9
Percentage of members to population: 16·2
Percentage of members and communicants to population: 20·1
Percentage of members and adherents to population: 48·9
Percentage of communicants, members and adherents to population: 52·8

BEDWELLTY AND EBBW VALE

Population: 30,982
Church communicants: 2,228
Nonconformist membership: 7,621
Nonconformist adherents: 15,034
Percentage of communicants to total number of communicants and members: 22·6
Percentage of members to total number of worshippers: 77·4

Percentage of communicants to population: 7·2
Percentage of members to population: 24
Percentage of members and communicants to population: 31·8
Percentage of members and adherents to population: 73·1
Percentage of communicants, members and adherents to population: 80·3

BLAENAVON

Population: 10,869
Church communicants: 813
Nonconformist membership: 2,366
Nonconformist adherents: 5,167
Percentage of communicants to total number of communicants and members: 25·6
Percentage of members to total number of worshippers: 74·4
Percentage of communicants to population: 7·5
Percentage of members to population: 21·8
Percentage of members and communicants to population: 29·3
Percentage of members and adherents to population: 69·3
Percentage of communicants, members and adherents to population: 76·8

ABER-CARN (Newbridge, and part of Mynyddislwyn and Mynyddislwyn Rural)

Population: 12,607
Church communicants: 1,321
Nonconformist members: 3,551
Nonconformist adherents: 7,211
Percentage of communicants to total number of communicants and members: 27·1
Percentage of members to total number of worshippers: 72·9
Percentage of communicants to population: 10·5
Percentage of members to population: 28·2
Percentage of members and communicants to population: 38·7
Percentage of members and adherents to population: 85·4
Percentage of communicants, members and adherents to population: 95·8

PONTYPOOL TOWN

Population: 6,126

Church communicants: 103
Nonconformist members: 1,517
Nonconformist adherents: 3,685.[1]
Percentage of communicants to total number of communicants and members: 6·4
Percentage of members to total number of worshippers: 93·6
Percentage of communicants to population: 1·7
Percentage of members to population: 24·8
Percentage of members and communicants to population: 26·5
Percentage of members and adherents to population: 85
Percentage of communicants, members and adherents to population: 86·7

Taking the old ironworks district as a whole, the following picture emerges:
Population: 232,922
Church communicants: 14,373
Nonconformist members: 57,500
Nonconformist adherents: 80,937
Percentage of communicants to total number of communicants and members: 20·0
Percentage of members to total number of worshippers: 80·0
Percentage of communicants to population: 6·2
Percentage of members to population: 24·7
Percentage of communicants and members to population: 30·9
Percentage of members and adherents to population: 50·4
Percentage of communicants, members and adherents to population: 65·6

It is instructive to compare the industrial areas with the rural areas of Monmouthshire:[2]
Population: 79,510
Church communicants: 10,041
Nonconformist members: 8,910
Nonconformist adherents: 19,349

[1] *Report of the Royal Commission on the Church of England and Wales and other religious bodies in Wales and Monmouthshire. Statistics of the Church of England and Nonconformists in Urban and Rural Areas*, i. 368–71.

[2] Abergavenny Urban, Abergavenny Rural, Caerleon, Chepstow, Llantarnam, Monmouth, Panteg, Usk, and the Rural Districts of Abergavenny, Chepstow, Magor, Monmouth, Pontypool, St. Mellons.

Percentage of communicants to total number of communicants and members: 53·0
Percentage of Nonconformist members to worshippers: 47·0
Percentage of communicants to population: 12·6
Percentage of members to population: 11·2
Percentage of communicants and members to population: 23·8
Percentage of members and adherents to population: 35·5
Percentage of communicants, members and adherents to population: 48·2

The figures for Newport illustrate a commercial and residential centre where the incidence of Welsh speaking was 3·6 per cent.
Population: 67,270
Church communicants: 3,823
Nonconformist members: 7,257
Nonconformist adherents: 17,534[1]
Percentage of communicants to communicants and members: 34·5
Percentage of members to worshippers: 65·5
Percentage of communicants to population: 5·7
Percentage of members to population: 10·8
Percentage of members and communicants to population: 16·5
Percentage of members and adherents to population: 36·9
Percentage of communicants, members and adherents to population: 42·5

Finally, the figures for Monmouthshire, including Newport.
Population: 299,156
Church communicants: 22,913[2]
Nonconformist members: 49,937
Nonconformist adherents: 106,328[3]
Percentage of communicants to communicants and members: 31·5
Percentage of members to worshippers: 68·5
Percentage of communicants to population: 7·7
Percentage of members to population: 16·7
Percentage of communicants and members to population: 24·4

[1] *Report of the Royal Commission on the Church of England in Wales and other religious bodies*, i. 380–1.
[2] Ibid., i, ii, Appendix B, p. 74.
[3] Ibid., *Nonconformist County Statistics*, pp. 376–7, 380–1.

Percentage of members and adherents to population: 52·2
Percentage of communicants, members, and adherents to population: 59·9

An examination of Appendix I shows that the picture in the industrial areas sixty years ago was by no means clear because of the very uncertain value that should be given to the figures relating to adherents; obviously this class made an appreciable difference to the picture, for in certain places it comprised the better part of the total population beyond communicants and members. Thus the figures for Aber-carn and Rhymney could have been arrived at by only one method, viz., the inclusion of church communicants (whose names and addresses were supplied to the Commission for every parish), chapel members and their children, and then all who had the remotest connexion with the chapels, together with their entire families. No other possible basis of computation could have brought into the religious picture the entire population of the Aber-carn area (12,607), with the exception of 524 people; and the same suspicion must surround the returns from Pontypool Town, and Bedwellty and Ebbw Vale. It should, of course, be emphasized once again that Nonconformity in general, and Welsh Nonconformity in particular, was able to reveal itself to its best possible advantage in 1905, the year to which the statistics presented to the Welsh Church Commission referred. The chapels were full as they had not been for half a century, and as they were not to be again to the present day. Moreover, it is known that this class of adherent disappeared very rapidly in the industrial areas after 1919 and soon virtually ceased to exist.

This leaves communicants and members, each class faithful in varying degrees, but, on the whole, the latter being more faithful than the former. Here again, the number of chapel members rose by thousands in 1904–5, and the statistics reflect this, while confirmations were not greatly affected by the revival. Consequently even the figures of communicants and certainly those of members in 1905 were more favourable than they were to be even five years later, when the usual reaction had set in and chapel membership had already fallen. The 'percentage of communicants and members to the total population' in Appendix I provides the only stable factor in the situation as it was in 1905, and even these figures were soon to be eroded. But the subsequent picture as the result of this analysis turns out to be what might have been expected, viz. that the Welsh-speaking areas led the English-speaking areas as they had done in 1851, and largely because of the strength of Welsh Nonconformity. Thus, Rhymney with 43·0 per cent., Aberdare with 37·8 per cent., Aber-carn with 38·7 per cent. of communicants and members to total population, led these industrial areas; but the industrial areas, with an average, under this particular analysis, of 30·9 per cent., did not have that marked lead over the rural areas with 23·8 per cent., but had a distinctly higher average than Newport, with its 16·5 per cent., and Monmouthshire as a whole, with 24·4 per cent. The general pattern for 1905 was similar to that of 1851, with the important exception that the percentages were lower in every case. This can be only a rough comparison between the two situations because of the unsatisfactory basis of the 1851 census.

The relation between the Established Church and Nonconformity has been of secondary importance in this study, but the result of the enumeration of 1905 showed that Nonconformity had still a substantial lead in the industrial areas with a ratio of 24·7 per cent. to 6·2 per cent., and with a greater preponderance of Nonconformity in the more Welsh-speaking areas, except in Rhymney where a more balanced picture was to be expected. The outstanding anomaly was that of Pontypool Town, with a ratio in favour of Nonconformity of 24·8 per cent. to 1·7 per cent. Again, as in 1851, south Monmouthshire restored the balance to some extent. The rural areas showed a slight preponderance of Anglicanism over Nonconformity (12·6 per cent. to 11·2 per cent.), while the ratio in Newport was 5·7 per cent. to 10·8 per cent. The over-all picture for the county was more favourable to the Established Church in 1905 than it had been in 1851, viz., 7·7 per cent. to 16·7 per cent.

This study began with the warning that the figures that are available for ecclesiastical purposes are all unsatisfactory to some degree or other. But they are the only figures to hand, and the best use must be made of them. They show a fairly solid core of church and chapel membership, decreasing, as one proceeds from the industrial areas of north Monmouthshire and north-east Glamorgan, from about 30 per cent. of the population, through the rural areas with about one quarter of the population, to the town of Newport, a little behind the rural areas in this matter. The study is incomplete: 1905 was an unsatisfactory year for reliable figures, and, in any case, the changes in society which affected church and chapel were already in motion before that year, but were checked somewhat by the religious revival of 1904–5; they quickly accelerated in the years before and during the First World War, and became apparent in their results after 1919. It was then that the religious aspect of the Welsh industrial scene was obviously approximating to what had been known of similar communities in England since 1851.

APPENDIX II

ROMAN CATHOLICISM IN A WELSH INDUSTRIAL SOCIETY

ROMAN Catholicism, in the areas and the period covered in this book, was confined almost exclusively to the Irish population which came to these parts in the wake of the industrial revolution. In 1773 there were 750 Roman Catholics throughout the whole of Wales;[1] and in 1813 those of the south-east were confined to Newport and the border districts such as Abergavenny, Llanarth, and Pershore. It appears that there was one Irish Roman Catholic in Merthyr Tydfil in 1798. There was an increase by 1815, and ten years later an Irish colony had grown up in Dowlais and around the Varteg ironworks. In 1838 the combined Roman Catholic population of Newport and Pontypool was 2,400;[2] Merthyr-Dowlais had 940,[2] and the 1851 census showed that there were 5,888 Irish people living in Monmouthshire and 3,646 in the Merthyr Tydfil Registration Union. The increase in the immigration of Irish people continued until the 1860s when it began to decline, and for the remainder of the period covered by this book the spread of Roman Catholicism in these parts depended solely on the high birth-rate among the Irish, who were concentrated largely in the old ironworks districts of Merthyr-Dowlais, Rhymney, Tredegar and the Pontypool district, in addition, of course, to Newport, which had the largest Irish population.

These Irish immigrants came to an area devoid of all provision for their worship. The first Roman Catholic church in the commercial and industrial areas was built in Newport, and it was from this town that the industrial communities were served. A mission was opened in Merthyr Tydfil in 1828, but by 1841 there were only two missions in the ironworks belt, the other being in Abersychan to serve the Varteg Irish. Merthyr had no chapel, but the Roman Catholics worshipped in a 'dark, low

[1] *Newport Catholic Magazine*, I, i, 6. [2] Ibid., I, i, 8.

loft, without ceiling, and gaping between the tiles of the roof, which, being gained by a ladder flung across a brook, extends over a portion of the foul public slaughter-house of a populous town', while their co-religionists 'near Pontypool' met in a room in the village inn. The priest in the former place eked out a livelihood by the sale of salt ('under the name and by the agency of one of his congregation') which he obtained at a low price from a friend in Ireland, and this commercial venture increased his stipend to £138. 16*s.* 0*d.* in 1841,[1] which made him 'passing rich' when compared with every Nonconformist minister and not a few of the clergy in these industrial areas.

The Irish colonies were undoubtedly the poorest section in the old ironworks districts. In 1827 a list of contributions from the Irish workers was proposed for the building of a church in Merthyr. It was suggested that £11. 0*s.* 6*d.* per month should be raised from about 300 Irish workers, some of them distributed as follows: Merthyr, 118; Rhymney and Bute, 52; Sirhowy, 11, and Tredegar, 7. The contributions were to be received at the various company offices where the men were paid, but it was pointed out that the majority of these workers were not directly employed by the ironmasters and so were not paid in their offices. A correspondent wrote to Bishop Collingridge: 'The people who are of the poorest description never will, and never can contribute.'[2]

Meanwhile the ecclesiastical reorganization was begun which was ultimately to change this state of affairs. In 1840 the Western Vicariate was divided into two and Dr. Thomas Joseph Brown, Prior of Downside, was consecrated titular Bishop of Apollonia, with charge of north and south Wales, Monmouthshire, and Herefordshire; and ten years later the diocese of Newport and Menevia was constituted, consisting of the south Wales counties with Brown as bishop. He was succeeded by Bishop Hedley in 1881, and when the diocese of Newport and Menevia was subdivided in 1898, Hedley became bishop of Newport. For a long time these Roman Catholic bishops had to rely upon members of monastic orders, particularly the Benedictines, for their clergy, because of the shortage of secular priests; thus in 1850 Bishop Brown's Chapter consisted entirely of members of this Order, and in 1881 Bishop Hedley had only 13 secular priests in his

[1] Ibid., vi, 7, 206–7. [2] Ibid. vi, 10, 296.

diocese.[1] As with the Established Church and Nonconformity the Roman Catholic Church had to rely upon rural areas for a supply of clergy; and as the churches and the chapels looked to rural Wales for their pastors, so did the Roman Catholic missions and parishes rely heavily upon Ireland.

The census of 1851 had shown that there were 5,888 Irish people living in Monmouthshire, concentrated largely in the Abergavenny, Pontypool, and Newport Registration Unions, and census Sunday of that same year showed an attendance of 4,460 worshippers in eight Roman Catholic churches in the county, of which Newport itself accounted for 2,200.[2] The Irish population in the Merthyr Tydfil Registration Union amounted to 4,467, and the church attendance on 31 March 1851 was 750.[3] These figures present surprises. Thus in Newport, where the Irish population was returned as 2,737 in 1851 the number of Roman Catholic worshippers was high, especially in relation to the seating capacity of the church which was returned as '300/600', but no doubt a number of masses on census Sunday accounted for the high figure of 2,200 worshippers, and children must have been counted as well. The Newport Irish population was the most concentrated in Monmouthshire, and where the Irish were more scattered the attendance figures and percentages were much lower than they were for Newport. The Abergavenny Registration Union which, it will be remembered, consisted of the rural areas around the town together with the greater part of industrial north Monmouthshire, returned a total of 1,733 Irish but only 294 Roman Catholic worshippers, while the Pontypool Registration Union contained 1,018 Irish and 330 Roman Catholic worshippers in a fairly concentrated area around Pontypool itself and Usk, which had had its place of worship since the end of the eighteenth century. These lower percentages were no doubt due to the scattered nature of the Irish communities and to the lack of churches in the industrial areas. But this important factor hardly accounted for the situation in the Merthyr Registration Union where there were 4,467 Irish people, largely concentrated in Dowlais, of whom only 750 worshipped on census Sunday in a densely populated district where a Roman Catholic church and school had been built in 1846. It is clear that the

[1] J. A. Wilson, *The Life of Bishop Hedley* (London, 1930), p. 99.
[2] H.O., 129/26/580.
[3] H.O., 129/26/582.

Roman Catholic Church had lost many of its communicants in these industrial areas but, unlike the Welsh communicants of the Established Church, they did not join Welsh Nonconformity but very probably went to make the growing unchurched proletariat in the industrial valleys. 'This apostacy [*sic*] happened because these poor strayed sheep had no shepherd.'[1] Bishop Hedley wrote in his first Pastoral Letter that the change from Irish country life to the new environment often resulted in a loss of faith: 'churches have multiplied, but the younger people do not fill them; schools have sprung up everywhere, but the children who go out from them are, in too large a proportion, lost to us when we lose sight of them.'[2] At the same time, much progress was made in the years after 1860 to provide churches in the industrial areas, so that by the end of the century these areas were adequately provided with places of worship where there were concentrations of Irish people. Such concentrations persisted in the old ironworks centres but were not characteristic of the coal-mining districts. Moreover, Irish immigration into these parts declined after 1860 and Roman Catholicism had to rely almost entirely upon the natural increase of the Irish population who had immigrated during the first half of the nineteenth century and, as is well known, this increase was prolific. The Roman Catholic Church made little, if any, headway among the non-Irish population. The cultural and social gap between the Irish and other communities, and especially between them and Welsh Nonconformists, was such that they had little to do with each other. Social contacts which might have led to, and have since resulted in mixed marriages, did not exist. The Irish way of life was in such startling contrast with that of the Welsh Nonconformist that they had little, if anything, in common; and when the various communities did meet the results were not always happy.

The attitude of Lady Charlotte Guest was characteristic, in a more sophisticated way, of the attitude toward Roman Catholicism in those days. Her husband's agent in Dowlais had married a Spanish Roman Catholic, and in 1851 he arranged to entertain the newly appointed bishop of Newport and Menevia (wrongly described in Lady Charlotte's diary as the 'Roman Catholic Bishop of Merthyr').[3] Both she and her husband regarded

[1] J. A. Wilson, op. cit., p. 103. [2] Ibid., p. 104.

[2] Earl of Bessborough (ed.), *Lady Charlotte Guest, extracts from her Jounal 1833–1852* (London, 1950), p. 254.

the visit of the bishop as a personal insult and a possible cause of trouble. She wrote in her diary for 18 January 1851: 'I felt I could not meet this man, here, on my own ground, my children's birthplace, and my own home of so many years standing, where every movement of ours is observed, and looked for, and commented on, and where in the present state of excited feeling on the Roman Catholic aggression any seeming favouring of the assumption on our part might do so much harm.'[1] The presence of the Roman Catholic bishop caused an awkward domestic situation when Lady Charlotte Guest refused to meet him, but Bishop Brown very diplomatically cut short his visit. It should be added that the wife of the Dowlais ironmaster was only slightly less put out by Puseyism in the Church of England and that her favourite ministrations were those which she received from the evangelical rector of Dowlais, Evan Jenkins.

The ecclesiastical and social influences of the Irish–Roman Catholic communities in the industrial areas of north-east Glamorgan and north Monmouthshire were very limited. The Irish produced no social or civic leadership in these industrial areas, and in local government they were too scattered to become politically significant. It was in the seaport towns such as Newport and Cardiff that these communities began to matter politically, because the concentration of Irish population in certain wards of these towns made possible what was virtually an Irish–Roman Catholic representation in local government. But ecclesiastically, both in the towns and in the industrial centres, Roman Catholicism was limited to the Irish population.

By the beginning of the present century there were 9,696 adult Roman Catholics in Monmouthshire and 5,356 under 15 years of age, while in Glamorgan the corresponding figures were 27,323 and 14,038, with 21 resident priests in the former, and 39 in the latter county. The old ironworks districts were still well represented, especially the Merthyr-Dowlais district which accounted for 6,720 Roman Catholics, and this was about half of the Roman Catholic population in the areas which have been dealt with in this book.[2]

[1] Ibid., pp. 254–5.

[2] *Royal Commission on the Church of England, and other religious bodies in Wales and Monmouthshire*, i, ii, Appendix L, pp. 128–9.

BIBLIOGRAPHY

A. MANUSCRIPTS

Bishop Copleston's letters to W. B. Knight and J. M. Traherne.

Josiah Thompson MS.

Records of the Church in Wales: Diocese of Llandaff.

Religious Census (1851) Returns.

T. Revel Guest MS.

B. PRINTED SOURCES: (1) ENGLISH

Annual Report of the Llandaff Diocesan Conference, 1884 ff.

Annual Report of the Llandaff Diocesan Church Extension Society, 1851 ff.

Annual Report and Minutes of the Committee of Council on Education (London, 1840).

Bruce, H. A., *On amusements, as the means of continuing and extending the education of the working classes* (Cardiff, 1850).

Census Returns, Glamorgan and Monmouthshire, 1801–1911.

Church Rates. Abstract of Returns to an Address of the Honourable The House of Commons, 10 August 1854 (London, 1856).

Church Rates. Abstract of Returns to an Address of the Honourable The House of Commons, 17 July 1855 (London, 1856).

Copleston, Edward, *A Charge to the Clergy of the Diocese of Llandaff* . . . (London, 1833, 1839, 1842, 1848).

Edmondes, Frederick W., (ed.), *Nineteenth Annual Meeting of the Church Congress held at Swansea on October the 7th, 8th, 9th, & 10th, 1879* (London, 1880).

Francis, James, *A Sermon to the working classes, preached in St. Paul's Church, Newport, on Sunday evening, April 21st, 1839* (Newport, 1839).

Hansard's Parliamentary Debates (Third Series, London, 1860).

Hughes, Joshua Pritchard, *A Charge to the Clergy of the Diocese of Llandaff* . . . (Cardiff, 1907, 1910, 1913).

Kenrick, G. S., *The population of Pontypool and the parish of Trevethin* (London, 1840).

Lewis, Richard, *A Charge to the Clergy of the Diocese of Llandaff* . . . (Cardiff, 1885, 1888, 1891, 1894).

Llandaff Diocesan Magazine, 1899 ff.

Monmouthshire Baptist Association Circular Letters, 1832 ff.

Newport Catholic Magazine, 1928–31.

Ollivant, Alfred, *A Charge to the Clergy of the Diocese of Llandaff*... (London, 1851, 1854, 1857, 1860, 1863, 1866, 1869, 1872, 1878, 1881).

—— *A proposal for the establishment of a Missionary Agency for the purpose of promoting the spiritual welfare of the mining population of his Diocese* (London, 1860).

—— *Address of the Bishop of Llandaff on the first appointment of Lay Readers for his Diocese, delivered in his chapel, April 27, 1870* (Cardiff, n.d.).

On the oaths taken in the Union Club. A dialogue between Thomas Cadogan, and David Nathaniel, colliers. By a Looker On (Newport, 1831).

Papers, Manifestoes, Petitions, etc., relating to the General Election of 1910 in the constituency of Merthyr Tydfil.

Royal Commission on the Church of England and other religious bodies in Wales and Monmouthshire. (London, 1910), 8 vols.

Royal Commission on Land in Wales and Monmouthshire (London, 1894–6).

Report of the Commissioners appointed by His Majesty to inquire into the ecclesiastical revenues of England and Wales (London, 1835).

Reports of the Proceedings of the Association of Welsh Clergy in the West Riding of Yorkshire (Carnarvon, 1852, 1853, 1854).

Reports from the Ecclesiastical Commissioners for England, 1846 ff.

Reports of the Commissioners approved to inquire into the organization and rules of Trade Unions and other Associations (London, 1867).

Reports of the Commissioners of Inquiry into the State of Education in Wales, appointed by the Committee of Council on Education (London, 1847), 3 vols.

Report and Minutes of Evidence of an Inquiry as to Disturbances in connection with the levying of Tithe-Rentcharge in Wales (London, 1887).

Report on the sanitary condition of Merthyr Tydfil (London, 1845).

Report to the General Board of Health on a preliminary enquiry into the sewerage, drainage, and supply of water and the sanitary condition of the inhabitants of the town of Merthyr Tydfil (London, 1850).

Report to the General Board of Health on a further inquiry held in the town of Bryn-Mawr in the County of Carmarthen [*sic*] (London, 1851).

St. Peter's Magazine, 1921–9.

Schedules of the Church in Wales Records, Diocese of Llandaff, 9 vols.

Substance of speeches delivered at Bridgend and Newport on the 29th and 31st October, 1850, at meetings called by the Lord Bishop of Llandaff, and in support of resolutions for establishing a society for providing additional superintendence and church accommodation within the Diocese of Llandaff (London, 1850).

Sumner, Charles Richard, *Charge to the Clergy of the Diocese of Llandaff*... (London, 1827).

The Established Church and Nonconformity in Wales. Proceedings of the Conference at Swansea, September 23rd and 24th, 1862 (London, n.d.).

Tithe Commutation Return by the Land Commissioners for England (London, 1937).

Van Mildert, William, *A Charge to the Clergy of the Diocese of Llandaff . . .* (London, 1821).

Williams, Thomas, *A letter to the Lord Bishop of Llandaff on the peculiar condition and wants of the Diocese* (London, 1850).

PRINTED SOURCES: (2) WELSH

Adroddiad Cyfundeb Annibynwyr Morganwg. Y Gymmanfa Ddwyreiniol, 1851–78, 1885–95, 1898, 1903, 1905, 1908–10.

Adroddiad Cyfundeb Annibynwyr Morganwg. Y Gymmanfa Ogleddol, 1901, 1904–10.

Adroddiad y ddwy gymmanfa ddeheuol, 1832–4, 1837–8, 1840–5, 1847–50, 1852, 1857–60.

Cylchlythyrau, Adroddiadau, a Rhaglenni Cymdeithasfaol Methodistiaid Calfinaidd Deheudir Cymru, 1846 ff.

Jones, William, *Hanes Cymmanfa y Bedyddwyr Neillduol yng Nghymru, o'i ddechreuad hyd y flwyddyn 1790, yn nghyda pharhad o hanes y Gymmanfa Dde-Ddwyreiniol o'r flwyddyn 1790 hyd 1831* (Caerdydd, 1831).

Llythyr Cymmanfa [Bedyddwyr] Mynwy, 1833 ff.

Llythyr Cymmanfa Bedyddwyr Neillduol Morganwg, 1833 ff.

Llythyr, yn rhoddi hanes yr ymraniad a gymerodd le yn ddiweddar yn eglwys yr Anymddibynwyr a arferai ymgynull yn Ebenezer, Sirhowy, o dan ofal y Parch. R. Jones (Crughywel, 1841).

Morris, Thomas, *Cynghor da mewn amser drwg* (Caerdydd, 1840).

Mynegai oddiwrth weinidogion yr Annibynwyr perthynol i Gyfundeb Dwyreiniol Morganwg (Abertawy, 1849).

Rheolai i sylwi arnynt gan Gymdeithas o Grefftwyr ac eraill a elwir Cymdeithas Unol y Blaenau, yn cyfarfod yn nhŷ George Davies, adnabyddus wrth arwydd Gwestfa y Milgi, yng nghweithfeydd haiarn Nantyglo, plwyf Aberystruth, Swydd Fynwy (Y Fenni, 1844).

PRINTED SOURCES: (3) NEWSPAPERS

South Wales Daily News.

The Aberdare Leader.

The Cardiff and Merthyr Guardian.

The Merthyr Express.

The Monmouth, Glamorgan, and Brecon Herald, or Star of Gwent.

The Monmouthshire Merlin and South Wales Advertiser.

The Pontypool Free Press and Herald of the Hills.

The South Wales Argus.

The Times.

Western Mail.

GENERAL BIBLIOGRAPHY

Addis, J. P., *The Crawshay Dynasty* (Cardiff, 1957).

Astle, John G. E., *The Progress of Merthyr Tydfil* (Merthyr Tydfil, n.d.).

Attwater, Donald, *The Catholic Church in Modern Wales* (London, 1935).

Barber, J. T., *A tour through South Wales and Monmouthshire* (London, 1803).

Beaven, E., *The history of the Welsh Sunday Closing Act* (Cardiff, 1885).

Bessborough, Earl of (ed.), *Lady Charlotte Guest, Extracts from her Journal, 1832–52* (London, 1950).

Boulard, F., *An introduction to Religious Sociology* (London, 1960).

Brennan, T., Cooney, E. W., Pollins, H., *Social change in South-West Wales* (London, 1954).

Cofnodion o hanes Eglwys Annibynol Saron, Tredegar (Tredegar, 1897).

Copleston, W. J., *Memoirs of Edward Copleston, D.D.* (London, 1851).

Coxe, William, *A historical tour of Monmouthshire* (London, 1801).

Davies, D. J., *The Tredegar Workmen's Hall, 1861–1951* (1951).

Davies, E. T., *Monmouthshire schools and education to 1870* (Newport, 1957).

Davies, Evan, *Revivals in Wales* (London, 1859).

Davies, John, *Bras-Linelliad hanesyddol o Gyfundeb Annibynol Dwyreiniol Morganwg o 1851 i 1878* (Caerdydd, 1879).

Davies, Walter, *General view of the agriculture and domestic economy of South Wales* (London, 1815), 2 vols.

Donovan, E., *Descriptive excursions through South Wales and Monmouthshire in the year 1804, and the four preceding summers* (London, 1805).

Ebbw Vale Literary and Scientific Institute. The history of a hundred years, 1849–1949 (Pontypool, 1949).

Edmunds, William, *Traethawd ar hanes plwyf Merthyr, o'r cyfnod boreuaf hyd yn bresenol* (Aberdar, 1864).

Edwards, David, 'Nodweddion Brodorol Dosbarth Gweithiol Gwent a Morganwg', *Y Traethodydd*, xii. 455–64 (Treffynon, MDCCCLVI).

Edwards, Wil Jon, *From the valley I came* (London, 1956).

Edwards, William, *Bapto a Baptiso* (Llanelli, 1858).

Elsas, Madeline (ed.), *Iron in the making. Dowlais Iron Company Letters, 1782–1860* (Cardiff, 1960).

Evans, Benjamin, *Bywgraffiad y diweddar Barch. T. Price, M.A., Ph.D., Aberdar* (Aberdar, 1891).

Evans, David, *The Sunday Schools of Wales* (London, n.d.).

Evans, E. W., *The miners of South Wales* (Cardiff, 1961).

Evans, John, and Britton, John, *A topographical and historical description of the County of Monmouth* (London, 1809).

Fowler, John Coke, *Church Pews, their origin and legal incidents* (London, 1844).

—— *On public libraries* (Swansea, 1871).

Glyn Congregational Church, Risca, Mon. Centenary 1841–1941. A brief history.

Gregory, Robert, *Side-lights on the conflicts of Methodism* (London, 1879).

Griffith, Gareth, and Lambert, John L., *New Bethel Congregational Church, Mynyddislwyn 1758–1958* (1958).

Griffith, John, *The Church in Wales. A speech at the Leeds Congress* (Cardiff, 1872).

Griffiths, R., *Hanes Eglwys Crist yn Zoar, Merthyr er ei dechreuad yn y 'Long Room', tu cefn i'r Crown Inn, yn y flwyddyn 1794, hyd yn bresenol* (Merthyr Tydfil, 1869).

Hughes, Ellis, *Cofiant y diweddar Barch. Evan Rowlands, Pontypwl, Mynwy* (Caerdydd, 1864).

Inglis, K. S., *Churches and the Working Classes in Victorian England* (London, 1963).

James, Charles Herbert, *Seven lectures on various subjects* (Merthyr Tydfil, 1892).

James, J. Spinther, *Hanes y Bedyddwyr yng Nghymru* (Caerfyrddin, 1893–1907), 4 vols.

—— *Traethawd ar fywyd ac athrylith Cynddelw* (Caernarfon, 1877).

Jenkins, John David, *Detholion o hanes yr Eglwys* (Caerdydd, 1880).

Jenkins, Llewellyn, a Thomas, Timothy, *Cofiant o'r diweddar Barch. Thomas Morris, Casnewydd-ar-Wysg* (Caerdydd, 1847).

Johnes, A. J., *An essay on the causes which have produced Dissent from the Established Church in the Principality of Wales* (3rd ed., London, 1835).

Jones, Anthony, *Chapel architecture in Merthyr Tydfil* (Merthyr Tydfil, 1962).

Jones, Daniel, *Eglwys Crist neu resymau dros ymadael ag Ymneillduaeth, ac ymuno a'r apostolig wir eglwys* (Caerfyrddin, 1856).

Jones, David, *Hanes y Bedyddwyr yn Neheubarth Cymru* (Caerfyrddin, 1839).

Jones Edmund, *A geographical, historical, and religious account of the parish of Aberystruth* (Trevecka, 1779).

Jones, Evan, *The dissent and morality of Wales* (London, 1847).

Jones, J. S., *Hanes Rhymney a Phontlottyn* (Dinbych, 1904).

Jones, Thomas, *Rhymney Memories* (Newtown, n.d.).

—— *Welsh Broth* (Newtown, n.d.).

Jones, T. Jesse, *Cofiant Canon William Evans, Rhymni* (Lampeter, n.d.).

—— *William Lewis, diweddar ficer Ystradyfodwg.* (Dolgellau, n.d.).

Lewis, E.D., *The Rhondda Valleys* (London, 1957).

Lewis, Henry (ed.), *Llanwynno Glanffrwd* (Caerdydd, 1949).

Lewis, Samuel, *A topographical dictionary of Wales* (4th ed., London, 1848), 2 vols.

Lewis, Thomas, *My Life's history* (Newport, 1902).

Lewis, Tom, *Hen Dŷ Cwrdd Cefn Coed y Cymmer* (1947).

Lloyd, John, *Old South Wales Iron Works* (London, 1906).

Malkin, Benjamin Heath, *The scenery, antiquities, and biography of South Wales* (London, 1807), 2 vols.

Manby, G. W., *An historic and picturesque guide from Clifton through the counties of Monmouth, Glamorgan and Brecknock* (London, 1802).

Mann, Horace, *Religious Worship in England and Wales* (London, 1853).

Morgan, John, *Four biographical sketches* (London, 1892).

Morgan, J. Vyrnwy (ed.), *Welsh religious leaders in the Victorian Era* (London, 1905).

—— *Welsh political and educational leaders in the Victorian Era* (London, 1908).

—— *The Welsh Religious Revival, 1904–5. A Retrospect and Criticism* (London, 1909).

Morgan, Kenneth O., *Wales in British Politics 1868–1922* (Cardiff, 1963).

Morgan, Llewellyn, *Hanes Wesleyaeth Cymraeg yng nghylchdaith Tredegar* (Monmouth, 1914).

Morgan, W., *Sylwadau ar resymau y Parch. D. Jones dros ymadael ag Ymneilltuaeth* (Llanelli, 1857).

Morgan, W. T., 'Disputes concerning seats in church before the consistory courts of St. David's', *Journal of the Historical Society of the Church in Wales*, xi. 65–89 (Cardiff, 1961).

Morris, David, *Hanes Tredegar o ddechreuad y gwaith haiarn hyd yn bresenol* (Tredegar, 1868).

Morris, J. H. and Williams, L. J., *The South Wales Coal Industry, 1841–1875* (Cardiff, 1958).

Niebuhr, H. R., *The social sources of denominationalism* (New York, 1960).

Owen, Evan, *Workmen's libraries in Glamorganshire and Monmouthshire* (Cardiff, 1895).

Parry, Edward, *Llawlyfr ar hanes y diwygiadau crefyddol yng Nghymru* (Corwen, 1898).

Parry, O., *Y dosbarth gweithiol yng Nghymru* (Caerfyrddin, 1865).

Phillips, John H., *An essay on the advantage of free libraries* (Cardiff, 1862).

Phillips, Thomas, *The Welsh Revival: its origin and development* (London, 1860).

Pococke, Richard, *The Travels through England* (Camden Society, 1888–9).

Port, M. H., *Six hundred new churches* (London, 1961).

Powell, Evan, *History of Tredegar* (Newport, 1902).

——*History of Carmel Baptist Church Sirhowy* (Cardiff, 1933).

Price, Evan, *The history of Penuel Calvinistic Methodist Church, Ebbw Vale* (Wrexham, 1925).

Pugh, Rex H., *A history of the Baptist Church, Abercarn* (Newport, 1932).

Rees, Thomas, *Hanes bywyd y diweddar Barch. David Thomas, Penmain, Swydd Fynwy* (Llanelli, 1842).

—— *Miscellaneous papers on subjects relating to Wales.* (London, 1867).

—— *History of Protestant Nonconformity in Wales.* (2nd ed., London, 1883).

Rees, Thomas, and Thomas, John, *Hanes Eglwysi Annibynol Cymru* (1871–5; 1891), 4 vols.

Richard, Henry, *Letters on the social and political conditions of the Principality of Wales.* (London, n.d.).

Richards, D. M., *Aberdare in 1837* (Aberdare, 1897).

Stephens, Tom, *History of Zion Baptist Church, Ponthir, Mon.* (1934).

Stonelake, Edmund, *Aberdare Trades and Labour Jubilee Souvenir, 1900–1950* (Aberdare, n.d.).

Thomas, D. J., *A short history of the Monmouthshire English Baptist Association* (Newport, 1857).

Thomas, E., *Crybwyllion hanesiol am Eglwys Silo, Tredegar* (ail argraffiad, Tredegar, 1858).

Thomas, John, *Sunshine on the 'Hills', being a narrative of a revival of the Lord's work at Tredegar, during the visitation of the cholera in the year 1866* (London, n.d.).

Thomas, John, *Jubili y diwygiad dirwestol yng Nghymru* (Merthyr Tydfil, 1885).

—— *Cofiant T. Rees, D.D., Abertawy* (Dolgellau, 1888).

Thomas, Joshua, *Hanes y Bedyddwyr ymhlith y Cymry* (ed. B. Davies, Pontypridd, 1885).

Thomas, Lleufer, *Labour Unions in Wales: their early struggle for existence* (Swansea, 1901).

Watson, Richard, *Anecdotes of the life of Richard Watson, Bishop of Llandaff* (London, 1818).

Wickham, E. R., *Church and People in an industrial city* (London, 1957).

Wilkins, Charles, *The history of Merthyr Tydfil* (Merthyr Tydfil, 1867).

Williams, A. H., *Welsh Wesleyan Methodism, 1800–1858* (Bangor, 1935).

Williams, C. R., 'The Welsh Religious Revival of 1904–5', *British Journal of Sociology* (1952).

Williams, David, *Cofiant y Parch. R. Ellis (Cynddelw)* (Caerfyrddin, 1935).

Williams, James, *Traethawd buddugol ar arferion drwg ieuenctyd y gweithfeydd, a'r moddion gorau i'w diwygio* (Merthyr, 1860).

Williams, John, *Cofiant y diweddar Barch. David Saunders, Merthyr* (Aberystwyth, 1842).

Williams, J. P., *Cofgolofn Jubili Eglwys Soar* (Rhymney, 1888).

Williams, J. Rufus, *Hanes athrofeydd y Bedyddwyr yn Sir Fynwy* (Aberdar, 1863).

Williams, J. R. D., *Parish of Rhymney, Monmouthshire. Centenary 1843–1943* (Cardiff, 1943).

Williams, William (Myfyr Wyn), *Atgofion am Sirhowy a'r cylch* (ed. D. M. Lloyd, Cardiff, 1951).

Wilson, Brian R., *Sects and Society* (London, 1961).

Wilson, J. Anselm, *The Life of Bishop Hedley* (London, 1930).

Young, David, *Origin and history of Methodism in Wales* (London, 1893).

INDEX OF PERSONS AND PLACES

PRINTED IN GREAT BRITAIN
AT THE UNIVERSITY PRESS, OXFORD
BY VIVIAN RIDLER
PRINTER TO THE UNIVERSITY